A GUIDE TO
THE PLAYS OF
BERTOLT BRECHT

Stephen Unwin has directed over fifty professional theatre productions, at the Traverse, the National Theatre, the Royal Court and the Almeida. He has directed at English National Opera, Covent Garden and Garsington Opera. He directed the post-war premiere of Brecht/Eisler's *The Decision* (Almeida Music Festival). He is Artistic Director of English Touring Theatre with whom he has directed a large number of classical plays, including *Hedda Gabler* (Donmar) and *King Lear* (Old Vic). He has co-authored three Pocket Guides: *Shakespeare, Twentieth Century Drama* and *Ibsen, Chekhov and Strindberg*. His most recent book is *So You Want to be a Theatre Director?*

A GUIDE TO
THE PLAYS OF
BERTOLT BRECHT

Stephen Unwin

Methuen

Published by Methuen 2005

First published in 2005 by
Methuen Publishing Limited
215 Vauxhall Bridge Road
London SW1V 1EJ

Methuen Publishing Limited Reg. No. 3543167

A CIP catalogue record for this book is available from the British Library

ISBN 0 413 77416 3

Typeset by SX Composing DTP, Rayleigh, Essex
Designed by Bryony Newhouse
Printed and bound in Great Britain by
St. Edmundsbury Press, Bury St. Edmunds, Suffolk.

IN MEMORY OF MARGOT HEINEMANN

CONTENTS

PREFACE

Brecht is a notoriously difficult writer. He lived in one of the bleakest periods of human history and his work is characterised by an active engagement in the taxing questions of his time. He has attracted an enormous amount of critical attention, about his plays, his theatrical theory, his complex relationship to politics and his private life, and any new study must tread warily. Several people – many of whom now sadly are dead – have acted as my guides. If I have failed to honour their work and experience I can only apologise; where I have succeeded, I owe them a debt of thanks.

The pre-war British Communists who dedicated themselves to their cause with such energy, commitment and rigour were the first British Brechtians and saw Brecht as one of their own. In my experience, one of the most impressive was Margot Heinemann (1913–92), to whom this book is dedicated. The historian Eric Hobsbawm described her as 'one of the most remarkable people of our time and a testament to its indestructible hopes'. Certainly, her lectures at Cambridge on 'Brecht on Shakespeare' in the early 1980s alerted me to an entirely different way of thinking about drama and society, and I hope her knowledge and inspiration can be heard in these pages.

I have also been influenced by a number of remarkable dissidents and exiles from Eastern Europe, whose lives were shaped – and often destroyed – by the very cause to which Brecht dedicated his life. The best knew that a distinction should be made between Stalinism and the pre-war European left, but a study of such an explicitly Communist dramatist needs to honour their experiences and respect their profound scepticism.

Then there is the large number of British theatre professionals with whom I have worked. I have great respect for many of them and have tried to honour their pragmatic, down-to-earth approach to this dauntingly intellectual writer. It is perhaps ironic that the theatre culture that has learned most from Brecht's political commitment is the one where his work is held in the least affection.

Finally, I have tried to honour the memory of the two men most responsible for the British appreciation of Brecht, John Willett (1917–2002) and Ralph Manheim (1907–92). Their outstanding edition of the *Collected Plays* is one of the great achievements in post-war British scholarship and it is to the credit of successive regimes at Methuen that their commitment to this project has been sustained over more than thirty years. I am particularly grateful to John Willett for his friendship and inspiration, and it is my fervent wish that he would have regarded this book as a logical extension of everything he achieved.

*

The book is divided into two sections. The first consists of seven chapters which outline the historical, cultural and theatrical context of Brecht's work, as well as providing an overview of his much debated theory. The second consists of an analysis of nineteen key plays, divided into six chronological groupings, each prefaced by a sketch of the writer's life at the time. The chapters on the individual plays contain a synopsis, an essay and a brief account of the play in performance. The book concludes with a chapter on Brecht's legacy and a chronicle of his life and times.

The central aim of the book is to focus on the plays themselves and describe the experience of seeing them in the theatre. If my emphasis is pragmatic, I am only following Brecht's favourite phrase from Hegel: 'The truth is concrete.'

Stephen Unwin, London, 2005

1 THE DARK TIMES

The life of the poet and playwright Bertolt Brecht (1898–1956) coincided with the most violent and dramatic half-century in German history. In everything he did, Brecht was concerned to create a new kind of art capable of reflecting the changing realities of the modern world. He wrote that he lived in 'dark times' and the briefest historical outline demonstrates this conclusively.

A German Half-Century

At the beginning of the twentieth century, Germany was a power capable of dominating Europe. She had come late to imperialism and her empire was limited in contrast to those of the other great European powers, especially Britain and France. Indeed, she had not been unified as a country until the Prussian victory over France and the crowning of the Kaiser in Versailles in January 1871. With unification came industrialisation, and Germany quickly started to threaten its competitors in terms of production, as well as world trade. Chancellor Bismarck's commitment to 'blood and iron' may have been reactionary but his country led the way in social welfare and the advancement of workers' rights. The first decade of the new century was one of peace and prosperity in Germany.

However, an increasingly aggressive foreign policy and an escalating arms race with Britain led inexorably to the outbreak of war in August 1914 and four years of unprecedented slaughter. If the First World War was traumatic for Britain, France and imperial Russia, it was catastrophic for Germany, which was fighting on two fronts against a powerful set of allies. Nearly two million Germans died and those who returned home after the surrender of November 1918 were leaderless, demoralised and angry.

Meanwhile, further east, the established order had been shaken to its foundations by the Russian Revolution of October 1917, in which the power of the Tsar, the aristocracy and the new middle classes was swept away. The 'ten days that shook the world' lit a beacon of hope for the poor and oppressed everywhere: not only did the Bolsheviks promise a better future for the industrial working class, they argued that all means should be used to achieve that goal. Lenin's October Revolution was a landmark event that inspired politicians, social reformers, philosophers, artists and intellectuals throughout the world. However, bloody civil war (1919–20) and terrible famine (1921) were the immediate results, and the newly formed Soviet Union struggled to make the kind of industrial 'leap forward' that its masters – and its survival – demanded.

*

Many of the thinkers who inspired the Bolshevik revolution were German, including of course Karl Marx and Friedrich Engels, who had always maintained that their ideas would first take root in Germany. Thus it was hardly surprising that the German Communists should attempt revolution in the 'Spartacus' risings in Berlin and other cities in 1918 and early 1919. These were brutally put down by a Social Democratic government supported by right-wing forces, and Rosa Luxemburg and Karl Liebknecht, the charismatic leaders of the newly founded German Communist Party, were assassinated. The German revolution had failed and this failure haunted the German left for another twenty years.

Within weeks of the signing of the Versailles Treaty in June 1919 a new German constitution was drawn up, but from the start the Weimar Republic was mistrusted. Fifteen different governments were elected between 1919 and 1928 and right and left fought each other in the streets as much as in parliament. The Allies had imposed crippling reparations on Germany and her economy was in deep trouble: post-war inflation was such that by November 1923 food was a hundred times more expensive than it had been in February 1920. When the Germans started to default on payments in 1923, French and Belgian troops invaded the Ruhr. However, the economy was stabilised by the reforming Chancellor Stresemann and the implementation of the Dawes Plan (1924), and there followed six years of relative economic stability.

This golden period was not to last. The New York Stock Exchange crash of October 1929 triggered the 'world economic crisis' and once again Germany suffered particularly badly. By 1930, five million Germans were out of work, providing rich soil in which far-right views flourished. The National Socialist Party (the Nazis) had been formed in February 1920 but their unsuccessful 'beer hall putsch' of November 1923 led to the party being banned. Adolf Hitler, its leader, was sentenced to five years in prison – but served only eight months – where he wrote his political manifesto, *Mein Kampf.* The Nazis were relaunched in February 1925 and grew rapidly, exploiting the economic and political chaos, as well as using violence, blackmail and political chicanery to make their way. In 1932 they gained control of the Reichstag, and Hitler was appointed Chancellor and President of the Third Reich on 30 January 1933.

Hitler's appeal to the German people was twofold: on the one hand he promised to restore to them their national identity; on the other he offered a new kind of streamlined modernity, valuable to the industrialists – whose financial support was so important to him – as well as creating jobs for the unemployed – whose mobilisation he needed. Citing Social Darwinism as their authority, the Nazis claimed that the Germans were 'the master race', destined for European, if not global, dominance. This was only possible in a totalitarian state, hostile to democracy, contemptuous of the rule of law and utterly committed to military prowess. Soon the secret police (the Gestapo) was founded and the first concentration camp (Dachau) was opened for enemies of the state. As Hitler's grip tightened, his regime persecuted anyone they regarded as inferior, subversive or 'not German'. A secret programme of euthanasia was launched and the Nuremberg laws of 1935 paved the way for the anti-Semitic violence unleashed on what became known as 'Kristallnacht', 9 November 1938.

*

Fascism was not confined to Germany. Mussolini had come to power in October 1922, promising to return Italy to its ancient glory and reform it of its Mediterranean backwardness. In July 1936 General Franco staged a military rebellion against the democratically elected government in Spain, triggering the Spanish Civil War (1936–8) in which Franco's Fascists – with German support – prevailed. The democracies – Britain, France and the United States – all produced home-grown, if less successful, Fascist parties, but their governments were slow to recognise the danger. By the end of the 'low dishonest decade', as W. H. Auden called the thirties, the future seemed to belong to the dictators.

The 'crisis years' also saw the emergence of a strong and articulate left-wing opposition. Artists and intellectuals from all over the world declared their support for the Spanish Republic, and called for a 'Popular Front' against Fascism. Volunteers travelled to Spain and joined the International Brigades – and many fought with great heroism. However, in Spain as elsewhere there was often a fatal split between Communists, Social Democrats and anarchists, and a tendency to dismiss Fascism as merely 'capitalism in crisis'; this sense of triumphant inevitability even led some German Communists to welcome the rise of the Nazis, who would, they thought, deal capitalism its *coup de grâce*.

Meanwhile, in 1924 Stalin had succeeded Lenin as General Secretary of the Communist Party and ruled with appalling brutality, ordering the destruction of the wealthy peasants (the kulaks), making impossible demands on industrial productivity and sanctioning the persecution and frequent execution of even the mildest critics of his regime. Of course, the full extent of Stalin's crimes was not known for many years, but the European Left was divided between those who were bitterly disillusioned with Communism and those who clung to the Soviet Union as the last bulwark against Fascism.

*

Hitler's vision was of a 'Greater Germany' that would dominate Europe, conquer France and Britain, and ultimately challenge American power. He declared that the German people required 'living space' (*Lebensraum*), and the annexation (*Anschluss*) of Austria in March 1938 and the occupation of the German-speaking area of Czechoslovakia (the *Sudetenland*) in October were just the first steps in gaining it. The German invasion of Poland in September 1939, which provoked Britain into war, was followed the next year by the rapid blitzkrieg conquests of Scandinavia (April), the Low Countries (May) and France (June). The planned invasion of Britain was never launched, but by the end of 1940 the German military machine seemed unstoppable.

The war reached a new pitch of brutality with the massive German attack on the Soviet Union in June 1941. To the Nazis, the Slavs were 'lesser beings' (*Untermenschen*) and they unleashed a new kind of all-out war, causing the deaths of more than twenty million Russians on the Eastern Front. From the winter of 1942, however, the tide began to turn and German defeats in Stalingrad, El Alamein, Italy and Normandy paved the way to the fall of Berlin, Hitler's suicide and finally the unconditional surrender of the Third Reich on 8 May 1945. After almost six years of war, three million German soldiers had been killed, many of the country's historic cities had been destroyed and its industrial base was in ruins.

The worst atrocities had taken place in secret. In early 1942 the Nazis had planned the mass murder (the 'Final Solution') of all the Jews of Europe, and developed a vast network of concentration and extermination camps to carry it out: Auschwitz-

Birkenau, Treblinka, Bergen Belsen, Sobibor and dozens of others. The liberation of these camps and the trials of the Nazi leaders in Nuremberg shocked the world with their accounts of unspeakable cruelty. Approximately six million European Jews had been murdered, along with five million Slavs, socialists, gypsies, homosexuals, Jehovah's Witnesses and other 'undesirables'. By May 1945 Germany was economically, culturally and, above all, morally bankrupt.

*

The victorious Allies quickly divided Germany into four zones of military occupation – Soviet, French, British and American – but the differences between East and West soon became evident. As early as March 1946 Churchill spoke of an 'iron curtain descending across the continent of Europe', splitting it into two distinct halves, one dominated by the Soviet Union, the other by the Western Allies. Berlin was a special case: a city divided into four sections in the midst of the Soviet zone. The Russians were unhappy about this and in late 1948 blocked land access to West Berlin and tried to starve the city into submission; the Berlin Airlift raised this siege, but a pattern for the future had been set. By 1949 the Soviet Union had acquired its own atomic bomb, triggering an arms race with the United States, and the long stand-off that came to be known as the Cold War had begun.

Germany was eventually divided into two new states, both founded in 1949. West Germany – the Federal Republic – was run on democratic lines and, within fifteen years, commentators were speaking of an 'economic miracle' having taken place. The successful implementation of the US-sponsored Marshall Plan (1947) for the redevelopment of Western Europe made this extraordinary turnaround possible. The creation in 1949 of NATO and the Council of Europe provided it with the best possible basis for territorial security and economic growth.

East Germany – a 'Republic of Workers and Peasants' – also came into existence in 1949, but there things were more complicated. The presence of Soviet troops and a puppet Communist government allowed few opportunities for the freedom that was transforming West Germany, and the economic weaknesses of the Communist system prevented her from making the kind of material advances that her citizens demanded. The hated Stasi (the secret police) was founded in 1950 and the DDR became one of the most authoritarian police states in the world. The death of Stalin in March 1953 brought hopes of change, but when a workers' uprising in East Berlin in June 1953 was brutally suppressed, the DDR was set on a path of steady decline.

The year 1956 saw new beginnings: Nikita Khrushchev, the new General Secretary of the Soviet Communist Party, denounced Stalin at the Twentieth Party Congress in June, while the use of Russian troops to put down an armed uprising in Hungary in November demonstrated that Communism's claims for universal popular support were untrue. Despite the building of the Berlin Wall in 1961, and the long years of the Cold War that followed, the darkest of the dark times were over.

Culture

In the thirty years before Hitler, culture in the German-speaking areas of Europe was astonishingly fruitful. Germany led the world in terms of workers' literacy and its middle classes were exceptionally well educated. Musical standards were unequalled, and in drama, poetry, painting and the other arts, German-speaking talent was everywhere to be seen.

Turn-of-the-century Vienna was a powerful magnet for artistic and intellectual talents: Sigmund Freud and Carl Jung explored the workings of the subconscious; Egon Schiele, Gustav Klimt and Alphonse Mucha created a new kind of painting, and Arthur Schnitzler wrote a series of plays remarkable for their social realism and frank sexuality. The composers Gustav Mahler and Richard Strauss created music of tremendous profundity – if on a classical model – while Anton Webern, Alban Berg and Arnold Schoenberg (the Second Viennese School) found a way beyond nineteenth-century certainties. Much of the best of twentieth-century German culture had its roots in Sezession Vienna.

The naturalistic revolution that had swept across late nineteenth-century Europe had left German culture relatively untouched. Her fine artists preferred psychological introspection and the dominant form was Expressionism. There were two main schools: 'Die Brucke' consisted of painters such as Ernst Ludwig Kirchner and Emil Nolde, while 'Der Blaue Reiter' included Wasily Kandinsky, Auguste Macke, Franz Marc and Paul Klee. Their extraordinarily rich, psychologically dense, brilliantly coloured canvases provided a powerful challenge to the dominance of Naturalism and Impressionism. Hugo von Hofmannsthal, Rainer Maria Rilke, Stefan George and Georg Trakl brought similar qualities to lyric poetry.

Naturalism had a deeper influence on the theatre: in the last quarter of the nineteenth century the Duke of Saxe-Meiningen had toured his company of actors in productions of the classics which were startling for their attention to naturalistic detail; in 1889 Otto Brahms had founded the Freie Bühne in Berlin in imitation of André Antoine's Théâtre Libre in Paris; in 1891 Gerhart Hauptmann's *The Weavers* had caused a scandal with its realistic portrayal of working-class life; and in 1913 Georg Büchner's *Woyzeck*, written in 1822, redefined what drama could be when it was finally premiered in Munich. Nevertheless, Germany produced nothing to rival the naturalistic masterpieces of Ibsen and Chekhov, and theatrical Expressionism – much influenced by late Strindberg – was the dominant form right through to the First World War, with playwrights such as Frank Wedekind, Carl Sternheim, Georg Kaiser, Arnold Bronnen and Hanns Johst all committed to a kind of theatre which ignored the conventions of the drawing room and the 'well-made play', and attempted to dramatise the inner life.

*

The impact of the First World War on German-language culture was enormous. One of the most remarkable developments was Dadaism, the playful anti-art movement that first emerged at the Cabaret Voltaire in Zurich in 1916, and then moved to Berlin and Paris after 1918; its key figures were Hans Arp, Kurt Schwitters and Hugo Ball. Meanwhile, figurative artists such as Otto Dix, Max Beckmann, George Grosz and Käthe Kollwitz used the suffering of the war and its survivors as their grim subject.

Germany's geographical position means that she looks east as much as west, and the cultural revolution which accompanied the political one in the Soviet Union had a profound impact on progressive German artists. Central to Communism was the notion that culture could raise consciousness and change people's lives, and the first few years of the Soviet Union saw remarkable cultural achievements in exceptionally difficult circumstances. Anatoly Lunacharsky, Lenin's Commissar for Education and the Arts, supported the post-revolutionary Soviet avant-garde and encouraged artists and designers such as El Lissitzky, Alexander Rodchenko and Vladimir Tatlin; their work embraced a whole range of formal innovations – film, photography, montage and newsprint – and provided a model for the subsequent boom in German political art.

Artists also looked west, above all to the USA, whose vibrant energy, dynamic economy and wide-open spaces seemed to provide an alternative to the carnage of old Europe, and the result was *Amerikanismus*, a wholehearted embrace of all things American: skyscrapers, railway trains, boxing rings, cigarette girls and so on. American literature was going through a golden age and popular writers such as F. Scott Fitzgerald, John Dos Passos, Upton Sinclair, Theodore Dreiser, Frank Wallace and Frank Norris were reaching massive readerships. The great American art form was the cinema, and among the finest achievements of the Weimar Republic were three film master-pieces – Robert Wiene's *The Cabinet of Dr Caligari* (1920), Fritz Lang's *Metropolis* (1927) and Josef von Sternberg's *The Blue Angel*

(1930) – all influenced by Charlie Chaplin, D. W. Griffiths and the early Hollywood giants. The 1920s was a decade of exceptional achievement in German literature. A number of major novels were published, of which Thomas Mann's *The Magic Mountain* (1929), Franz Kafka's *The Castle* (1926) and Joseph Roth's *The Radetzky March* (1930) were perhaps the most remarkable. Dozens of other important writers such as Heinrich and Klaus Mann, Erich Maria Remarque, Hermann Broch, Robert Musil, Stefan Zweig, Anna Seghers, Ernst Döblin, Erich Kästner and Franz Werfel also produced significant novels, essays and short stories, often reacting against the certainties of nineteenth-century realism and inventing new forms to reflect the new realities.

In the theatre the dominance of Expressionism prevented most dramatists – with the important exception of Brecht – from engaging in a world transformed by war, and even the best plays of the period – Karl Kraus's *The Last Days of Mankind* (1919), Ernst Toller's *Man and the Masses* (1920) and Marieluise Fleisser's *Pioneers in Ingolstadt* (1927) – struggled with its legacy. Instead, the German theatre was shaped by a number of outstanding directors and designers. Influenced above all by the innovators of the Soviet theatre – Nikolai Okhlopkov, Sergei Tretiakov, Alexander Tairov and Vsevolod Meyerhold – Berlin became a hothouse for radical theatre of all kinds: Max Reinhardt worked on a series of groundbreaking productions at the Deutsches Theater, Erwin Piscator ran an exceptionally influential company at the Volksbühne and Leopold Jessner explored the use of technology in his versions of the classics at the Staatstheater.

Germany retained her musical pre-eminence and was the home of many fine orchestras and musicians. However, following the First World War, some retreated into classical certainties while others looked abroad, whether to Sergei Prokofiev, Béla Bartók and Igor Stravinsky, or to jazz, gospel and American popular music. This internationalism provided a stimulating environment for a new generation of radical composers including Ernst Krenek,

Hans Pfitzner, Kurt Weill and Erich Korngold. The Kroll Opera House in Berlin under Otto Klemperer became a centre for experimental stagings of repertoire operas and saw the premieres of several important new pieces; and Paul Hindemith ran a festival of new music, first at Donaueschingen, then at Baden-Baden, committed to developing a style of music (*Gebrauchsmusik*) with a socially useful element.

The late 1920s were the golden years of the Weimar Republic. Especially in the big cities, there was a new permissiveness in attitudes towards women's rights, sexuality and individual self-expression, and Berlin became famous for its nightlife, its bars and its cabarets, where prostitutes mingled with poets, Christians drank with anarchists and Communists fought with nationalists. The sharp-tongued and politically charged cabaret sketches of Kurt Tucholsky, Walter Mehring, Erich Kästner and others savaged the hypocrisy of their fellow citizens with devastating wit and style, and it is in this brief period of apparent stability that the popular image of Weimar Germany – especially Berlin – as a place of pleasure-seeking freedom finds its truest reflection.

*

The economic crisis of 1929 polarised artists and intellectuals. The political indifference and frivolity of the preceding decade was frowned on and writers were expected to express their preferences. Most chose the left and some of the most remarkable became Communists; others, such as the poet Gottfried Benn and the playwright Hanns Johst, moved to the right. Splits emerged in cultural allegiances too, with some advocating active engagement in politics and others retreating into nostalgia for a vanished world. One of the results was a renewed interest in theoretical aesthetics, and the Frankfurt School provided a forum for an elaborate discussion of the relationship between politics and culture. Its leading figures were Walter Benjamin, Theodor Adorno and Georg Lukács. Unfortunately, the simultaneous rise of Soviet cultural conservatism and the promotion of 'Socialist Realism' by

Stalin's Cultural Commissar A. A. Zhdanov led to an increasing coarsening of the debate.

Out of this maelstrom emerged a movement known as the New Objectivity (*Die Neue Sachlichkeit*), a conscious reaction against the extremes of Expressionism and a fascination with the clean lines of modernity. Architecture was at the cutting edge of this, and the late 1920s and early 1930s saw Le Corbusier and Mies van der Rohe producing their best work. Under Walter Gropius, the Bauhaus became an influential centre for the finest in modern design, which was increasingly understood to be instrumental in the way that people lived their lives. This movement had an impact on all aspects of Weimar culture and was a heroic last attempt at rationality before madness descended.

*

Except for kitsch, anti-Semitic rants and monuments to German victories, the Nazis had very little use for culture – 'When I hear the word culture I reach for my revolver,' said Goering. Music was tolerated (as long as the musicians were not Jewish) and Hitler's favourite film-maker, Leni Riefenstahl, made two documentaries, *The Triumph of the Will* (1937) and *Olympia, Parts One and Two* (1938), whose role as Nazi propaganda is almost eclipsed by their artistic and technical skill. The great figures of Weimar culture, however, were dismissed as 'metropolitan' (often used as a euphemism for Jewish) and the Nazis staged exhibitions of 'decadent art' (*Entartete Kunst*), as well as organising mass burnings of books by writers they despised. Some made compromises with the new regime or simply stopped working. Others committed suicide or died at the hands of Nazi thugs. Many fled abroad – to Moscow, London, New York or Los Angeles – where they attempted to articulate the best aspects of German culture and imagine a better future for their homeland. Exile was especially bitter for poets, novelists and playwrights, who found themselves cut off from their readers, their publishers and their audience.

*

German culture after 1945 was in profound shock and the challenge for artists was not just to respond to the disaster of the Nazi period but also to find a way forward. Berlin, Prague and Vienna had lost their positions as artistic capitals and the centre of gravity had moved westwards. Reassembling the cultural apparatus was a complicated process: many of the theatres had been destroyed, most of the artists and managers who had stayed in Germany were fatally compromised and, of those who had fled, many were reluctant to return to the country that had rejected them. In East Germany the new Communist government developed a cultural policy which invested heavily in the arts but was restrictive in what it deemed 'constructive'. Many artists were condemned as 'formalist' and the regime was increasingly committed to the dead hand of 'Socialist Realism' as the only form appropriate for the working class.

*

Such was the world into which Bertolt Brecht was born and produced his extraordinary work. His complex, moving plays provide us with the most acute reflections of the 'dark times' through which he lived.

2 BRECHT: PLAYWRIGHT, POET AND ARTIST

Brecht's Life

Eugen Bertolt Brecht was born on 10 February 1898 in the south German city of Augsburg. His father, Berthold (1869–1939), was a paper manufacturer and Brecht enjoyed a comfortable middle-class childhood. His mother, Sophie (1871–1920), however, died of breast cancer at the age of forty-nine and he was a sickly youth, sensitive and withdrawn.

Brecht attended a good school, the Königlich-Bayerisches Realgymnasium, matriculated as a medical student at Munich University in 1917 and worked as a medical orderly in Augsburg immediately after the end of the First World War. He soon wrote two plays, *Baal* (1918) and *Drums in the Night* (1918–20), and in 1919 fathered an illegitimate son, Frank, by his first love, Paula Banholzer. He left university without a degree in 1921 and, in 1922, married the opera singer, Marianne Zoff, with whom he had a daughter, Hanne. While working as a dramaturg at the Munich Kammerspiele, he wrote his third play, *In the Jungle of the Cities* (1921–4) and was awarded the prestigious Kleist Prize. In 1924 he directed his first production, an adaptation with Lion Feuchtwanger of Christopher Marlowe's *Edward II*.

In 1924 Brecht moved to Berlin. He had met the left-wing Austrian actress Helene Weigel the previous year and they had a son, Stefan, in November 1924. In the same year he began working with Elisabeth Hauptmann, an American-German scholar. He became Assistant Director at Max Reinhardt's Deutsches Theater and joined the 'dramaturgical collective' at Erwin Piscator's ground-breaking Volksbühne. In 1924 in Berlin he wrote *Man equals Man*, started to read Karl Marx in 1926 and published his first volume of poetry, *The Devotions*, in 1927. He divorced Zoff in 1927, married Weigel in 1929 and their second child, Barbara, was born in 1930.

In 1927 Brecht met the composer Kurt Weill with whom he wrote several music-theatre pieces, including *The Rise and Fall of the City of Mahagonny* (1927–9) and *The Threepenny Opera* (1928). He also met the composers Paul Hindemith, Paul Dessau and Hanns Eisler, and wrote with them – and Kurt Weill – a series of *Lehrstücke* (learning plays), including *The Decision* (1930) and *The Mother* (1930–1). In 1930 he met the young Berlin Communist, Margarete Steffin, who became the closest of his lovers. In the dying years of the Weimar Republic he wrote *Saint Joan of the Stockyards* (1930–1), as well as the film script for *Kuhle Wampe* (1932).

On 28 February 1933, the day after the Reichstag Fire, the Brechts fled Germany for their own safety. They went first to Paris, where Brecht wrote his last major work with Kurt Weill, then moved to Denmark where he lived with Weigel, their two children and Steffin. There he met the Danish journalist, Ruth Berlau and began his remarkable *Journals*. He spent three months in London and visited New York to oversee the Theatre Workshop production of *The Mother*. He wrote his only novel, *The Threepenny Novel* (1934), two anti-Fascist masterpieces, *Señora Carrar's Rifles* (1937) and *Fear and Misery of the Third Reich* (1935–8), and the radio play *The Trial of Lucullus* (1939). He also started work on three of his greatest plays – *The Good Person of Szechwan* (1938–42), *Mother Courage and her Children* (1939) and *Life of Galileo* (1937–9; 1945–7) – as well as producing some of his key theoretical texts and much of his finest poetry.

With the growing likelihood of war, the Brechts moved to Sweden in April 1939, and in 1940 sought refuge in Finland, where he wrote *Mr Puntila and his Man Matti*. In April 1941 they left for Los Angeles, via Moscow, where Steffin died of tuberculosis.

Brecht found it difficult to find paid employment in Hollywood but contributed to the screenplay for Fritz Lang's film *Hangmen Also Die* (1942). He also wrote three plays about the war, including *The Resistible Rise of Arturo Ui* (1941) and *Schweyk in the Second World War* (1941–3), as well as perhaps his most popular play, *The Caucasian Chalk Circle* (1943–5). Having been interrogated by the House Un-American Activities Committee in October 1947, Brecht left the United States for Switzerland, where he directed an adaptation of Sophocles' *Antigone* (1948) and wrote his last major play, *The Days of the Commune* (1948–9).

In October 1948 – after fifteen years in exile – Brecht returned to Berlin. In January 1949 his production of *Mother Courage and her Children*, with Helene Weigel in the title role, received its Berlin premiere at the Deutsches Theater. As a result of its extraordinary success, Brecht and Weigel were asked to found the Berliner Ensemble, where he directed renowned productions of *Mr Puntila and his Man Matti* (1949), *The Mother* (1951) and *The Caucasian Chalk Circle* (1954). He also adapted a number of classical plays – Lenz's *The Tutor* (1950), Shakespeare's *Coriolanus* (1952), Molière's *Don Juan* (1954) and Farquhar's *The Recruiting Officer* (1955) – as well as writing one of his greatest collections of poems, the *Buckow Elegies* (1953). In 1954 the Theater am Schiffbauerdamm – where *The Threepenny Opera* had premiered twenty-six years previously – became the permanent home of the Berliner Ensemble. In 1955 Brecht was awarded the Stalin Peace Prize.

Brecht died on 14 August 1956. He is buried in Berlin near his favourite philosopher, Hegel. His gravestone bears the simplest of inscriptions: 'Brecht'.

Influences

Brecht had a notoriously libertarian attitude to intellectual property and his work is rich with influences from an astonishing range of sources.

Despite being a lifelong atheist, Brecht had a strong feeling for the language of the Lutheran Bible, and his style often echoes with the simplicity and directness of its parables. He admired the austere realism of Roman literature – especially Tacitus and Horace – and was fascinated by oriental poetry and theatre. He was also influenced by late medieval art, especially Breughel and Hieronymus Bosch, and his early work was indebted to the fifteenth-century French poet, François Villon.

Brecht had a lifelong interest in the great Elizabethan and Jacobean English dramatists: Marlowe, Webster and, above all, Shakespeare – writers well known in Germany, but often interpreted through the filter of romanticism. He returned to Shakespeare constantly and there are numerous references to him in the *Diaries*, the *Journals* and many of the letters. His theoretical work contains fascinating insights into Shakespeare's theatre and his influence is evident in almost everything he wrote. He also worked on adaptations of Marlowe's *Edward II* and Webster's *The Duchess of Malfi*.

The free-speaking, hard-nosed materialism of English literature was a long way from the cult of the romantic genius that characterised so much nineteenth- and early twentieth-century German literature, and chimed with Brecht's own view of the role of art. His admiration for English writers extended beyond the golden age of Shakespearean drama and he turned to John Gay for *The Threepenny Opera* (1928), Rudyard Kipling for *Man equals Man* (1924) and George Farquhar for *Trumpets and Drums* (1955).

Brecht's attitude towards German romantic drama was highly ambivalent. He admired the young Schiller and adapted Goethe's *Urfaust*, but was suspicious of their status. While he recognised that their best plays were full of social and political energy, he saw how the Nazis exploited their innocent nationalism for their much more sinister ends. Instead, he identified an alternative tradition in German drama, rich with politics and rooted in experience, evident in the plays of Heinrich von Kleist, Georg Büchner and Jakob Lenz: these are Brecht's German forebears.

Brecht's view of nineteenth-century drama was ambivalent. He was intrigued by Strindberg and Bernard Shaw, regarded Maxim Gorky as a 'comrade', admired the plays of Gerhart Hauptmann and was affected by the French urban poets, Rimbaud, Verlaine and Baudelaire. However, he tended to dismiss nineteenth-century culture as 'bourgeois' and showed very little interest in the great masters of naturalistic drama, especially Ibsen and Chekhov. It was as if Brecht felt that the nineteenth century was too recent to be useful.

*

Brecht's plays consistently defy categorisation and central to the development of his aesthetic is the integration of popular, even 'low', elements within his overall artistic and intellectual structure. This interest dates back to his youth, and he acknowledged the impact of the annual autumn fair in Augsburg, with its sideshows, booths and panoramas. As a student he performed with the Bavarian political clown Karl Valentin and loved raucous ballads and sentimental songs. He read detective stories in vast quantities, watched American films (especially Charlie Chaplin) and enjoyed all kinds of junk fiction. He admired Rudyard Kipling – often dismissed as an apologist for the British Empire – and was profoundly affected by that great comic novel about the ordinary soldier, Jaroslav Hašek's *The Good Soldier Švejk*.

By his own admission, Brecht stole from everywhere. He forced the old into powerful contradiction with the new, and montage, parody and quotation are evident throughout his work. It is this magpie quality that explains the rich texture and multi-dimensionality of many of his greatest plays.

Collaborators

Brecht had an enviable talent for friendship and an appreciation of his work must take into account the many collaborators who contributed so much to it. These included designers, writers, actors, directors, musicians and others: the editors of the *Collected Works* credit their contributions, and I have followed their lead. Brecht surrounded himself with a circle of dedicated women. The most important was his wife, the great actress Helene Weigel (1900–71), who created many of his finest roles: Pelagea Vlassova, Mother Courage, Señora Carrar and the Governor's Wife. She also helped him set up the Berliner Ensemble and was its Intendant (Chief Executive) until her death. Brecht relied, too, on Elisabeth Hauptmann (1897–1973), who provided him with a background in English literature and acted as his lifelong editor, secretary and textual collaborator. Margarete Steffin (1908–41) was a working-class actress in Berlin when she met Brecht in the late 1920s; she quickly became the closest of his lovers, working with him on several of his most important plays before her untimely death. In 1933, Brecht met the Danish actress and journalist Ruth Berlau (1904–74), with whom he had a passionate affair (in 1944 she gave birth to his child, who died in infancy); she collaborated with him on several projects and was responsible for the superb photographs that document his productions at the Berliner Ensemble. Criticisms have been levelled at Brecht about the way he treated these women – and there were others, often younger, after the war – and he has sometimes been dismissed as a male chauvinist, who stole what they had to offer and gave nothing in return. However, such views neither explain their devotion to him, nor detract from the great contributions they made to his work.

Brecht developed his aesthetic beliefs with the help of a wide range of writers and thinkers. The most significant were his friends, the independent-minded philosopher and theoretician Karl Korsch (1886–1961), who introduced him to Marxism, and the great left-wing intellectual and philosopher Walter Benjamin (1892–1940), who helped give his aesthetic innovations a theoretical shape. He also learned about the role of art in modern society from the Marxist sociologist Fritz Sternberg (1895–1963) and Brecht's public arguments with the socialist critic Georg Lukács (1885–1971) – although not strictly speaking a collaborator – helped him formulate his views on working-class art. Brecht worked closely with four remarkable composers. His collaboration with Kurt Weill (1900–50) resulted in his greatest hit, *The Threepenny Opera*, as well as his first opera, *The Rise and Fall of the City of Mahagonny*. His lifelong friend Hanns Eisler (1898–1962) was the most politically minded of Schoenberg's disciples and his formidable music is central to *The Mother* and *The Decision*. Brecht also worked with the leading German composer of the 1920s, Paul Hindemith (1895–1963), and contributed to his festivals of New Music in Donaueschingen and Baden-Baden. Finally, Paul Dessau (1894–1979) wrote incidental songs for *Mother Courage* and *The Good Person of Szechwan*, as well as the score for Brecht's second opera, *The Condemnation of Lucullus*.

Brecht also collaborated with three talented stage designers. The first was his friend from schooldays in Augsburg, Caspar Neher ('Cas') (1897–1962), who designed many of his productions before the war and, after a fourteen-year gap, returned to Berlin to work on *Puntila*, *The Mother* and *Life of Galileo* for the Berliner Ensemble. Two others became important after the war: Teo Otto (1904–68), who had designed the premieres of several of his plays at the Zurich Schauspielhaus during the war, and Brecht's own 1948 production of *Mother Courage* in Berlin; and Karl von Appen (1900–81), who spent the war years in a concentration camp and was responsible for Brecht's famous production of *The Caucasian Chalk Circle* in 1954. These two contributed almost as much to the highly distinct look of the Berliner Ensemble's work as Neher himself. Although Brecht never worked with George Grosz (1893–1959) on any productions, his remarkable designs for *The Good Soldier Svejk* at the Volksbühne and his extraordinary paintings and drawings provided Brecht with a powerful visual correlative.

Brecht's plays are notoriously difficult to direct in that they require such a sophisticated understanding of the author's intentions. Of course, he was a formidable director in his own right, and although others usually directed his early plays, his presence in rehearsals meant that this was often in name only. He co-directed a number of productions with his lifelong friend, Erich Engel (1891–1966), collaborated with the Romanian director, Slatan Dudow (1903–63), and worked with the Swiss director, Benno Besson (b. 1922). The great political director Erwin Piscator (1893–1966) had been Brecht's mentor in 1920s Berlin, and remained a lifelong colleague and friend. Brecht's assistant directors and disciples at the Berliner Ensemble – Manfred Wekwerth (b. 1929), Joachim Tenschert (1928–92) and Peter Palitzsch (1918–2004) – became some of the foremost figures in post-war German theatre.

Brecht's productions before the war and at the Berliner Ensemble featured many of the finest German-speaking actors and actresses of his generation: indeed, Brecht was responsible for making many of them famous. As well as Weigel, these included Ernst Busch (1900–80), Therese Giehse (1898–1975), Oskar Homolka (1898–1978), Angelika Hurwicz (1922–99), Fritz Kortner (1892–1970), Lotte Lenya (1898–1981), Peter Lorre (1904–64), Carola Neher (1900–42), Leonard Steckel (1900–71) and Ekkehard Schall (b. 1930). Brecht also enjoyed a close relationship with the British actor Charles Laughton (1899–1962) and worked with him on the English translation of *Life of Galileo*, which Laughton performed in Los Angeles in 1947.

Brecht was neither a solitary genius writing plays and developing theories in isolation, nor an artistic giant surrounded by pygmies: collaboration is at the heart of the 'Brecht Circle' and integral to its enduring strength. Some have suggested that this demonstrates a lack of creative individuality; others have defended it on the grounds of Brecht's attitude towards shared endeavour and intellectual property. The fact is, however, that collaboration was essential to his way of working and should be recognised as such.

A Theatre for the Modern World

As well as writing some of the most remarkable plays of modern times, Brecht revolutionised the art of the theatre itself. Like all the best playwrights – Shakespeare, Molière, Ibsen – he was a practical man of the theatre. He understood how the theatre worked and was committed to making it into a relevant, provocative and dynamic art form.

German artistic life has always had a tendency towards intellectual pronouncements and Brecht's own theoretical bent needs to be seen as part of this tradition. It should be stressed, however, that Brecht was highly sceptical of abstraction and it is unfortunate that this most tactile and sensuous of playwrights is so often caricatured as an incomprehensible intellectual with his head in the clouds. His experimentation did not take place in isolation and was part of a much broader attempt to create a new kind of theatre, capable of reflecting the 'dark times'; furthermore, many of his ideas were drawn from elsewhere, above all Shakespeare and other classical writers. In other words it is essential to place Brecht's various theoretical pronouncements in context, and take them with a pinch of salt. His attempts to describe his ideas – 'alienation effect', 'epic theatre', '*Gestus*' and so on – can seem like so many confusing terms which I have tried to clarify in the next few chapters.

Brecht was determined that the 'audience shouldn't hang up its brain with its coat and hat'; he wanted to create a kind of theatre that could not only reflect reality but help to change it and argued that poetry, character, music, design, and theatricality – everything – should be used to realise this all-important goal:

> The modern theatre mustn't be judged by its success in satisfying the audience's habits but by its success in transforming them. It needs to be questioned not about its degree of conformity with the 'eternal laws of the theatre' but about its ability to master the rules governing the great social processes of our age; not about whether

it manages to interest the spectator in buying a ticket – i.e. in the theatre itself – but about whether it manages to interest him in the world.

Language and Poetry

Brecht was not just a great dramatist and theatre director, he was also a literary figure of real stature. His plays are written in an idiosyncratic language, poised somewhere between realism and aphorism, analysis and dream. It draws on a wide range of registers: Luther's Bible, junk fiction, peasant proverbs, Expressionist poetry, folk ballads, Americana, literary sonnets, haikus, Shakespearean blank verse, Victorian slang and Brecht's own unrhymed free verse; its eclecticism is fundamental to its strength.

Brecht wrote lyric poetry throughout his life and some argue that this was his greatest talent. It is free of abstraction and is simple and direct; it is also remarkably eloquent. It takes a range of forms: sonnets, epigrams, ballads, elegies, children's songs, satirical verses and so on. He also wrote a large number of theatre poems, which should be read alongside the plays and which contribute enormously to our understanding of his approach to the theatre.

This poetry carries a powerful physicality. In his essay 'On Rhymeless Verse with Irregular Rhythms' (1939) Brecht distinguished between two versions of a line in the Bible, arguing that 'pluck out the eye that offends thee' was weaker and less dramatic than 'If thine eye offend thee, pluck it out'. From this sprang a notion of 'gestic' poetry, a language built out of vivid actions and material objects. At its finest, Brecht's use of language reveals that beauty is to be discovered in material objects and argues – like the Greek philosopher Epicurus – that life's meaning is to be found in the everyday things of the world. One example is in *The Good Person of Szechwan*:

I had never seen the city at dawn. These were the hours when I used to lie with my filthy blanket over my head, terrified to wake up. Today I mixed with the newsboys, with the men who were washing down the streets, with the ox-carts bringing fresh vegetables in from the fields. It was a long walk from Sun's neighbourhood to here, but with every step I grew happier. I had always been told that when one is in love one walks on air, but the wonderful thing is that one walks on earth, on tarmac. I tell you, at dawn the blocks of buildings are like rubbish heaps with little lights glowing in them; the sky is pink but still transparent, clear of dust.

The second is in *Mother Courage*:

Kattrin, polish the knives, there's the pumice. And you, stop hanging round like Jesus on the Mount of Olives, get moving, wash them glasses, we'll have fifty or more of cavalry in tonight and I don't want to hear a lot of 'I'm not accustomed to having to run about, oh my poor feet, we never run in church'. Thank the Lord they're corruptible. After all, they ain't wolves, just humans out for money. Corruption in humans is the same as compassion in God. Corruption's our only hope.

This is writing with a profound physical presence.

Occasionally, Brecht's work expresses a particular kind of regret, that the darkness of the times will not allow him to be more sensual, that the political situation has prevented him from being able to write about the simple pleasures of life:

Some of us have now decided
To speak no more of cities by the sea, snow on roofs, women
The smell of ripe apples in cellars, the senses of the flesh, all
That makes a man round and human.

Thankfully, Brecht's own sensuality stopped him from always obeying this injunction, and he remained fascinated by the physical and the tangible.

The extraordinary thing is that despite all the horrors of his time

Brecht continued to believe in the value of poetry and argued that art still had a role, however bleak the world seemed. One of his simplest and most effective poems expresses this perfectly:

> In the dark times
> Will there also be singing?
> Yes, there will also be singing
> About the dark times.

Translations and Further Reading

Brecht's German is notoriously difficult to translate and some commentators feel that no one has managed to render his peculiarly allusive language satisfactorily.

Brecht's first English translator was the American scholar and theatre aficionado, Eric Bentley, whose fine, if somewhat collo-quial, translations were published by Grove Press. British readers are fortunate to have had John Willett and Ralph Manheim as joint editors of Methuen's eight volumes of *Collected Plays*. Their superb editions (quoted throughout this book) provide the reader with the best possible account in English. They also produced definitive volumes of the *Poems, Letters, Songs from the Plays, Short Stories* and *Journals*. British theatres have sometimes looked to commission fresh translations, often from well-established writers such as Howard Brenton, David Hare and Frank McGuinness, and these are detailed in the individual chapters on the plays.

The best biographies of Brecht are by Frederic Ewen (1967) and Klaus Volker (1979). Probably the two most important studies in English are Keith Dickson's *Towards Utopia* (1978) and John Willett's *Brecht in Context* (1984). The same author's *Theatre of Bertolt Brecht* (1967) is invaluable, as is *The Cambridge Companion to Brecht* (1994). Fredric Jameson's *Brecht and Method* (1998) provides a stimulating if occasionally opaque view. Two controversial volumes are Martin Esslin's *A Choice of Evils* (1959) and John

Fuegi's *The Life and Lies of Bertolt Brecht* (1994); both need to be read alongside more balanced studies. Margot Heinemann's essay, 'How Brecht Read Shakespeare', in *Political Shakespeare* (1994) provides a superb introduction to Brecht's views on Shakespeare, but a more comprehensive study is long overdue.

Two of the most important works on Brecht were published in his own lifetime: Walter Benjamin's individual essays have been collected under the title *Understanding Brecht* (1998), and the debates on aesthetics between Brecht and Georg Lukács, originally published in *Das Wort* in the 1920s and 1930s, have been reproduced in *Aesthetics and Politics* (1977).

3 POLITICS, ECONOMICS AND A NEW MORALITY

It is only possible to understand Brecht's view of the world by seeing him in the context of his time. An interest in the way society operates, how its wealth is distributed, its justice is exercised and its opportunities are made available runs right through his work. Karl Marx had declared that it was not enough to interpret the world, the point was to change it, and this imperative is central to Brecht's restless engagement in politics.

A Political Maelstrom

Brecht came to politics comparatively late. Like many of his generation his response to the First World War was a kind of anarchist despair, lacking in political analysis or prescriptions for a better future. In February 1919 he served briefly on the Workers Council in Augsburg as an Independent Socialist, but was not involved in the 1919 German revolution. He spent his early twenties in a highly personal and deeply poetic reverie, cut off from the great upheavals of the time. His subsequent political education was piecemeal and dependent on friendship as much as on study. An important turning point came in 1926 when he started to read Karl Marx. His commitment to Communism was triggered by seeing the Berlin police – under Social Democrat control – break up a banned demonstration on May Day 1929.

For radicals of Brecht's generation, the Russian Revolution of October 1917 was the defining moment in the struggle of the poor of the world to improve their lot. Support for revolutionary Communism meant a commitment to creating a better society, in which wealth is equally shared, the means of production are owned by the state, private industry is shut down and the state takes on dictatorial powers for the good of the working class as a whole. The Communists argued that such a radical change could only come about through a revolution and that if the ruling class was not prepared to give up its power and privileges voluntarily, force would be necessary.

Brecht's growing commitment to Communism was hardly unique. He was part of a mass movement which saw Communism – and the USSR in particular – as embodying the hopes and dreams of a better world. Critics have accused the European Communists of turning a blind eye to the brutality of Stalin's dictatorship and failing to criticise the Soviet Union for its manifest failings. However, Russia in the 1920s and 1930s was run on extraordinarily restrictive terms and its worst violence and oppression took place in secret. One of the great strengths of the Communist movement was the almost religious commitment of its cadres and it is a terrible irony that the state that should have provided the lodestar for all their efforts was a dictatorship almost as cruel as the Fascists whom they so properly despised.

Brecht's own relationship with Communism was complicated. Although he argued that only Communism could improve the lot of the poor, his temperament and instincts resisted the single-minded commitment that the revolutionary movement required and it is telling that he never formally joined the party. As the disaster of Stalin's rule became clear, he found himself in a difficult position, having to defend 'really existing socialism' (as it was called) while at the same time wanting to maintain his own independence. Some have argued that his political beliefs coarsened his poetic talent; others have criticised him for holding them while also enjoying silk shirts and cigars. The fact is that by the late 1930s Brecht was deeply disillusioned by the Soviet Union and dismayed by its betrayal of socialist ideals; if he kept his reservations largely to himself, it was because he saw the Soviet Union as the best hope against Fascism.

*

It has sometimes been said that Brecht's critique of Fascism was so coloured by the standard Communist interpretation of it as capitalism in its death throes that it has limited value. However, by 1939 Brecht had the evidence of his own eyes: not only had Hitler come to power with the active support of large parts of industry, big business and finance, but the German economic recovery was a direct result of his preparations for war.

The fact is that Hitler's twelve-year reign was devastating to Brecht. The Nazis were not merely a threat to his life, they drove him into exile, far away from his home, his theatres, his readers and his friends. Despite Brecht's commitment to Communism, he recognised the need for an alliance with the Social Democrats and acknowledged the extent of Hitler's working-class support. He also predicted his catastrophic warmongering with deadly accuracy.

Some say that Brecht overlooked the most heinous aspect of Hitler's rule: its virulent anti-Semitism. Others have even accused him of anti-Semitism himself. However, this is to ignore the evidence: he was married to a Viennese Jew, many of his closest friends and collaborators were Jewish and he made his disgust at anti-Semitism abundantly clear on several occasions. If he saw anti-Semitism as only one of the many disturbing elements of life under the Nazi regime, he was simply reflecting the realities of the time.

All the same, it must be accepted that Brecht failed to grasp the blind hatred that drove the Nazis and their supporters, and nowhere does his work describe the murderous brutality of the regime at its worst. He was preoccupied with articulating and supporting the opposition to Fascism and Hitler's exploitation of a mystical, almost atavistic sense of German nationalism was beyond his historical frame of reference.

From his early days, Brecht was mesmerised by the energy and exuberance of high capitalism, even as he criticised its cruelty and destructive power, and his six years in America allowed him to observe its mechanisms at close quarters. He did not thrive in Hollywood, however, where it seemed that artists needed to prostitute their talents to survive; instead, he used his time there to articulate German opposition to Hitler and plan his return.

*

Brecht's attitude towards East Germany was complex. As an established champion of the Left and one of Germany's most successful writers, he felt that the DDR deserved his support. The East German regime encouraged him in this view by giving him his favourite theatre in Berlin as the base for his well-funded Berliner Ensemble. His public involvement in politics tended to be limited to questions about culture, but in private he became increasingly critical of the state. These tensions reached a crisis point in the days following the suppression of the workers' demonstration in East Berlin on 17 June 1953, which Brecht said 'alienated the whole of [his] existence'. He publicly expressed his 'solidarity' with the regime, while satirically wondering in an unpublished poem whether, it would be easier 'for the government / To dissolve the people / And elect another'. As a result, in his last years, Brecht withdrew into an increasingly isolated position, going through the motions required of a leading figure in East Germany, while concerning himself above all with questions of artistic form.

The position of the West European Communists following the Second World War was difficult. They tended to emphasise – rightly – the enormous extent of the Soviet Union's contribution to the defeat of Fascism, while ignoring the annexation of Eastern Europe that Stalin regarded as his prize. Many felt that only the Soviet Union could prevent the re-emergence of Fascism and put the possibility of another European war firmly in the past. It was 1956, the year of Brecht's death, in which Khrushchev denounced Stalin's crimes at the Twentieth Party Congress and Soviet troops were used to put down a popular uprising in Hungary, that led many European Communists to leave the party for good.

Economics

The First World War unleashed economic forces that were new in kind and in extent. By 1923 the German economy was crippled by soaring unemployment and runaway inflation, only temporarily relieved by Chancellor Stresemann's financial reforms of 1924. However, the American stock market crash of October 1929, and the Great Depression which followed, hit Germany particularly badly. This posed a direct challenge to Communists, who had long argued that the 'world revolution' would begin once capitalism had collapsed under the weight of its own contradictions; they now had to work out whether the hardship caused by the depression was a price worth paying for the radicalisation of the poor that would surely follow in its wake.

The rebirth of the German economy under Hitler was seen by many Communists as conclusive evidence that Fascism was merely capitalism by another name, and the large profits made by leading industrialists showed that the word 'socialism' in National Socialism was a lie. The war between Germany and the capitalist West was sometimes dismissed as a struggle for economic advantage between national economies, and the profound philosophical and moral differences were glossed over. However, the sight of capitalism (above all the United States) profiting from the ravages of the Second World War posed a new kind of challenge to the Communist prophets of doom.

Socialists have always argued that writing which fails to grasp the centrality of the 'cash nexus' cannot be regarded as realistic. As early as 1922, Brecht expressed frustration with his own ignorance of economic affairs. His reading of Karl Marx gave him the key concepts – 'base', 'superstructure', 'means of production', 'exploitation of labour' and so on – that he needed and, thus armed, he set out to write a new kind of drama that could explain capitalism's mysterious workings and suggest a strategy for its overthrow.

The results were mixed. Brecht failed to dramatise the market economy in terms that were readily comprehensible or useful, and the best passages in *Saint Joan of the Stockyards* – his most direct attempt to do so – are those concerned with individual responses to the market, not an attempt at dramatising its impersonal forces. To be fair, drama is not good at the abstract and the theoretical, and Brecht's lack of success is unsurprising. He did, however, manage to incorporate financial realities into his portraits of everyday life, often quite brilliantly – the arms dealer in *Drums in the Night*, the SA Man in The Chalk Cross (from *Fear and Misery of the Third Reich*) and the poor fisherman's widow in *Señora Carrar's Rifles* are just a few examples. The impact of economics on the individual becomes particularly sophisticated in his mature work, which shows characters caught by the restraints of economic determinants: Mother Courage and Shen Teh, Galileo and Matti are all shaped and distorted by their financial circumstances, and their stories cannot be understood without reference to their financial situation.

A New Morality

Brecht was deeply sceptical of received notions about how human beings should behave towards each other and regarded bourgeois morality with disdain. He knew that talk about morality often papered over a lack of interest in the living conditions of the poor and one of his most telling mottoes, from *The Threepenny Opera*, is 'Food first, morals later'.

Brecht's plays describe the world from the point of view of those at the bottom. The results are often startling, above all for the lack of heroism or idealism: Baal, Galy Gay, Mother Courage, Schweyk, Shen Teh and Grusha are all intent on their own survival, oblivious to higher abstractions. Brecht's purpose was to show that his characters are scarred by the distortions imposed on them. He hoped that by doing so, his audience would draw its own conclusions about the new kind of morality which needed to be constructed.

Brecht rejected the Social Democrat, 'gradualist' approach to improving the conditions of the working class, preferring the Leninist claim to 'the whole cake, not just a larger slice'. He was sceptical about the value of charity and philanthropy (see *Saint Joan of the Stockyards*), which he regarded as ways of alleviating the symptoms of poverty – and salving the consciences of the ruling class – without confronting the root causes. He was also convinced that the poor could never receive justice under capitalism unless, as he argued in *The Caucasian Chalk Circle*, the system of justice is itself corrupt.

Perhaps the most contentious area of Brecht's morality was his acceptance of violence as necessary to the transformation of society. This reflected the standard Leninist view that some changes are so urgent that only armed revolution can bring them about. Some say that Brecht goes a step further and glorifies violence; others suggest that he is simply being realistic about the way the world works. However, history has not been kind to Brecht and the terrible crimes and cruelties enacted in the hope of a better world cast a dark shadow over even his finest achievements.

Brecht's moral vision can be bewildering. After all, surely the women in *The Mother* who bring Vlassova hot soup to comfort her after the death of her son are doing a good deed? Similarly, surely Kattrin in *Mother Courage* banging the drum to warn the town of Halle of its imminent destruction is an act of extraordinary heroism? Brecht's argument, however, is that all such actions should be seen in relation to their context – even the sacrifice of the Young Comrade in *The Decision* needs to be judged relative to the cause for which he is fighting – and the construction of a new moral code must start from reality, not abstract principles. The effect is startling and challenging, and is, Brecht would argue, the precondition for a better world.

At the heart of Brecht's morality was a simple and unflinching commitment to the cause of the ordinary man: how could peasants, workers and the unemployed survive and improve their lot in a world controlled by the rich and powerful, preoccupied with lining their pockets and extending their power? He argued that their situation could only change if the world changed, and his shifting contradictory political views reflect his commitment to that demand. Brecht can be criticised on many counts; but in thinking about his politics and morality it is well to remember the words of one of his greatest poems, 'To Those Born Later' (1938–9):

> You who will emerge from the flood
> In which we have gone under
> Remember
> When you speak of our failings
> The dark time too
> Which you have escaped.

4 ART AND CULTURE

The upheavals of the first half of the twentieth century drove German artists and intellectuals into a profound re-examination of the fundamental values of art itself. Brecht was one of the key figures in this process, and his views on art and society are an essential accompaniment to the plays themselves. A discussion of these views must start with some definitions.

Naturalism

The term 'Naturalism' is best used to describe the late nineteenth-century artistic movement which insisted that the ordinary things of life – money, railway stations, alcohol, divorce and so on – were worthy subjects for art, and that novels, paintings and plays could analyse and describe the world with the same degree of objectivity as that being achieved by science. The Naturalists, led by the novelists Balzac and Zola and the playwrights Ibsen and Chekhov, argued that behaviour was the product of environment and regarded the surface of the world as the key to understanding its complexities. Naturalism was an extraordinary revolution with enduring consequences and Brecht's work would have been impossible without its pioneering achievements. His reaction against it needs to be seen as a rejection of its subject – bourgeois life – more than as an abstract disapproval of its artistic form.

Expressionism

'Expressionism' describes the artistic movement that swept across Germany and northern Europe in the first years of the twentieth century, largely in reaction against Naturalism. Its leading figures abandoned any pretence at objectivity and attempted to express their dreams and visions, their fears and desires, with as much intensity and power as possible. Expressionism was the dominant artistic form in the Germany of Brecht's youth and he could not escape its influence. However, it is possible to argue that Brecht's early plays – before the watershed of *Man equals Man* (1924) – are nothing less than a working out of the young artist's complex relationship with its pervasive power. Above all, he challenged the Expressionists' solipsistic self-indulgence and their tendency to exalt the mythological above the concrete, the abstract above the factual and the individual above the social.

Realism

'Realism' is the most useful term in any discussion of Brecht's aesthetics. Realism needs to be distinguished from Naturalism in that it is an attitude to the world, rather than an artistic style. Brecht's own definition is this:

> On the question of Realism: the usual view is that the more easily reality can be recognised in a work of art, the more realistic it is. Against this I would like to set up the equation that the more recognisably reality is mastered in the work of art, the more realistic it is.

Thus Brecht's Realism poses uncomfortable questions about the material basis of life ('Who built the Great Wall of China?' asks one of his finest poems) and is sceptical about the motives of those in power. It refuses to accept the hypocritical moralising of the middle classes and recognises that survival is the most important motivation for the poor and wretched. Furthermore, Brecht's Realism is morally relative and acknowledges that the ends sometimes justify the means and that, as Mother Courage says, 'a short anger changes nothing but a long anger can change the world'. It also recognises that the processes of history are contradictory, but that the future is still up for grabs. Most controversially, Brecht defined Realism as a kind of art that told stories from the perspective of the revolutionary working class.

Socialist Realism

Brecht's aim of creating a new kind of revolutionary socialist art, in tune with working-class experiences and rooted in the material facts of everyday life, should be distinguished from the artistic movement – or rather, propaganda – that emerged in the Soviet Union in the 1930s, the officially sanctioned 'Socialist Realism'. Whereas Brecht's work is full of contradiction, challenges pre-conceived opinions and is resolutely unsentimental, Socialist Realism reduces everything to the simplest terms (peasants and workers are good, everybody else is bad – except for the leader and the party) and numbs the viewer with its banalities. Brecht was aware of this orthodoxy and struggled – especially after his return to Stalinist East Germany – to free himself of its restrictive embrace.

Modernism

The most important international artistic movement of Brecht's youth was Modernism – that extraordinary flowering of challenging work that appeared across Europe in the first quarter of the twentieth century, exemplified above all by the paintings of Pablo Picasso, the poetry of T. S. Eliot and the novels of James Joyce. Brecht's relationship to Modernism was complicated.

Driven by the desire to create a new, socially useful kind of drama, he dismissed its literary self-consciousness. At the same time he opposed narrow definitions of artistic form and rejected the view that only the nineteenth-century 'realist' novels could provide a model for progressive working-class art. With his unique combination of committed political content and radical popular form, Brecht occupies a strange position in the Modernist hall of fame.

Amerikanismus

One of the most surprising phenomena to emerge from the German defeat in the First World War was *Amerikanismus*, a fascination with all things American. This was largely a reaction to the repressive nature of Wilhelmine Prussia, held responsible for the disaster of the First World War. It was also driven by a genuine interest in a culture which appeared young, dynamic and forward-thinking. *Amerikanismus* permeated almost every aspect of the arts, and an interest in the 'new world'.

Brecht's fascination with the 'heroic' phase of American capitalism is both ironic and self-evident. Although America represented everything that as a socialist he despised, it gave him a milieu in which to locate his tales of individual struggle unencumbered by the niceties of European bourgeois society, and some of his most robust plays take place in fantastical American settings: *In the Jungle of the Cities*, *Saint Joan of the Stockyards* and *The Resistible Rise of Arturo Ui* are all set in a mythical Chicago, while his only full-length opera, *The Rise and Fall of the City of Mahagonny*, is set in a Las Vegas-type, Wild West free-for-all. However, Brecht's love affair with America could not survive actually living there, and with the notable exception of his bitterly satirical song cycle *The Hollywood Elegies* (1942), all of his work written after arriving in California is set elsewhere.

The New Objectivity

One of the strongest influences on Brecht's aesthetics was his identification in the 1920s with the 'New Objectivity' (*Neue Sachlichkeit*). This international movement was driven by a reaction against the excesses of Expressionism and celebrated instead the crisp, clear lines of modernity. Inspired by America, it developed its own distinct European identity, and flowered in Weimar Germany, above all in the work of the Bauhaus School of Architecture and Design, in the radical productions at the Kroll Opera in Berlin, in Paul Hindemith's festivals of new music, and in the photo-collages and fine art of John Heartfield and others. With the increasing politicisation of Weimar culture, the New Objectivity became identified with the left-wing reaction to Fascism's appeal to the irrational, and provided the theoretical and aesthetic foundation of the entire post-war movement in design. The best book on the movement is John Willett's *The New Sobriety* (1978).

From the late 1920s – especially after reading Karl Marx and writing *Man equals Man* – this striving for objectivity became central and Brecht increasingly sought ways of encouraging in the audience an attitude of critical distance towards what is being presented. This is the fundamental aim of the alienation effect and the central formal achievement of the *Lehrstücke*. The explicit use of contradiction and dialectic in his greatest plays derives from the same pursuit.

Brecht's notion of objectivity needs to be distinguished from the Olympian objectivity of Goethe and the high classical tradition: Brecht is not sitting above the fray, musing over the paradoxes of life, like a philosopher in his ivory tower; instead, his insistence on objectivity is inextricably allied to his commitment to creating a better world and the one is meaningless without the other.

Existentialism

Perhaps the most significant philosophical response to the catastrophe of the Second World War and the growing disillusionment with Communism was Existentialism. This held that all human effort was in vain and that the meaning of life lay in the bare facts of existence. The key figures were ex-Marxists such as Jean-Paul Sartre, Albert Camus and Simone de Beauvoir, as well as playwrights such as Eugene Ionesco and Samuel Beckett (later dubbed 'absurdists').

Brecht tended to regard this movement with some disdain, preferring a more constructive, rational approach to the turmoils of society. Critics have sometimes drawn connections between Brecht's theatre and that of the Existentialists, based only on superficial aesthetic similarities. His late poems do, however, betray a private disillusionment with state Communism and, occasionally, touch the despair that was the basis for existential thinking. It is tantalising that among the papers found on Brecht's desk after his death was an edition of Samuel Beckett's *Waiting for Godot* with Brecht's inconclusive pencil jottings in the margins.

The Charge of Formalism

In the 1930s, Brecht found himself engaged in a fascinating argument about left-wing aesthetics and the issues raised are still debated today. In essence, the great Marxist critic Georg Lukács accused Brecht of artistic formalism, a decadence which was more interested in artistic innovation than in reaching out to a popular, working class audience. In many ways this was nothing less than orthodox Marxism's critique of the perplexing nature of Modernism.

This led to a lively – and sometimes bad-tempered – discussion in which Brecht defended himself robustly. He declared that the working class, the engine of the revolution, had least to lose in abandoning the old ways and was uniquely suited to appreciate radical art. More important, he turned the charge of formalism against his accusers, arguing that the artistic forms he was exploring were dictated by the new content and not the other way round, and it was those who laid down blueprints about artistic form who were the real formalists. This is a debate in which Brecht's position feels the more amenable to a modern, liberal sensibility.

As time goes by, however, the terms of this debate look increasingly complex. First, it is unfair to caricature Lukács, as some have, as a Stalinist apparatchik, keen on the banal art produced by the dead hand of Socialist Realism; in fact, he was championing the great nineteenth-century novelists – Tolstoy, Balzac, Dickens and so on – whose enduring popularity across all classes has outshone Brecht's. Second, although Brecht's work is accessible in comparison with the difficult masterpieces of high Modernism, there is something self-serving about Brecht's confident declaration that his *Lehrstücke* were written for the 'workers'; they were in fact designed for working-class revolutionaries and left-wing intellectuals at a moment of political crisis.

5 TOWARDS A MARXIST THEATRE

Throughout his life, Brecht was involved in developing a new kind of theatre, which could reflect the modern world and speak to contemporary audiences. As a Marxist, he was concerned that the theatre should not simply, as Hamlet says, 'hold a mirror up to nature', but should expose the workings of the world and provide an indication of how they could be changed. By drawing on – and reacting against – a wide range of both classical and contemporary models, Brecht created a new kind of Marxist theatre, classical in its ambition but resolutely modern in its form and content.

Shakespeare

Brecht admired Shakespeare more than any other dramatist, above all because of the way he dramatised the great changes of fifteenth- and sixteenth-century England – from the feudal to the modern, the medieval to the Renaissance, and the monarchical to the republican – in plays that are theatrically gripping, rich with human detail and politically coherent. It was the directness and fluidity of Shakespeare's theatre, which moves from place to place and across classes and worlds without let or hindrance, that appealed to Brecht most; indeed, some would say that everything that is meant by Brecht's theatrical practice is evident in Shakespeare, and that his greatest achievement was adapting Shakespeare's dramaturgy for the modern world.

Despite describing Shakespeare's plays as 'drama for cannibals' (because of their unblinking violence), Brecht admired their tough materialism and anti-sentimental realism, and adapted them for his own purposes. He cheerfully admitted to stealing from Shakespeare, and was happy to adapt and rewrite him for his own purposes (even declaring that Shakespeare wrote for 'a theatre full of alienation effects'!). It is telling, however, that right at the end of his life he admitted that it would be possible to stage *Coriolanus* as it is, 'relying solely on good direction'.

Working-Class Art

Brecht felt that the sympathetic presentation of the urban working class was essential to a new kind of socialist art. Of course, he was not the first dramatist to do so: Shakespeare himself wrote about the 'poor naked wretches' (*King Lear*), as did a number of important German dramatists such as Heinrich von Kleist, Georg Büchner and Gerhart Hauptmann. Brecht was also inspired by more contemporary writers such as J. M. Synge, Sean O'Casey and Maxim Gorky, whose plays depict working-class characters with great humanity.

Brecht's aim was particular, however: he wanted, above all, to show the working class at a moment when there was an opportunity for them to better their position. He was not interested in presenting the poor just as poor, and when he did show a poor person blind to the possibility of change, he wanted to show it negatively. Again, it is important to remember that Brecht believed in the Marxist notion of class struggle: that the working class was involved in a continuous conflict with the property-owning classes, and the dramatisation of this lies at the heart of all his work.

It must be emphasised that Brecht's view of the working class was very different from the banal hero-worship which was such a feature of Socialist Realism. His work is free of such propagandist simplifications, and where he did present explicitly left-wing workers (as in *The Mother*, *Fear and Misery of the Third Reich* and *Señora Carrar's Rifles*) it was usually to distinguish them from those members of the same class – soldiers, policeman or reactionaries – who confronted them. It was the divisions in the working class that interested Brecht, not their solidarity, even as he argued that only unity could help them improve their lot.

Folk Art

Like many Marxists, Brecht had a complex attitude towards the peasantry. He recognised that they had an important role to play in creating a new society and believed – with Lenin – that only an alliance of the proletariat and the peasantry could spark a revolution that could withstand the forces of reaction; however, he was realistic, even pessimistic, about their conservative tendencies. Furthermore, while Brecht knew that a socialist theatre would need to draw on the motifs and techniques of folk art, he accepted that he was in competition with totalitarian regimes – both Fascist and Communist – who had promoted the idea of 'the people' (*das Volk*) and praised folk art accordingly. His essay, 'Notes on the Folk Play' (1940), draws some of these ideas together.

Brecht's view of the peasantry developed: in *The Mother* they are slow to recognise the value of the proletariat in their struggle with the landowners, but are persuaded of it eventually; in *Señora Carrar's Rifles* a peasant woman's instinctive caution is challenged and changed by her experiences; in *Mother Courage* and *The Caucasian Chalk Circle* they are capable of narrow-minded short-termism and envious brutality, but play an essential role in resolving the injustices of the world. As Brecht's work matured, he came to portray them with greater complexity: indeed, in his notes to *Mother Courage* he wrote that an actor playing a peasant should play an individual peasant and that urban audiences will only understand the class of the peasantry when they see what connects the very different people that make up that class.

Brecht drew on the forms of folk art cautiously, but successfully, above all in *Mr Puntila and his Man Matti*, with its Scandinavian legends, earthy peasant jokes and rural atmosphere, and *The Caucasian Chalk Circle*, with its panoramic portrait of south Russian peasant society. He also borrowed from sophisticated assimilations of folk art, such as Grimmelshausen's *Simplicissimus* (1668) for *Mother Courage* and J. M. Synge's *Riders to the Sea* (1904) for *Señora Carrar's Rifles*.

The Oriental Theatre

The young Brecht was fascinated by the Orient. This is evident in his inclusion of a Malay character in *In the Jungle of the Cities* and the Sacristan Wang in *Man equals Man*. It was deepened when, in the late 1920s, Elisabeth Hauptmann introduced him to Arthur Waley's (1889–1966) English versions of ancient Chinese and Japanese plays (some of which she then translated into German). Brecht was struck by their economy of means and their lack of interest in illusion: like the Elizabethan theatre, he realised, the oriental theatre is utterly frank about practical realities and presumes on the audience's imaginative cooperation throughout.

The influence of the oriental theatre can be most keenly felt in the *Lehrstücke*, many of which – *The Decision*, *The Exception and the Rule*, *He Who Says Yes* and *He Who Says No* – have oriental settings. It is also evident in Brecht's mature plays – for example, *The Good Person of Szechwan*, *The Caucasian Chalk Circle* and *Turandot* – and in his last years Brecht was drawn to the ancient Chinese philosophy of Lao-tzu, as well as the contemporary teachings of the Chinese Communist leader Mao Tse-tung.

This fascination with Chinese culture must be distinguished from the orientalism evident in more recent assimilations of Asiatic theatre, such as the work of Peter Brook or Ariane

Mnouchkine. Indeed, in his notes to *The Good Person of Szechwan*, Brecht expressed his anxiety about 'chinoiserie', a form of cultural imperialism which he despised. His aim was something quite distinct: a dramatic style of clarity, delicacy and elegance, which provokes the audience into comment on what it is being shown, and dissects the world even as it presents it.

Anti-Aristotelian Theatre

Brecht's essays often speak dismissively of the 'Aristotelian drama', a reference to *The Poetics*, in which the Greek philosopher attempted to describe the function and form of art. Brecht read Aristotle selectively, however, distrusting 'empathy' and the 'classical unities', while ignoring Aristotle's emphasis on the importance of 'story' and 'thought'.

It should be pointed out that Aristotle's 'unities' – the whole play should take place in one place, with a consistent dramatis personae and over the course of one day – have been more influential in European classical theatre (particularly French and German drama) than in Britain, where Shakespeare's informal attitude to time, place and action has predominated. Furthermore, although Brecht described his own theatrical practice as 'anti-Aristotelian', it would have been more accurate if he had spoken about creating the antithesis to 'the well-made play', a common description of a kind of bourgeois nineteenth-century drama he despised. In brief, Brecht's critique of Aristotle should be taken with a pinch of salt.

The Reaction Against Stanislavski

The work of the Russian theatre director Konstantin Stanislavski (1863–1938) is often seen as antithetical to everything Brecht stood for: psychological, empathetic, bourgeois and so on. Certainly,

Brecht's early work consciously rejects Stanislavski and his later plays deliberately eschew fixed notions of character, place and action.

However, not only did Brecht come to recognise the fundamental strengths of what Stanislavski achieved at the Moscow Art Theatre (see, for example, his notes on 'Some of the Things that can be Learnt from Stanislavski', 1952), but his mature work draws on many of the key elements in Stanislavski's approach to acting – class, age, environment, objective, obstacle and so on. The fact is that Brecht had little objection to naturalism as such, but he wanted the subject of that naturalism to be seen as subject to the possibility of change.

Intriguingly, as is evident from a letter in 1936, Brecht worked for a few days with Lee Strasberg, the father of the American 'method' school of acting, on Brecht's most explicitly didactic and anti-illusionist piece, *The Decision*. It is a shame that no other record of this collaboration exists. It certainly suggests that the differences between Brecht, Stanislavski and Lee Strasberg have been exaggerated.

Laughter and Learning

In 'A Short Organum for the Theatre' (1948), Brecht declared:

> Let us therefore cause general dismay by revoking our decision to emigrate from the realm of the merely enjoyable, and even more general dismay by announcing our decision to take up lodging there.

Of course, the 'merely enjoyable' has a serious role to play and Brecht's notion of entertainment carries within it its own pedagogical value; in his view, nothing opens the mind as readily as laughter and only a relaxed spectator is capable of thinking about the familiar in new ways. Brecht was reacting against German culture's tendency for high seriousness and he realised that solemnity is antithetical to rational thought.

Laughter and pleasure are fundamental to many of Brecht's characters: sometimes – as in the high jinks in *Man equals Man* or the black comedy of *Arturo Ui* – their commitment to fun is deliberately forced and their 'jolliness' is a cover for something more sinister; at other times, as in *The Threepenny Opera* or *The Rise and Fall of the City of Mahagonny*, the relentless pursuit of pleasure is presented as part of the non-stop moneymaking machine of capitalism, while Brecht's embrace of his characters' gargantuan appetites casts its own ironical shadow.

Brecht used laughter as a weapon against the self-important strutting of those in power and his plays are full of portraits of their absurdity: the Merchant in *The Decision*, the Gods in *The Good Person of Szechwan*, the Very Old General in *Mother Courage* and so on. He used the same technique in his approach to Hitler: he pasted into his *Journals* a sequence of photographs of Hitler, having been told about the fall of Paris, dancing like a hyperactive child; Charlie Chaplin's film *The Great Dictator* (1940) satirised the same tendency, and a demystification of the dictator that reveals his essential buffoonery lies at the heart of *Arturo Ui*.

As he matured, Brecht's emphasis on fun was slowly replaced by the notion of 'cheerfulness'. In formulating this, he contrasted the relaxed, practical approach of the craftsman with the tension and effort of the ruler. Cheerfulness, he argued, encourages a pragmatic approach to problem solving: rational and forward-looking, effective and to the point. This is evident in Vlassova's attitude to her son in prison in *The Mother*, in the first scene of *Life of Galileo*, in Matti's growing distance from his master and in the resolution reached in the first scene of *The Caucasian Chalk Circle*. Shen Teh in *The Good Person of Szechwan* summarises this brilliantly:

> There are still friendly people, for all our wretchedness. When I
> was little once I was carrying a bundle of sticks and fell. An old man
> helped me up and even gave me a penny. I have often thought of it.
> Those who have least to eat give most gladly. I suppose people just
> like showing what they're good at; and how can they do it better

than by being friendly? Crossness is just a way of being inefficient. Whenever someone is singing a song or building a machine or planting rice it is really friendliness.

Of course, this friendliness needs to be distinguished from the smiling peasants and cheerful workers of totalitarian propaganda, all happy to be pulling in the same direction for the good of the country – and its dictator. On occasions, such as the Prologue to *The Caucasian Chalk Circle*, Brecht does not entirely avoid this cliché; at its best, however, this friendliness is seen as the most useful characteristic of shared problem solving.

The Emphasis on Sport

One of the features of the New Objectivity was an interest in sport. Large-scale sporting events seemed to encapsulate American modernity: they attracted huge numbers of working-class spectators, featured athletes chosen for their skill and strength, not background or social standing, and celebrated youthful energy and physical prowess.

Sport inspired Brecht in two ways. He enjoyed how it showed the clash between competing forces, working within certain clearly defined rules, but driven by energy and skill. He was also intrigued by the way spectators watch sport: with interest and detachment, not just enjoying the excitement of the outcome, but appraising the skill that the sportsmen use to achieve their aims. Brecht wanted to encourage his audiences to watch the theatre in the same way.

In the 1920s, this gave Brecht a model for a new kind of theatre. The Prologue to *In the Jungle of the Cities* sets the scene:

You are about to witness an inexplicable wrestling match between two men and observe the downfall of a family that has moved from the prairies to the jungle of the big city. Don't worry your heads about the motives for the fight, concentrate on the stakes. Judge impartially the technique of the contenders, and keep your eyes fixed on the finish.

Then, in the mid 1920s, he struck up a friendship with the German heavyweight boxer, Paul Samson Korner, and helped him write his memoirs (there is a fine photo of the two together, the epitome of Brecht's anti-romantic view of literary activity); Galy Gay in *Man equals Man* was given his nickname – 'The Human Fighting-Machine' – and the soldiers in Brecht's 1931 production walked around athletically on stilts. In 1926, in 'The Emphasis on Sport', Brecht declared, 'we pin our hopes to the sporting public.' Caspar Neher's sets for *The Little Mahagonny* used a boxing ring as its central metaphor and the same emphasis can be detected in the *Lehrstücke* too.

If Brecht's own interest in sport started to wane in the 1940s, it was evident in the work of his disciples, and Manfred Wekwerth and Peter Palitzsch's great production of *Arturo Ui* in 1959 was an astonishingly athletic event.

A Smokers' Theatre

Brecht loved cheap cigars and photos show him wreathed in blue tobacco smoke (tobacco was surely one of the causes of his early death). Cigars, these photos seem to imply, allow the proletarian writer to taste the exclusive luxuries of the capitalist. Brecht joked that cigars were 'part of my means of production' and even smoked them throughout the HUAC hearings – which surely befuddled his interrogators as much as his evasive answers. The soldiers in *Man equals Man* bribe Galy Gay with cigars and the promise of a better way of living that they offer. It could even be argued that Brecht's plays are like these cigars: pungent, provocative and antisocial, but also elegant, stimulating and intensely pleasurable.

In the early 1920s Brecht developed the notion of a 'smokers' theatre' and, in one of his more extravagant statements, declared:

> I even think that in a Shakespearean production one man in the
> stalls could bring about the downfall of Western art. He might as
> well light a bomb as light his cigar. I would be delighted to see our
> public allowed to smoke during performances. And I'd be delighted
> mainly for the actors' sake. In my view it is quite impossible for the
> actor to play unnatural, cramped and old-fashioned theatre to a
> man smoking in the stalls.

It is difficult to imagine this being possible in the modern theatre,
but it does give a strong indication of Brecht's desired relationship
between the audience and the stage: the spectator watches the
action with all the objectivity, scepticism and analytical skill of a
cigar-smoking chess player considering his opponent's latest move.

The Learning Play

In the late 1920s and early 1930s Brecht developed a kind of drama
that he called the *Lehrstück*, or learning play. Drawing on the
oriental theatre, but also European models such as Bach chorales,
German romantic drama and popular culture, these elegant, small-
scale pieces use music, direct narrative and simple dramatic action
to convey a powerful point. They are much more sophisticated
than the Soviet 'agit-prop' plays of the early 1920s and are nothing
less than an attempt to create a new kind of pedagogical, liturgical
drama, aimed as much at the participants (often workers' choirs
and other amateur groups) as at the audiences. Although the
mature Brecht moved beyond the limitations of the *Lehrstücke*,
their economy of means, radical content and formal daring had a
big impact on his subsequent work, and their legacy can be seen in
his greatest masterpieces. In his last years he even referred to them
as the model for the theatre of the future.

The eight *Lehrstücke* are *Lingbergh's Flight* (1928–9), *The Baden-
Baden Lesson on Consent* (1929), *He Who Says Yes, He Who Says No,*

The Exception and the Rule (all 1930) and *The Horatians and the Curatians* (1934), as well as two of his greatest works, *The Decision* (1930) and *The Mother* (1930–1). They feature music by all four of Brecht's composers: Kurt Weill, Paul Dessau, Hanns Eisler and Paul Hindemith.

Plays for the Decade

The standard defence of great art is that it expresses and illuminates certain 'eternal truths' about mankind and allows us to come to a deeper understanding of what it means to be human. Artists who have subscribed to this view have been concerned to create works of art which speak to all people at all times, regardless of background, culture, religion or class.

Marxists tend to dismiss such claims and contend that notions of 'universality' merely render all experience the same and negate the possibility of change. Brecht argued that his plays – particularly those with the most direct political engagement – should be seen as products of their time, only relevant in particular circumstances: it was 'plays for the decade' that were needed, he said, not attempts at immortality. It was even imagined that, as a result, they might have broad appeal:

> People are always telling us that we mustn't simply produce what the public demands. But I believe that an artist, even if he sits in strictest seclusion in the traditional garret working for future generations, is unlikely to produce anything without some wind in his sails. And this wind has to be the wind prevailing in his own period.

Brecht's point is that only the writer involved in the world can help to change it; one might add, ironically, that only then does his work stand a chance of speaking to future generations as well.

This emphasis on the useful and the relevant – even when conveyed through a parable, or glimpsed as part of history – runs through all of Brecht's work. It was in this spirit that he wrote a new Prologue for *Señora Carrar's Rifles* following the Republic's defeat in the Spanish Civil War, created an introduction set in the ruins of defeated Berlin for his version of *Antigone* and set the first scene of *The Caucasian Chalk Circle* in the contemporary Soviet Union. These innovations contextualise the story as an action with a specific use; similar innovations should perhaps be applied by other writers to Brecht's plays today.

Playing Things Historically

Brecht knew that it was impossible to create a new kind of drama suitable for the modern world without a profound feeling for history and an understanding of his work requires a grasp not only of the times in which he lived, but also of his own reading of the past. This had at its heart Hegel's theory of the dialectical processes of history, in which conflict between classes leads inexorably, and often bloodily, to a better society. This does not preclude the tragic but, like classical tragedy, places individual experience within a broader context. Personal suffering (the deaths of Pavel in *The Mother*, the Young Comrade in *The Decision* or Kattrin in *Mother Courage*) does not prevent – indeed, it sometimes contributes to – a wider good.

Such an emphasis on history means that notions of 'eternal truth' and 'human nature' should be replaced by an analysis of behaviour which is specific to environment and changes according to the context in which it appears. Thus a discussion about character that does not take into account the historical forces which have shaped it cannot be convincing, and the telling of a story which does not include the conditions under which it takes place cannot be revealing. Brecht spoke about 'playing things historically' and one of the most important objectives of the Brechtian theatre is to show how the actions and arguments of the individual are created by the circumstances that surround him.

As part of his analysis of historical process and change, Brecht was particularly interested in discovering those places in the drama – the 'useful junction points', as he called them – where the clash between periods and belief systems is most evident, such as the feudal and the Renaissance in *Life of Galileo* or the bourgeois and the revolutionary in *The Mother*. Of course, such analysis runs the danger of simplification, but highlighting these moments encourages the audience to see the drama historically, and helps them place individual actions within a broader context, as part of a continuous process of change.

A Theatre for the Scientific Age

A central part of Communism's appeal was its commitment to scientific rationalism as a way of cutting through the mysticism inherent not just in organised religion, but in the existing social order. It is not surprising, therefore, that Brecht was keen to create a 'theatre for the scientific age'.

The left-wing director Erwin Piscator had attempted something similar at the Volksbühne in Berlin, with large-scale productions using a range of modern technology: projectors, treadmills, revolving stages and so on. His successes included Ernst Toller's *Hoppla, We're Alive!* (1927) and a dramatisation of *The Good Soldier Švejk* (1928). His aim was to present an image of modern man swamped by the machines of the modern world.

Brecht's view was different. It was not dependent on machinery, and he tried to show the complexities of the scientific age with the simplest of means. More important, with the notable exception of *Saint Joan of the Stockyards*, he was not interested in portraying the alienation caused by technology, nor in celebrating the advancement of science for its own sake. Instead, he wanted his audience to learn the great lesson of science – the scientific method – and encouraged an approach to social problems that was practical, rational and free of assumptions – like Galileo asking the professors to look through the telescope and make up their own minds, or Azdak awarding the child to the woman who is most evidently capable of caring for him.

Brecht's attitude to science became increasingly political and latterly he became interested in discovering who would benefit from its achievements: the rich and the powerful, or the poor and the oppressed. Galileo's great speech of warning, written after the dropping of the atomic bomb, gives a strong sense of Brecht's own concerns:

> You may in due course discover all there is to discover, and your progress will nonetheless be nothing but a progress away from mankind. The gap between you and it may one day become so wide that your cry of triumph at some new achievement will be echoed by a universal cry of horror.

It is not surprising that in his last years Brecht was contemplating a play about Albert Einstein.

Complex Seeing

As his political analysis matured, Brecht became increasingly interested in encouraging what he called 'complex seeing'. By this he meant something more dynamic than despair at the myriad contradictions of the world; instead, he wanted to make these contradictions visible and show the causal link between wealth and poverty, money and power, and expose the different sides of the argument in such a way as to encourage debate.

Thus, in *The Caucasian Chalk Circle*, Brecht was keen to show that his working-class heroine Grusha was a 'sucker' in following her 'natural' maternal instincts; she would have been much better off if she had ignored the abandoned Michael. Similarly, he wanted to make plain that Azdak is not a canny peasant judge with sympathies for his own class – instead, he is deeply corrupt. Furthermore, Brecht argued, it is only in conditions of such corruption that the working class stand any chance of being given real justice. These observations are counter-intuitive and go beyond notions of 'common sense' or 'nature': Brecht's theatre, with its commitment to objectivity, tries to help audiences understand their society in such a way that they might want to try to change it, and 'complex seeing' is the precondition for any such change.

6 KEY CONCEPTS OF BRECHT'S THEATRICAL THEORY

Brecht's theatrical theory presents the reader and practitioner with a series of terms which can be bewildering. In approaching them, it is important to remember not only how deliberately provocative Brecht could be, but also the German tradition of aesthetic theory, with its tendency for the abstract and the intellectual.

Brecht's most important theoretical works are 'The Messingkauf Dialogues' (1940) and 'A Short Organum for the Theatre' (1948). Other essays are to be found in John Willett's collection *Brecht on Theatre* (1957), Marc Silberman's *Brecht on Film and Television* (2000) and Tom Kuhn and Steve Giles's *Brecht on Art and Politics* (2004).

The Alienation Effect

From the outset, Brecht tried to create a kind of theatre which would encourage the audience to look at what was being presented in such a way that they would draw conclusions about the society in which they lived. In 1940 he wrote,

> So the question is this: is it quite impossible to make the reproduction of real-life events the purpose of art and thereby make something conducive of the spectators' critical attitude toward them?

The result was the 'alienation effect' (*Verfremdungseffekt*, sometimes translated as 'estrangement'), one of the most misunderstood terms in the Brechtian vocabulary.

Essentially, the alienation effect is achieved when the audience is encouraged to re-examine its preconceptions and to look at the familiar in a new way, with an interest in how it can and should be changed. This requires the actor both to inhabit his character and remember that he is showing it to the audience. The danger with identification, Brecht argued, was that it prevented the actor from commenting on his character and stops his performance from having an active purpose. It also prevents the audience from looking at the action with any degree of critical distance. Crucially, Brecht wanted his actors to be clear about what each scene – and each moment in each scene – was trying to show and made the understanding of the play's intentions fundamental to the performance.

To this end Brecht asked his actors to tell their story with as much objectivity as possible. Just as witnesses of a car crash or a murder or a football match might describe what they saw, drawing attention to the decisive moments, asking the listeners to look at what happened from a variety of perspectives, helping them come to their own judgements, so in rehearsal Brecht encouraged his actors to present their stories in the third person, prefacing each speech with 'he said . . . she said . . .'. At other times he asked them to draw attention to particularly important moments in their story, adding 'instead of responding like this, he responded like that'. These were all just exercises, but could have a powerful effect on the performance.

The alienation effect requires a different approach from directors and designers too. Brecht wanted them to ensure that what is presented has quotation marks round it: 'this is what happened', 'this is who got hurt', 'this is who won the battle' and so on. They should tell the story in such a way that the individual elements can be seen as temporary and subject to change – a long way from a theatre that presents its audience with unshakeable 'eternal truths'. He often asked his actors to be involved in the practical presentation of the play – moving chairs, putting on new costumes and so on – in full view of the audience. The effect of this is twofold: it helps the actor present each moment with clarity and allows him to demonstrate his own attitude to what is being shown.

The alienation effect has become rather fetishised among students of Brecht and the phrase should be used carefully. Apparently, when Helene Weigel was asked whether an English production of *Life of Galileo* had created the alienation effect, she replied that 'it was just a silly idea that Bert came up with to stop his actors from overacting'. Not only does Brechtian acting require extraordinary emotional fluency, but the best actors and directors today regard the alienation effect as little more than carefully observed realism, presented in fragmentary form. Brecht's own summary can be found in a 'Short Description of a New Technique of Acting which Produces an Alienation Effect' (1951), and at greater length in paragraphs 43–54 of 'A Short Organum for the Theatre'.

Epic Theatre

The second key notion in Brechtian theory is the 'epic theatre'. By his own admission, Brecht took much of his inspiration for this from Shakespeare, whose plays are built out of a series of self-contained episodes and jump from location to location unconfined by the Aristotelian unities of time and place. Brecht's work eschews the smooth inevitability of nineteenth-century drama and he argued that only the epic theatre could express the bewildering disjointedness of modern life. Of course, the idea was not new and the epic style is evident wherever art deliberately pastes together conflicting elements, be it the Elizabethan theatre, popular culture, photomontage or Dadaism. Brecht's great achievement was to borrow from all these predecessors and develop a theatrical technique of his own.

The essential point of the epic theatre is that stories are told through a collage of contrasting scenes, whose content, style and approach are deliberately incongruous. A new kind of artistic unity is built out of such conflicting elements: interruptions are encouraged, text is set against action, music is given its own reality, scenery is cut away, unconnected scenes follow on from each other and so on. The point is that by exposing the audience to such diversity, they are encouraged to think independently and come to their own conclusions. Thus the epic theatre is nothing less than dialectics in practice.

It is a common mistake to imagine that the epic theatre refers only to large-scale historical dramas. Of course, Brecht was interested in writing such plays, and many of his plays cover an epic sweep of history and refer to actual events. However, the term describes a technique more than a genre: *The Mother* and *Fear and Misery of the Third Reich* are as much epic theatre as *Mother Courage, Life of Galileo* or *The Caucasian Chalk Circle*.

Brecht tried to define the epic theatre on many occasions. Perhaps the most complete account can be found in 'The Street Scene (A Basic Model for an Epic Theatre)' (1950), 'The Messingkauf Dialogues' and 'A Short Organum for the Theatre'. Walter Benjamin's 'What is Epic Theatre?' in *Understanding Brecht* is exceptionally revealing.

Contradictions

Brecht recognised that the key to drama lies in the conflict of opposites: one group wants one thing, another wants the opposite and the conflict between the two resolves itself in a third position. He felt that identifying such contradictions was an essential part of the theatre's role.

In the early work this is expressed in an insistent clash of registers: the sentimental followed by the cynical, the intellectual by the sensual and so on. The effect is to relativise any argument that is pursued and to undermine any feeling that is expressed. If the result was sometimes negative, it cleared the way for Brecht's understanding of the way that the contradictions inherent in society manifest themselves within the individual.

In his mature work, however, this interest in contradiction and dialectic becomes more positive, and Brecht's reading of Voltaire and classical Chinese philosophy made it into an exercise in clear thinking: 'on the one hand this, on the other hand that' was, he felt, the approach that stood most chance of approximating to the truth of the world. Apparently, while directing *The Caucasian Chalk Circle* with the Berliner Ensemble, he exasperated his colleagues by continually exposing the contradictions implicit in every decision – including his own – and challenging them accordingly.

All of Brecht's greatest characters are constructed on contradictory principles: the 'good woman' Shen Teh has to become the bad man Shui Ta in order to survive; Mother Courage sacrifices her children in order to make a living; Galileo abandons pure scientific pursuit because of its implications; and Puntila, who is generous when drunk, reverts to brutality when sober. The point is that these contradictions are not the result of poor characterisation – rather, they are realistic portraits of the way that real people behave in a contradictory world.

Gestus

One of the most difficult terms in the Brechtian vocabulary is *Gestus*. At its most superficial, this is close to the English word 'gesture': the pointed finger, the shrugged shoulder, the turned back and so on. However, *Gestus* also refers to something deeper: a physical embodiment of the relationships between people in society. Each *Gestus* captures a particular set of interlocking attitudes and the sum total of these provides the audience with a chart of the society that is portrayed.

Understanding the *Gestus* of any particular moment is an essential task in directing or acting in one of Brecht's plays. Thus the way that Galileo teaches Andrea about the orbit of the earth around the sun has a different *Gestus* from the way that he presents the Doge with a telescope. Similarly, in *Mother Courage*, the way that Courage, all alone, hauls the cart round the stage for the last time, still looking for business, is a very particular *Gestus*: a poor production would make this image as pathetic as possible; Brecht's by contrast, expressed a very troubling *Gestus*, which showed a woman determined to continue living off the war, even though it had robbed her of everything.

The fact that *Gestus* does not readily translate into English suggests that it is a term perhaps best avoided: professional directors and actors find that detailed attention to social relationships and a commitment to expressing them in three dimensions produce much the same effect.

Telling the Story

Despite his rejection of *The Poetics*, Brecht unwittingly agreed with Aristotle's emphasis on the importance of the story: 'Everything', he wrote, 'hangs on the "story"; it is the heart of the theatrical performance.' Brecht knew that the audience wants to find out what happens next and his best plays are rich with dramatic tension: 'Will Galileo repent in the face of the Inquisition?', 'Will Grusha cross the bridge before the Ironshirts reach her?', 'Will Kattrin succeed in saving the city of Halle?' and so on.

Dramatic storytelling shows that the things of the world are subject to change, and articulating that process of change and development – of history itself – is an essential element in the Brechtian theatre. Everything that takes place on stage should serve the story, and a production which does not tell the story is one that has failed to learn from Brecht's example. It is interesting to see from his working notes just how important story outlines were to Brecht's method of playwriting: much of his preparation consisted of pure story, free of opinion, character or even meaning.

Brecht was eager, however, to distinguish between traditional dramatic storytelling – 'this happens because that happened' – and the epic style – 'this happens and then that happens'. His plays are built out of discrete, dynamic units of action, which deliberately do not flow one into the other and he writes with an almost biblical simplicity which avoids smoothness and allows the joins to be visible. This distinction is described in 'The Modern Theatre is the Epic Theatre' (1927).

Brecht's emphasis on dramatic action deliberately avoids interpretation: it is the presentation of 'unvarnished raw material' ('The Messingkauf Dialogues') that allows the audience to make its own connections. A space is created in which the audience can gain some sense of how the events came about, and how the society that made them can be changed.

Playing One Thing After Another

A common criticism of Brecht's plays is that they are long-winded and boring. Certainly the full scale ones benefit from judicious cutting and even the finest can, at times, seem overextended.

One reason for this is Brecht's emphasis on 'playing one thing after another'. This means, above all, a way of acting and directing which allows the individual moments to be played for all their worth and gives the audience the space to look at each element individually, instead of being swept along uncritically by the action. Brechtian productions tend to find detail in small social 'gests', whose inclusion illuminates the way that the society operates. These details – paying the servants, bowing to royalty and so on – should not be glossed over, but they can slow down the dramatic action as a result.

In his finest work (*The Decision, The Mother, Life of Galileo, Mother Courage* and *The Caucasian Chalk Circle*) Brecht achieved an extreme economy of means – stripped of rhetoric, dramatically taut, simple and elegant – and they are at their best when played fast. One of the last things Brecht wrote was a note to the actors of the Berliner Ensemble on their first visit to London in August 1956:

> The English have long dreaded German art as sure to be dreadfully ponderous, slow, involved and pedestrian . . . So our playing must be quick, light and strong. By quickness I don't mean a frantic rush: playing quickly is not enough, we must think quickly as well. We must keep the pace of our run-throughs, but enriched with a gentle strength and our own enjoyment. The speeches should not be offered hesitantly, as though offering one's last pair of boots, but must be batted back and forth like ping-pong balls.

It should be pinned up in the rehearsal room of anyone attempting to stage Brecht today.

7 STAGING BRECHT

Brecht's plays are notoriously difficult to stage and working in a 'Brechtian' style is littered with pitfalls. He was a very great director in his own right and an understanding of his practical work in the theatre can help us grasp the plays themselves.

Model Books

The Berliner Ensemble produced a series of model books, which documented several of Brecht's productions, including *Antigone* (1948), *Señora Carrar's Rifles* (1952), *Life of Galileo* (1958) and *Mother Courage* (1958). These were edited by Ruth Berlau, featured her production photographs, and contained extensive commentary by Brecht and his assistants. They are now out-of-print collectors' items, but most of the texts are included in the Methuen editions of the plays.

The model books were published to give subsequent directors insights into the thinking behind the plays and their productions. Brecht was aware that they could be constricting and discussed this in 'Does Use of the Model Restrict the Artist's Freedom?' (1949). However, the plays were written to be performed in a very particular way, and their meaning is only released when the author's theatrical intentions are understood. The model books provide an extraordinary range of insights, which a good director should find useful, even if he uses them mainly as a way of refining his own ideas.

Stage Design

Brecht had a keen interest in fine art, and his plays and poetry often express a powerful and highly original visual imagination. His practical work as a director appealed to the eye as much as to the ear and one of the most distinctive features of his productions was their exceptional beauty.

It is a common mistake to imagine that Brecht's rejection of naturalism meant that his productions were abstract or void of human detail. In fact, they almost always featured entirely naturalistic elements – a fragment of wall, a door, a piece of furniture and so on. The crucial point is that these elements were arranged in such a way that they told the story and embodied the dramatic action. Furthermore, they felt provisional and capable of being changed – literally, by actors and technicians, but metaphorically also, by history and social change.

At times, Brecht and his designers went a step further and presented the 'stage as a stage', stripped of all scenery, with the actors visible throughout: 'The theatre', he wrote, 'must acquire *qua* theatre the same fascinating reality as a sporting arena during a boxing match. The best thing is to show the machinery, the ropes and the flies.' This has two effects: it encourages the audience to look imaginatively and it provokes them into thinking critically. Once again, Brecht was inspired by Shakespeare's theatre, which did not use scenery as such, but relied on costumes and props for its visual impact and entered into an unspoken contract with the audience about what the theatre could not show – and what it could.

One of the most striking of Brecht's scenic innovations was the use of a 'half curtain', a thin white curtain hung on a tension wire stretched across the front of the stage, which fluttered shut at great speed between scenes, while changes of scenery took place behind. Occasionally text would be projected on to it, or an actor would step forward and a song would be sung; the important thing was that it cut through the illusion of the previous scene and wiped the slate clean for the new image which was about to be drawn on it.

Brecht was fascinated by stage design and wrote about it on several occasions, including two remarkable eulogies for Caspar Neher: the essay 'Stage Design for the Epic Theatre' (1951) and his poem 'The Friends' (c.1948):

> The war separated
> Me, the writer of plays, from my friend the stage designer.
> The cities where we worked are no longer there.
> When I walk through the cities that still are
> At times I say: that blue piece of washing
> My friend would have placed it better.

John Willett's *Caspar Neher, Brecht's Designer* (1986) reproduces the most important drawings, but a full-length monograph in English is long overdue. No books in English on Karl von Appen or Teo Otto are currently available.

Lighting

Central to Brecht's theatrical aesthetic was the use of brilliant white light to illuminate the action. This gave his productions tremendous visual clarity, in which everything was held up for analysis, like a body on a dissecting table. In the early days he even used car headlights and several of his productions with the Berliner Ensemble used white cycloramas that further intensified this effect.

By refusing to light the king more brightly than the servant, Brecht was making a political as well as an aesthetic point, and his productions gained a kind of even-handedness as a result, a sense that there is no 'hierarchy of reality'. Brecht's poem 'The Lighting' (1950) expressed this vividly:

> Give us some light on the stage, electrician. How can we
> Playwrights and actors put forward
> Our images of the world in half darkness? The dim twilight
> Induces sleep. But we need the audience's
> Wakeful-, even watchfulness. Let them
> Do their dreaming in the light. That little bit of night
> We now and then require can be
> Indicated by moons or lamps.

As so often, the technical simplicity of the Elizabethan theatre provided him with a useful model.

Brecht also asked for the source of the lights to be made visible ('No one would expect the lighting to be hidden at a sporting event'). This practice was anathema to the naturalistic theatre, but is fundamental to the breaking of the illusion that Brecht regarded as the first step to achieving his audience's critical attention. It has become standard practice in most European theatres as a result.

Music

Music plays many roles in Brecht's theatre. At its simplest, it intensifies the emotional effect and drives the story on, and is often strikingly emotional and dramatically exciting. However, music is also essential to the alienation effect, in that it interrupts the flow of the action, provokes a fresh look at what is happening and highlights the emotions in such a way that they are quotable and consumable. Finally, music provides an ironical commentary on the action, drawing attention to sentimentality, horror, self-importance and so on, and showing them up as stock emotions which should be subjected to rational argument.

Brecht worked with four great composers – Kurt Weill, Hanns Eisler, Paul Dessau and Paul Hindemith – who independently developed a distinctly Brechtian sound. This drew from a wide range of influences – popular music and jazz, as well as folk elements and classical motifs – but the diversity of its origins was always preserved. The colours are clear and emotional but the orchestration is deliberately thin, with each instrument clearly distinguishable from the other. Brecht was suspicious of the 'beautiful voice' and his performers were asked to sing in such a way that the words came immediately to the fore.

Brecht insisted that the different musical sections should be separated from each other and from the action, and found ways of presenting them as clearly defined musical numbers, as his poem 'The Songs' (1950) demands:

> Separate the songs from the rest!
> By some symbol of music, by change of lighting
> By titles, by pictures now show
> That the sister art is
> Coming on stage.

Brecht was reaching back to a pre-romantic notion of musical theatre, in which arias are clearly separated from recitative, and favourite numbers are inserted and repeated regardless of dramatic logic.

The original recordings of *The Threepenny Opera* and *The Rise and Fall of the City of Mahagonny* with Lotte Lenya are still available. Deutsche Gramophon released David Atherton's recording of *The Little Mahagonny*, *Happy End* and *The Berlin Requiem* in 1976, and Decca produced a modern recording of *The Threepenny Opera* in 1990, with René Kollo, Ute Lemper and Milva. In addition, Ute Lemper has produced two volumes of songs by Kurt Weill. Harder to find is the music of Hanns Eisler, although Decca's *Entartete Musik* series is trying to redress that, as is the reissue of the old East German recordings on the Berlin Classics label. Even rarer is Paul Dessau's music for Brecht, which is currently unavailable on CD.

Brecht's songs have been recorded in English in a piecemeal fashion. The most interesting collection is Robyn Archer's two volumes of *Songs for Bad Times*, conducted by Dominic Muldowney with the London Sinfonietta. Jeremy Sams's updated lyrics for the Donmar Warehouse's production of *The Threepenny Opera* were recorded in 1994.

Props and Costumes

Marxists believe that people's lives are shaped by the food they eat, the chairs they sit on and the clothes they wear. Thus a central part of the materialism of Brecht's theatre was his attitude towards props and costumes. One of the novel aspects of the Berliner Ensemble's work was the attention paid to the detail and quality of these traditionally neglected elements of the live theatre.

Many of the key moments in Brecht's plays are dependent on material objects to make their meanings clear: Galileo teaching Andrea about the movements of the earth, the sun and the moon, with the help of a chair, an apple and a toothpick; Mother Courage haggling with the Cook over the price of a starved capon; or Azdak drawing a chalk circle on the floor and placing the child between his natural mother and the serving girl who has looked after him, so as to find out which woman should be granted custody.

In his mature productions Brecht was fascinated by the evidence of work, the grain and patina of frequent use, and insisted that every prop, costume or piece of furniture should carry some sense of how it has been used, and this emphasis on the worn and the weathered was highly valued. Brecht elaborated on this in a number of poems, including 'Weigel's Props' (1950):

> Just as the millet farmer picks out for his trial plot
> The heaviest seeds and the poet
> The exact words for his verse so
> She selects to accompany

Her characters across the stage.

All

Selected for age, function and beauty
By the eyes of the knowing
The hands of the bread-baking, net-weaving
Soup-cooking connoisseur
Of reality.

If at times this interest in the material was almost fetishistic, it
ensured that his productions were vivid, realistic and meaningful.

The Literalisation of the Theatre

Brecht often used signs, symbols and written texts in his productions,
as described in his essay 'The Literalisation of the Theatre' (1931):

> As he reads the projections on the screen the spectator adopts an
> attitude of smoking-and-watching. Such an attitude on his part at
> once compels a better and clearer performance as it is hopeless to
> try to 'carry away' any man who is smoking and accordingly pretty
> well occupied with himself.

Such signs seldom express the playwright's own thoughts: instead,
they provide the audience with a series of contradictory postures
which, taken together, help the audience deconstruct the texts that
shape society.

Moral tableaux are an important part of popular culture –
wickedness punished, goodness rewarded and so on – and Brecht
was keen to exploit their techniques as a way of upending such
moral certainties and creating new ones. As a young man he had
been struck by the stalls at the Augsburg fair, with their graphic
depictions of human foibles and failures, and their written slogans,
sometimes taken from the Bible, to accompany the story. He also
learned from contemporary art: the Cubists had cut out texts from
newspapers and placed them in their paintings, as did John

Heartfield in his political collages, and quotations and references were fundamental to several Modernist novels, above all James Joyce's *Ulysses* and John Dos Passos's *USA*.

This literalisation appeared in many different productions: Caspar Neher's provocative signs in *Drums in the Night*, the slogans in *Mahagonny*, the placards in the *Lehrstücke*, the captions on the curtain for *Life of Galileo* in Los Angeles and the location signs hanging over the stage during Brecht's production of *Mother Courage* at the Deutsches Theater in Berlin.

Direct Address

The term 'direct address' describes the moment when an actor steps out of the action and talks directly to the audience – usually in character, but sometimes as the actor himself – recognising that they are there and denying the naturalistic convention of the 'fourth wall'.

In Brecht, direct address is used in a variety of ways, sometimes to provide a straightforward narrative voice (such as the Singer in *The Caucasian Chalk Circle*); at other times characters talk directly to the audience in the first-person 'confessional' mode (such as Wang in *The Good Person of Szechwan*); it is also used to provoke a particular understanding of the play (as in the verse of *The Decision* or *The Mother*). It is a mistake, however, to imagine that direct address is always solemn or didactic; in fact, the effect is often comic, giving the audience an opportunity to step back from the drama and look at what is being presented in a fresh way, enjoying a new perspective and laughing at what went before.

Caricatures of Brecht's theatre sometimes cite the use of direct address as an odd and somewhat sterile innovation; the fact that it is fundamental to nearly all pre-romantic – and, most obviously, Shakespearean – theatre is usually forgotten.

Stage Pictures

One of the chief characteristics of Brecht's work as a director was the way that each unit of dramatic action told the story in visual terms. Brecht argued that it should be possible to tell what is going on dramatically at any single moment – 'gestically', in fact – by looking at a production photograph. The model books feature sequences of photographs which demonstrate this vividly.

Achieving this effect depended on months of detailed rehearsals, in which every physical detail – of gesture, position and setting – was precisely realised, but in a way which was continuously developing and changing. Brecht used to say that the actors' movements should be kept to a minimum, so that every move carried meaning, and his stage groupings often consisted of small clusters of people presented in dynamic connection with each other, whose physical relationship reflected the underlying social realities. Although the result can at times feel stylised, it is also highly theatrical. Brecht argued that it was nothing less than a new kind of realism.

Brecht's designers, especially Caspar Neher, developed an approach to stage design – sometimes called 'scenography' – in which the designer was responsible for more than simply the inanimate objects and produced drawings of suggested groupings of actors, often adopted by the director. Their exceptionally vivid but anti-decorative style drew on pictorial art, especially primitive and popular visual art, as well as religious iconography, and is described in some detail in Brecht's remarkable essay 'Alienation Effects in the Narrative Pictures of the Elder Breughel' (1934).

Staging the Classics

Brecht had a dual approach to producing the classics of the past: on the one hand he felt that they should be seen as the products of their age, thick with prejudices and ideologies, and difficult to appropriate for the kind of progressive drama that he was keen to create; on the other hand, he was acutely aware of their innate qualities and wanted to explore how they could be reworked for his own purposes. He struggled with this dilemma throughout his life and it is a debate that the modern theatre is still unable to resolve satisfactorily.

Brecht recognised that the reputation of the classics can prevent readers and audiences from grasping their true qualities. Thus he wrote, in 'Classical Status as an Inhibiting Factor' (1954), of how important it was to come to terms with their real greatness and not approach them with 'respect of a false, hypocritical, lip-serving kind'. His struggle with this question of classical status got him into all sorts of scrapes, especially in culturally conservative East Germany.

Poverty of Means

Brecht was keen to show that productions of great beauty did not have to be extravagant and that simple means could create elegant effects. He described this in his poem 'The Masters Buy Cheap' (1950):

> The decors and costume of the great Neher
> Are made of cheap material.
> Out of wood, rags and colour
> He makes the Basque fisherman's hovel
> And imperial Rome.

It should not be imagined, however, that Brecht's plays can be staged cheaply: the great plays were written for a large company of actors, ample rehearsal time, decent production budgets and so on. The Berliner Ensemble received generous government subsidy and it is perhaps ironic that Brecht's emphasis on poverty of means has been most imitated in the best-funded European theatres. Nevertheless, it is a lesson that should not be forgotten in a time of shrinking production budgets.

Simplicity

Brecht's theatre has a reputation for fearsome complexity. At its heart, however, he was involved in a search for simplicity. His last poem 'And I Always Thought' (c.1956) expresses this perfectly:

> And I always thought: the very simplest words
> Must be enough. When I say what things are like
> Everyone's heart must be torn to shreds.
> That you'll go down if you don't stand up for yourself
> Surely you see that.

8 FOUR EARLY PLAYS

1918–1924

In 1917, the year of the Russian Revolution, Brecht matriculated as a medical student at the Ludwig-Maximilian University in Munich. He did rudimentary military service as a medical orderly in Augsburg and, following the German defeat, served briefly as an Independent Socialist member of the town's Soldiers' Council.

In 1919 Brecht met the great Bavarian clown Karl Valentin (1882–1948) and became involved in his political cabaret in Munich. This gave him insights into the satirical possibilities of popular drama. He also attended theatre seminars held by Artur Kutscher, the biographer of Frank Wedekind (1864–1918). Brecht admired Wedekind enormously – his *Lulu* and *Spring Awakening* had shocked pre-war German audiences with their unabashed portraits of sexuality – and attended his funeral in 1918. Another seminal influence was Georg Büchner (1813–37), whose *Woyzeck* had received its belated world premiere in Munich in 1912 and had shown German dramatists that tragedy could have a working-class hero. Inspired by all this, Brecht visited Berlin in 1920 and 1921, quickly introduced himself to the leading figures in the theatre, and observed rehearsals held by Max Reinhardt (1873–1943) and others.

From these early years Brecht showed the talent for friendship and collaboration – as well as for self-promotion – that was to play such an important role in his subsequent success. This is evident in the early *Diaries* (1920–2), which mythologise his youthful experiences and his circle of friends. The most important figure from this time was the painter and stage designer Caspar Neher. The *Diaries* also include descriptions of two of his lifelong friends, George Pfanzelt, the 'Orge' to whom *Baal* is dedicated, and Otto Müller ('Müllereisert'), the medical student who eventually signed Brecht's death certificate. At times the atmosphere is incestuous and sometimes borders on the homoerotic. Yet Brecht's enormous appetite for women is abundantly clear: in 1913 he fell in love with Paula ('Bi') Banholzer, who bore him his first son, Frank, in 1919; in 1922 he married the opera singer Marianne Zoff and their daughter, Hanne, was born in 1923; and there were numerous other girlfriends.

Brecht's first creative efforts were songs and ballads – often echoing popular stories and themes – which he would perform to simple tunes that he wrote for the guitar. He also wrote occasional essays and theatre criticism of local newspapers. His first play, *Baal*, a tale of sensational amorality and greed, was written in 1918 and is much influenced by Büchner and Wedekind. It was quickly followed by a series of light-hearted and highly enjoyable one-act plays: *The Respectable Wedding, The Beggar or the Dead Dog, He Drives out the Devil, Lux in Tenebris* and *The Catch* – all probably written in 1919. These were followed by two full-length plays: the 'comedy' *Drums in the Night* (1918–20), first performed at the Munich Kammerspiele in 1922, and his first Chicago play, *In the Jungle of the Cities* (1921–3), premiered at the Residenztheater in Munich in 1923.

Brecht left Munich University in 1921 without a degree and managed to get work as a dramaturg at the Munich Kammerspiele between 1922 and 1924. There he collaborated with the well-established novelist and playwright Lion Feuchtwanger (1884–1958) on an adaptation of Christopher Marlowe's *Edward II*, which he directed at the Munich Kammerspiele in the spring of 1924. Later in the same year he wrote *Man equals Man,* a transitional piece that bridges the Expressionism of his early plays with the objectivity of his Marxist work.

Expressionism was the dominant artistic form of pre-First World War Germany and it was difficult for Brecht to shake free of its influence. From the outset, however, he reacted against its introverted excesses and it was in these early years that he first glimpsed his own mature style:

> I can compete with the ultra-Modernists in hunting for new forms and experimenting with my feelings. But I keep realizing that the essence of art is simplicity, grandeur and sensitivity, and that the essence of its form is coolness.

Readers and theatregoers looking for the characteristics of the 'Brechtian theatre' in these early plays will be disappointed: the theatrical form is influenced by Büchner and Wedekind, the language by Rimbaud, Verlaine, the Bible and popular literature, and those innovations that do exist are largely instinctive. The plays do, though, exhibit Brecht's characteristic cynicism and anti-romanticism: a dry-eyed and unshockable scepticism from a writer who was alive to the injustices of the world but had not yet discovered a system of analysis to provide the basis for changing it. Some argue that it is in these early plays that Brecht's genius is most liberally on display; it is perhaps truer to say that without these extraordinary pieces of juvenilia his later work would lack the poetical intensity, theatrical vividness, and social and psychological acuteness that make it so memorable.

BAAL
[Baal]

1918

THE STORY

Baal is being entertained (1) by the literary middle classes who praise him loudly and read out his poetry. He drinks too much and makes a pass at Emilie, his publisher's wife. Eventually they turn on him and the critic says, 'You mean nothing to me. You mean nothing to literature.' Soon Baal is in his attic (2), talking to the adolescent Johannes, who is in love with Johanna. Having declared that his parents are 'a thing of the past', Baal advises him, 'You have to have teeth for it, then love is like biting into an orange, with the juice squirting into your eye.' In a roadside inn (3), Baal boasts to lorry drivers about Emilie, his latest conquest; she soon arrives, as does Johannes with Johanna in tow. Baal insists that they drink together but Emilie tries to protect them from him: so Baal sings a song in praise of lavatories instead. His friend Ekart tells him he should turn his back on women and Baal gets a lorry driver to kiss Emilie – who is in love with Baal.

It is sunrise in the attic (4). Baal has slept with Johanna and she wants to know if he still loves her. He has no answer, so she leaves and drowns herself in the river. Two sisters visit Baal; they are undressing when the landlady comes in and gives him his notice. That evening Baal is drinking heavily and goes off to get himself a woman. He comes back with Sophie, and finds that Johannes has crept into his room. So he throws him out and seduces her. Baal meets a religious tramp (5): they discuss dead trees and women's pale bodies. One spring evening (6) Sophie and Baal are lying on the grass: she has been with him for three weeks and is worried about her mother. In a seedy club (7) Baal sings an obscene song; in the uproar he locks himself in the lavatory and escapes through the window. Baal and Ekart are out (8) walking through green fields: 'My body's light as a little plum in the wind.' In a village inn

(9) Baal tells farmers that he wants to buy one of their bulls – but only to get a drink out of them. He says that he wants the bulls from seven villages brought to him, to make an 'impressive sight'. Baal and Ekart leave and the local parson pays for their drinks: 'Eleven gins, your reverence'.

A group of woodcutters (10) are looking at the dead body of their workmate, Teddy. They decide to drink his gin, but cannot find it; so they blame Baal for stealing it. He tells them off: 'Sit down. Look at the sky growing dark between the trees. Is that nothing? There's no religion in your blood.' Baal and Ekart are in a hut in the rain (11); Baal tells him that he is a 'bad man, like me, a devil'. Sophie is pregnant (12) and although Baal wants nothing to do with her she adores him: 'I'd love his corpse. I even love his fists.' Ekart advises her to leave him and, when she refuses, he fights with Baal; but soon they sneak off leaving Sophie alone. They go to a rough bar (13) with two bottles of stolen champagne, which they share with beggars and prostitutes. Ekart declares that he is not going any further, but they leave together: 'We'll wash ourselves in the river.' The water is warm (14) and Baal declares his love for him: 'I don't care for women any longer.' On a windy night (15), Ekart is asleep in the long grass and Baal sings him his new poem; he wants to know if Ekart's girlfriend is more beautiful than he is. Soon (16) Baal is sitting among the hazel shrubs. A young woman has come to see Ekart; she says she is in love with him, but Baal drags her off into the thicket to rape her. Baal and Ekart are sitting under the maple trees in the wind (17); Baal reads out his new song, 'Death in the Forest'. Ekart says that Baal has not had a woman for a long time; Baal gets up and laughs. In an inn (18) Johannes, Ekart and a friend are drinking heavily, despairing of Baal. Johannes has gone mad with grief for Johanna. Baal arrives and sings a song; he is jealous of Ekart's relationship with a waitress and stabs him with a knife.

Alone in the forest (19), Baal walks off into the distance. Two policemen are looking for Ekart's murderer (20); as they go, Baal emerges: 'So he's dead? Poor little animal! Getting in my way.

Now things are getting interesting.' Baal is ill in bed (21). Men playing cards notice that he is dying; he wants them to stay but they have work to do. So he crawls out of the hut to look at the stars. Woodcutters (22) complain about Baal and shudder, remembering how he died. One of them says, 'I always want to know what goes on in a man's head then. I'm still listening to the rain, he said. I went cold all over. I'm still listening to the rain, he said.'

ABOUT THE PLAY

The single biggest influence on Brecht's debut was Georg Büchner's unfinished masterpiece *Woyzeck* (1836). This fragmentary tragedy of a soldier who murders his wife shaped a whole generation of German dramatists when it was finally premiered in Munich in 1913. It was the first play to make an ordinary man its hero and its jagged, earthy language gave a whole new direction to German drama. *Baal* also shows the influence of Frank Wedekind, whose biographer, Artur Kutscher, had taught Brecht at university and whose work had caused such a stir in pre-war Germany. Finally, the play's dense, poetic language echoes with the bleak lyricism of the French medieval poet François Villon and the blunt intensity of the Lutheran Bible, especially the Psalms, as well as the more modern urban visions of Rimbaud, Verlaine and Baudelaire.

Eight years later, Brecht claimed that 'the dramatic biography called *Baal* treats of the life of a man who really existed'. However, other than various autobiographical hints – not least its explicit references to Brecht's friend 'Orge' Pfanzelt – no real-life model has been found. Instead, Brecht turned to the pagan god Baal, worshipped by the Israelites of the Old Testament in orgies of sexual excess and cruelty, which allowed him to explore the nature of all-consuming sensuality, destructive greed and antisocial energy.

Brecht went to the heart of the matter in the Prologue to the 1918 version of the play:

Baal is neither an especially comic character nor an especially tragic one. Like all wild animals he is serious. As for the play, the author has managed to find a message in it: it sets out to prove that you can have your cake if you are prepared to pay for it. And even if you aren't. So long as you pay ... The play is the story neither of a single incident nor of many, but of a life.

He expanded on this in the 1926 Prologue:

You see before you Baal the abnormality trying to come to terms with the twentieth century world. Baal the relative man, Baal the passive genius, the whole phenomenon of Baal from his first appearance among civilized beings up to his horrific end, with his unprecedented consumption of ladies of high degree, in his dealings with his fellow-humans. This creature's life was one of sensational immorality.

Baal shows all this and more.

The play has an extraordinary erotic intensity, which verges at times on the pornographic. Baal's intimate friendship with Ekart is implicitly – almost explicitly – homosexual and climaxes with Ekart's murder. Baal's relationships with women are extraordinarily abusive, almost rapacious: the middle-class Emilie, the childlike Joanna, the two sisters who come to visit Baal in his attic room, the young girl Sophie, whom he picks up in the street and impregnates, and Ekart's anonymous girlfriend are all women who are prepared to sacrifice themselves to Baal's voracious sexuality and who adore him even as he despises them. Some have detected in this Brecht's own misogyny; others recognise the truth of Brecht's psychological insights into a particular kind of brutally frank heterosexual relationship.

Baal also features two groups of anonymous working men: the lorry drivers and the woodcutters. They are unwashed and impolite, men unrestrained by propriety and entirely free of the political consciousness that was such a feature of the working-class characters in Brecht's later plays. There are various other lowlife characters: prostitutes, a tramp, drunks and so on, each written with energy and colour. These are an essential part of the play's peculiarly powerful atmosphere, as is the dreamlike landscape through which Brecht's misshapen central character wanders: the middle-class dining room, Baal's attic on a starlit night, the lorry drivers' inn and so on. Some scenes even bear titles that read like the names of Expressionist paintings: 'Whitewashed Houses with Brown Tree Trunks', 'Spring Night Beneath Trees' and so on.

The choice of such an antisocial central character runs contrary to Brecht's subsequent commitment to Communism and the need for social cooperation, and so it is unsurprising to find him, many years later, approaching the play from a distinctly revisionist point of view:

> Baal is a play which could present all kinds of difficulties to those who have not learnt to think dialectically. No doubt they will see it as a glorification of unrelieved egotism and nothing more. Yet here is an individual standing out against the demands and discourage-ments of a world whose form of production is designed for exploitation rather than usefulness. We cannot tell how Baal would react to having his talents employed; what he is resisting is their misuse. Baal's art of life is subject to the same fate as any other fate under capitalism: it is attacked. He is anti-social, but in an anti-social society.

Intriguing as this is, there is something disingenuous about such *post hoc* rationalisation; perhaps more honest is Brecht's note in 1939 explaining why he gave up trying to turn *Baal* into a learning play:

> Today I at last realised why I have never been able to produce the little *Lehrstück* on the adventures of *Bad Baal the Antisocial Man.* Asocial people have no part to play. They are merely the possessors of the means of production and of other sources of livelihood, and that is all they are.

It seems that Brecht needed to write about antisocial people before he could construct a kind of drama in which the society they are kicking against could be seen as capable of change. His first play has all the strengths of a young prodigy's remarkable debut, but greater claims for it should be resisted.

IN PERFORMANCE

Baal was first performed on 8 December 1923 at the Altes Theater, Leipzig, in a production directed by Alwin Kronacher, with Brecht attending many rehearsals. It was subsequently performed at the Deutsches Theater in Berlin (for a single matinée performance given by the radical Junge Bühne) on 14 February 1926, in a production co-directed by Brecht and the actor Oskar Homolka – who also played the title role – with scenery by Caspar Neher. Brecht composed his own melodies for the songs. The influential critic Walter Kerr saw it and dismissed 'the gifted Brecht' as 'a frothing plagiarist'.

The British premiere took place at the Phoenix Theatre, London, on 17 February 1963, with Peter O'Toole as Baal; it was directed by William Gaskill and designed by Jocelyn Herbert. The US premiere was in 1965 at the Martinique Theater, New York, in Eric Bentley's translation.

BBC Television filmed *Baal* with David Bowie in the title role in 1982.

DRUMS IN THE NIGHT
[Trommeln in der Nacht]

1918–20

THE STORY

Act One (Africa) takes place in the home of Karl and Amalie Balicke. They are worried about their daughter Anna, who is mourning her fiancé Andreas Kragler, reported 'missing in action' two years previously. Balicke warns Anna that he must be dead, and that she should marry Friedrich Murk, a colleague who made his fortune in the war, instead. When Murk arrives, however, we discover that he and Anna are already sleeping with each other (although she does not love him) and that she is expecting his child. Murk invites them all to join him at a celebration at the Piccadilly Bar. A journalist friend, Babusch, arrives with news that the Spartacus rebellion has broken out and that there is unrest on the streets. A red moon is rising when a man in 'muddy dark blue artillery uniform' appears in the door: it is Kragler. He explains that he has been a prisoner of war in Morocco, but Balicke tells him bluntly, 'You've been away for years. She's waited for years. Now time's up and you've had your chance.'

For Act Two (Pepper) the action moves to the Piccadilly Bar. The red moon is shining and crowds are gathering around the newspaper offices. Anna wants Murk to kiss her, but he refuses: 'Half Berlin's looking.' When she insists, he calls a waiter to witness it. Balicke wants to drink to the 'happy couple'; as they do, Kragler enters. Murk wants him thrown out, but Babusch says he should be allowed to speak. Kragler is just about to embrace Anna, when they are interrupted by the waiter, Manke, followed by the Balickes and Babusch. Murk returns with a prostitute, Marie, and asks if they have 'settled this third-rate farce'. They patronise Kragler and offer him a drink, but he wants Anna to go with him. They try to buy his boots (and pay him off) and their abuse reaches a frenzy, when suddenly the 'Internationale' is heard outside.

Manke defends Kragler and Anna, and Marie tells Murk that he is drunk. However, Anna still does not want to go with Kragler. Balicke reminds Kragler of his poverty and Anna is determined to abort Murk's child by taking too much black pepper. Machine-gun fire can be heard outside; Babusch says, 'It's starting. The masses are stirring. Spartacus is rising. The slaughter continues.'

Act Three (The Ride of the Valkyries) takes place on a street leading to the newspaper district. Marie is tagging along after Kragler, who ignores her. Two middle-class men need to urinate, but are afraid that the revolutionaries will shoot them if they are caught. The 'entire Ride of the Valkyries' appears: Manke behaves as if he were intoxicated and talks in riddles, Babusch is worried about the revolutionaries, Murk is desperately drunk and Anna goes off in search of Kragler. 'The lover has already vanished, but his beloved hastens after him on wings of love. The hero has been brought low, but his path to heaven is already prepared,' says Manke. 'But the lover's going to stuff his beloved down a sewer and take the path to hell instead' is Babusch's sinister reply.

Act Four (The Dawn is Turning Red) takes place in a small schnapps distillery, where Glubb, the left-wing proprietor, is singing 'The Ballad of the Dead Soldier'. Various lowlife characters are drinking and smoking. A worker comes in for a drink – he is one of the revolutionaries. Augusta, a prostitute, criticises one of her clients for demanding a cheap price, 'now we've lost the war'. Kragler and Marie turn up. A drunk sings raucously, and Kragler challenges Glubb: 'Did you say injustice, brother Red? What sort of a word is that? Injustice! A whole lot of little words like that they keep inventing, and blowing in the air, and then they can put their feet up and one gets over it. And big brother clouts his little brother on the jaw, and the cream of society takes the cream off the milk, and everyone gets over it nicely.' A newspaper seller comes in with the latest news of the revolution, but there are no takers. Kragler staggers off towards the newspaper district.

Act Five (The Bed) takes place on a wooden bridge; there is much shouting and a bright red moon. Babusch wants Anna to go home; what is more, he has run out of cigars: 'They're flinging torn-up papers in the puddles, screaming at machine-guns, shooting in each other's ears, imagining they're building a new world.' Kragler, Glubb and the others arrive, and Anna tells Kragler that she is 'with child'. He is incredulous: 'I was lying in the filth. Where did you lie while I was lying in the filth?' He throws lumps of earth at her and the others hold him down. They try to take him away, but he wants to stay with his 'wife'. The men jump on Anna, as if to kill her, and they hear artillery in the distance as the revolution is put down. Kragler declares that he is 'fed up to here. It's just play-acting. Boards and a paper moon and the butchery offstage, which is the only real part of it.' He picks up a drum and bangs on it, mocking the Spartacists, but the newspapers and himself too: 'The bagpipes play, the poor people die, the houses fall on top of them, the dawn breaks, they lie like drowned kittens in the doorway. I am a swine and the swine's going home.' In an astonishing last sequence, he 'throws the drum at the moon, which was a lantern, and drum and moon together fall into the river, which is without water'. He takes Anna off to 'bed, the great, white, wide bed' and, as 'a white, wild screaming comes from the newspaper buildings', the two walk away together.

ABOUT THE PLAY

Ever since the *Oresteia* the story of soldiers returning home from the war has had a powerful hold on the dramatic imagination, and in the 1920s the word *Heimkehr* (homecoming) was used to describe an entire genre of post-First World War German drama and literature. The same theme appears in several of Brecht's plays, but is at its most powerful in *Drums in the Night*, written in the aftermath of the German surrender in 1918 and the subsequent failure of the Spartacist revolt.

Many years later Brecht declared, 'Of all my early plays the comedy *Drums in the Night* is the most double-edged' and his judgement is acute: on the one hand it is a conventional five-act drama, with a beginning, a middle and an end, a central character, love interest and 'character roles', which uses all the technique of exposition, development and climax of the nineteenth-century naturalistic 'well-made play'. As such it is reminiscent of Carl Sternheim's turn-of-the-century satires on the hypocrisies and absurdities of the German bourgeois family. Brecht's great innovation was to set these nineteenth-century certainties against the immense tragedy of the war and the uprising that followed it. It is this historical perspective that justifies the play's savagely ironical references to Wagner, as well as its revolutionary socialist imagery.

One of Brecht's most accomplished early poems was the viciously satirical 'Ballad of the Dead Soldier', which he set to his own melody on the guitar. It tells of a soldier being dug out of his grave and sent back to the front to provide cannon fodder. It appears in Act Four of *Drums in the Night* and resonates throughout the play, particularly in the story of its central character, the soldier Andreas Kragler. Exhausted by his terrible experiences at the front, presumed dead by everyone at home, Kragler is a walking representative of the inchoate mass of the defeated German Army, dead to the world, brutalised by its experience, angry and confused, returning home to haunt the bourgeois society that had demanded its sacrifice. Furthermore, he is not merely the unpleasant reality that society needs to face if it is to avoid bitterness and violence; he is also a member of the apolitical, antisocial 'underclass' that must be inspired by the revolutionaries who claim to act in his name. His cynicism is comprehensive, but it is the logical conclusion of his experiences.

The Balickes, by contrast, are a satirical portrait of the German bourgeoisie: self-serving, hypocritical, complacent and ignorant. Balicke himself is bullish and domineering, more interested in reputation than in substance; his wife is vain and idle, hypocritical and unattractive. When we first meet their daughter, Anna, she seems to be their antithesis: faithful to her young love, a Penelope awaiting the return of Odysseus. However, we soon discover that she has outpaced her parents in cynicism and is already sleeping with her proposed fiancé, the deeply distasteful Murk. Her betrayal of Kragler is more than simply sexual, or even romantic; she is attracted to Murk for his fortune, made during the war, presumably in the arms trade. Her wish to maintain romantic relations with Kragler while staying engaged to Murk makes her one of the least attractive characters in the play and her attempt to abort Murk's child hardly redeems her. Babusch, the journalist, is another man who stayed at home during the war and his hands, though unblooded by the trenches, are blackened by the poisonous ink of the mendacious newspapers for which he writes.

The play has its fair share of 'lowlife': the unfortunately named socialist innkeeper Glubb, the prostitutes Marie and Augusta, the revolutionary worker who drops in for a drink, and the independent-minded waiter, Manke. Although, according to Lion Feuchtwanger, the play's original title was *Spartakus*, the Spartacist uprising of 1918–19 is not its central subject; instead it can be heard off stage like an unstoppable, malevolent force that will devour them all. Brecht's own view, it seems, is sceptical in the extreme; the very fact of its presence in the play, however, shows his eagerness to create a kind of theatre which could dramatise the great social upheavals of his time.

One of the most extraordinary moments in the play is its ending. It is as if Brecht is trying to resolve his dispute with Expressionism and provides a foretaste of the anti-illusionist style which was to become the hallmark of his work. Kragler's reunion with Anna, it seems, is only possible in a world in which all certainties are torn up and every possibility is examined. Art has a role in all this and, if the world is to be changed, the forms of art need to change with it.

Drums in the Night is not entirely successful. It is, however, an essential early step for a young writer determined to describe the world that surrounded him in a way that was quite new and stepped free of the clichés and closed-mindedness that had caused his central character such suffering.

IN PERFORMANCE

Drums in the Night was first performed on 29 September 1922 at the Munich Kammerspiele, in a production directed by Otto Falckenberg (with Brecht attending many rehearsals). The influential critic Herbert Ihering declared that 'overnight the twenty-four-year-old poet Bert Brecht has changed the literary face of Germany'. The play was then performed at the Deutsches Theater in Berlin on 20 December 1922, with Alexander Granach as Kragler, directed again by Falckenberg, but with Brecht even more vocal in rehearsals. Caspar Neher designed this production and Brecht described the scenery and its effect:

> Pasteboard screens some six feet high represented the walls of the rooms, with the big city painted in childish style behind them. Every time Kragler appeared the moon glowed red a few seconds beforehand. Sounds were thinly hinted. In the last act the 'Marseillaise' was performed on a gramophone. The third act can be left out if it fails to work fluently and musically and to liven up the tempo. It is a good idea to put up one or two posters in the auditorium bearing phrases such as 'Stop that romantic staring'.

As a result of *Drums in the Night*, Brecht was awarded the highly prestigious Kleist Prize for a young dramatist in 1922.

The play had to wait till August 1961 for its English-language premiere, at the Arena Theater in Albany, USA. The British premiere was not until 1969, at the Victoria Theatre, Stoke-on-Trent. It is very seldom performed today, except by students.

IN THE JUNGLE OF THE CITIES
[Im Dickicht der Städte]
The fight between two men in the great city of Chicago

1921–4

THE STORY

It is August 1912 (1) and George Garga, a poor migrant from the prairies, is behind the counter at Maynes's Lending library in Chicago. Schlink, a Malayan lumber dealer, enters and, with the help of his followers – Skinny, Worm and Baboon – proceeds to humiliate Garga. They know everything about him and have even made friends with his girlfriend Jane. By the end of the scene, Garga is in a state of nervous breakdown, strips off his clothes, gives them to Schlink and runs out, crying, 'I want my freedom.'

Two weeks later (2) Garga goes to Schlink's office to collect his clothes. He is surprised to discover that his sister, Mary, is now working for Schlink. To his astonishment, Schlink treats him well and hands over ownership of his entire lumber business. Garga immediately orders the entire stock to be sold twice over, to two different buyers. He also fires Schlink's men and offers to sell his sister to Skinny. The Salvation Army is heard outside and Garga offers to give them the house, but only if Schlink spits in the Salvation Army preacher's face. At the end of the scene, Garga goes off with his new followers and Schlink leaves with Mary.

That evening (3), in a filthy attic, Garga's parents, Mae and John, are with their friend Manky. They are worried about their children and Manky bemoans the insecurity of life in America. Garga appears, well dressed, ready to take them out to dinner, but tells his mother that he is unhappy. When she asks him how she will live, now that he has no job, he becomes even gloomier, but she refuses to move to the South with him. Soon Worm appears, looking for Garga, who has now left, and tells them that Mary is working as a prostitute in a Chinese hotel. Schlink also turns up, denies any knowledge of Mary's profession and offers to work for them, now that their 'breadwinner' has deserted them. They accept his offer and offer him a bed; his reply is 'I am a simple man, don't expect words from my mouth. I've only teeth in it.' Two days later (4), in the Chinese hotel, Baboon is telling Skinny of his despair at Schlink's strange behaviour. Jane is now also working as a prostitute, and Mary is desperately in love with Schlink – but he never touches her. Jane worries about Garga, who has disappeared: 'There's an east wind. The Tahiti-bound ships are weighing anchor.'

A month later (5), in the same hotel, Worm is in the hall, Garga is in a filthy bedroom and Manky and Baboon are in the bar: they are all appalled by what has happened. Mary comes in and sees Garga: they are both disgusted with each other. Schlink arrives, Mary tells him how much she loves him and Garga confronts him: 'Whatever is human to me, you devour like chunks of meat. You open my eyes to possible sources of help by choking them off. You use my family to help yourself. You live on my reserves. I'm getting thinner and thinner. I'm getting metaphysical. And on top of everything, you vomit all this in my face.' Garga serves drinks and Schlink offers to marry Mary, but she prefers Manky's offer and goes off with him instead. Garga insists that Schlink give him the last of his money; soon he is drunk and disappears with Jane.

At the end of September (6) Schlink and Mary are in the woods beside Lake Michigan. He declares his love for her, but she feels her capacity for love has 'turned to bitter fruit'. 'My courage', she says, 'has gone with my innocence.' As they go off into the undergrowth, Manky appears with a pistol, looking for Mary. He leaves, they return and she demands payment for what happened ('You took me so quickly,' she says, 'as if you were afraid I'd get away') but Schlink refuses.

Garga's living room is full of new furniture (7) and John, Mae and Manky are dressed up in new clothes for Garga and Jane's wedding dinner. Schlink comes in to offer his congratulations, but Garga informs him that 'our acquaintance is at an end'. However, Schlink hands him a letter from the attorney-general concerning the double sale of the lumber and Garga realises that he will be sent to jail. Schlink leaves triumphantly, but the others are in despair, the only option being unthinkable: living off Mary's immoral earnings. Garga drafts a letter to the local newspaper accusing Schlink of rape and molestation, and says that he intends to send it from jail: 'For him the day of my release will be marked by the howling of the lynch mobs.'

Two years later (8) Schlink is in his office, dictating a letter to Mary, saying that he will never again have anything to do with her or her family. A man comes in to warn him that Garga has told a newspaper that he has committed a number of crimes and charges him a thousand dollars for the tip-off. Meanwhile (9), Worm, Baboon, Jane, Mary and the Salvation Army preacher are gathered in a bar across the street from the prison. Worm tells a story about the resilience of a dog, while outside, as Garga predicted, a lynch mob is hunting for Schlink. Soon, Garga enters with Maynes and three other men, having just got out of jail. He wants Jane to go home with him, but she refuses and leaves with Baboon. Garga tells his men that 'the yellow weed [Schlink] must never again be allowed to take root in our city'; he also assures his sister that he still loves her, 'soiled and wasted' as she is. She tells him that 'when I've made money I don't want to save, I throw it down the sink'. At this the preacher, who has been drinking, goes into a back room and shoots himself. Left alone together, Mary tells Garga that she still misses Schlink. The lynch mob is getting louder and Schlink enters and persuades Garga to leave with him.

It is two o'clock on a November morning (10), and Schlink and Garga are in a deserted tent in the gravel pits of Lake Michigan. Schlink says that they are 'comrades in a metaphysical contact' and even declares his love for him, adding that in the real jungle things are much simpler. Garga, however, declares that he, the younger man, has won the fight – 'the important thing is not to be stronger, but to come off alive. I can't defeat you, I can only stamp you into the ground' – and says he is leaving for New York. Schlink is left alone and Mary enters, offering him a hiding place; but he kills himself as the lynch mob cuts its way into the tent.

A week later (11) Garga, his father and Mary are in Schlink's old office. The lumberyard has been burned down and the business is up for sale. Mary and her father, John, are planning to stay together. Manky comes in, wanting to buy the business; Garga offers it to him for 'six thousand, if you'll take the woman too'. A contract is signed and Garga sets off to New York alone.

ABOUT THE PLAY

The young Brecht was fascinated by the *Amerikanismus* craze that swept across Germany in the 1920s. This was a reaction against Germanic heaviness and was inspired by the frontier spirit of American society and the dynamic, meritocratic nature of the New World. Brecht was also morbidly attracted to the dark side of American capitalism: the dog-eat-dog mentality which he identified as a prerequisite for success.

In the Jungle of the Cities is one of Brecht's most self-consciously literary works and quotes directly from its many sources. The most important one is the American socialist Upton Sinclair, whose best-selling novel about the Chicago poor, *The Jungle*, had appeared in 1904. Brecht was also inspired by the Danish novelist, J. V. Jensen, whose *The Wheel* was first published in German in 1921. In addition, the nineteenth-century French poets Verlaine, Rimbaud and Baudelaire – especially Rimbaud's *A Season in Hell* (1873) – provided Brecht with a model for a new kind of urban poetry. Finally, as ever, the influence of Shakespeare and the other Elizabethans can be detected.

The play is set in an entirely mythical Chicago, a vision of the ultimate big city that, as Sinclair pointed out, with its tall skyscrapers and its struggle for survival, resembles a jungle. The atmosphere is resolutely anonymous, cold, bleak and harsh. It is also remarkable for its ethnic diversity – the Malay lumber dealer, the Chinese hotel, the talk about Tahiti, the racist mob – even if, ultimately, this adds up to little more than mere poetical exoticism.

The play's characters are caught in a fight to the death, redolent of social Darwinism at its crudest. In the Prologue Brecht describes it as a 'fight between two men in the great city of Chicago':

> You are in Chicago in 1912. You are about to witness an inexplicable wrestling match between two men and observe the downfall of a family that has moved from the prairies to the jungle of the big city. Don't worry your heads about the motives for the fight, concentrate on the stakes. Judge impartially the technique of the contenders, and keep your eyes fixed on the finish.

Many years later, Brecht acknowledged the impact of seeing a bad production of Friedrich Schiller's early play *The Robbers*:

> There is a most furious, destructive and desperate fight over a bourgeois inheritance, using partly non-bourgeois means. What interested me about this fight was its fury, and because it was a time (the early 1920s) when I appreciated sport, and boxing in particular, as one of the 'great mythical diversions of the giant cities on the other side of the herring pond', I wanted my new play to show the conclusion of a 'fight for fighting's sake', a fight with no origin other than the pleasure of fighting and no object except to decide who is 'the best man'.

The result is a drama of a strange, haunting intensity.

In the Jungle of the Cities is dominated by its two protagonists: Schlink, a Malay lumber dealer, and George Garga, an assistant in a Chicago bookshop. Since the point is that these two characters are locked in a conflict which has no rational cause, it is unwise to apply the usual question of psychological motivation. What is fascinating, however, is the complex, and at times perplexing, routes that both men take in their fight to the death. At first, Garga seems to be the weaker one: he is quickly outmanoeuvred by Schlink and seems destined for defeat. Schlink's decision to hand his business over (2) is as perplexing to us as it is to Garga. Schlink's plan, however, is initially successful and the delivery of the attorney-general's letter (7) seems to nail Garga once and for all. By this time, however, Garga has drawn on deeper resources, and his denunciation of Schlink's behaviour towards his sister, and the provoking of the lynch mob, is the knockout punch. All of this is executed with extraordinary sangfroid, and one of the striking things about these two men is their philosophical attitude to misfortune and their growing camaraderie in the bitter struggle in which they are engaged.

Although Brecht refuses to provide any motivation for this fight (in itself a metaphor for the mysterious energy of high capitalism), he does paint his two central characters in very distinct colours. The fifty-one-year-old Schlink is an isolated figure, an exotic stranger in the American urban jungle. He surrounds himself with a bizarre group of undomesticated and utterly unreliable men, each with his own animal nickname (Worm, Skinny, Baboon and so on). His experiences as a brutalised 'yellow man' working on the Yangtze have scarred him for ever and drive him to his own destruction. His sexuality is violent and he seems incapable of any kind of emotional attachment. His lonely death is inevitable and only his involvement in the fight animates him. The much younger Garga, by contrast, is a traditional migrant from the wide-open prairies into the crowded city, and lives with his mother and father in dire poverty. His sister works as a prostitute and his girlfriend is only interested in him when he does well. This sense of family and roots, satirical as Brecht's presentation of it may be, ultimately makes Garga the more attractive of the two.

The play's tone is brutally masculine, full of macho talk and bravura. Its imagery is drawn from traditional male pursuits – boxing, hunting and whoring – and the women in the play are defined above all by the availability of their bodies. In its portrayal of the central love-hate relationship, the play has distinctly homoerotic, masochistic overtones. Nevertheless, beneath the surface, the play has a strange, oblique emotional intensity, nowhere more vividly than in Brecht's portrait of Garga's sister Mary, whose obsessive, unrewarded love for Schlink provides perhaps the most moving passage of the play:

I lay in bed with a man who was like an animal. My whole body was numb, but I gave myself to him, many times over, and I couldn't get warm. He smoked stogies in between, a seaman. I loved you every hour I spent between those papered walls, I was so obsessed that he thought it was love and wanted to stop me. I slept into the black darkness. I don't owe you anything, but my conscience cries out to me that I've soiled my body, which is yours even if you scorned it.

Despite its poetic extravagance, this is psychological writing of the highest quality.

In the Jungle of the Cities is one of Brecht's most difficult plays. Its action is strange, contradictory and meandering. Its use of language is sometimes florid, at other times elliptical and occasionally downright impenetrable. Brecht's disclaimers about psychological motivation do not make its characters any easier to understand. Furthermore, by presenting the heroic phase of American capitalism as a jungle in which the fittest survive, a boxing match in which one man takes satisfaction in the destruction of the other, Brecht poses the modern reader – particularly the believer in progress and civilisation – with a profound challenge. 'This is how the city works,' he seems to be saying, 'and anything else is weakness.'

The play's great strength lies in the intensity and theatrical flair with which Brecht conveys the cannibalistic energy of capitalism; and by the time he came to attempt a Marxist critique of it he had already laid bare the thrills and spills of its unlocked energies.

IN PERFORMANCE

The play was first performed at the Munich Residenztheater on 9 May 1923, where it was entitled simply *In the Jungle*. It was directed by Erich Engel, with scenery by Caspar Neher. The same team produced the play at the Deutsches Theater in Berlin on 29 October 1924, under the title *Jungle (Downfall of a Family)* and Fritz Kortner played Schlink. Carl Ebert directed a revised version at the Hessisches Landestheater in Darmstadt in December 1927.

The New York premiere took place in 1960 and the British one was at the Theatre Royal, Stratford East, in 1962. Peter Stein directed a famous production at the Munich Kammerspiele in 1968, with Bruno Ganz as Garga. The play is hardly ever staged today, except in university drama departments.

MAN EQUALS MAN

[Mann ist Mann]

Collaborators: Emil Burri, Slatan Dudow, Elisabeth Hauptmann, Caspar
Neher, Bernhard Reich

1924–6

THE STORY

One morning (1) Galy Gay, an Irish porter, tells his wife that he is
going out to buy a fish. Four soldiers, Jesse, Polly, Uriah and Jip,
draw up outside the Pagoda of the Yellow God (2). They are
desperate for beer and decide to rob the pagoda. They break a
window, Jip loses his helmet inside and the other three climb in to
fetch it. Wang the bonze appears and Jip walks in through the door.
The soldiers smash the place up, but Jip's hair gets stuck as he comes
out. Uriah cuts it off, but now Jip is 'a walking wanted notice' and he
is left to sit in a leather palanquin. On a country road (3) Sergeant
Fairchild nails a 'wanted' poster to a shed: he wants to know what
happened at the pagoda. He stops the soldiers and warns them, 'It
would be better for you if you had been summarily shot in your
mother's wombs than if you turn up at my roll call tonight without
your fourth man.' Galy Gay arrives, carrying things for Widow
Begbick and complaining. She is desperate for sex, but he just wants
to buy a fish; she persuades him to buy her cucumber instead. The
soldiers decide that he is their man – 'someone who can't say no' –
and bribe him with the promise of a cigar.

In Begbick's canteen (4) soldiers are singing a rousing song.
Jesse, Polly and Uriah arrive with Galy Gay, explain that they need
his help and dress him up as a soldier. He agrees, but at a cost in
cigars and beer. Begbick is anxious about the 'wanted' poster, but
the men are more worried that it will rain and that Jip will be
discovered. What is more, Begbick explains, when it rains,
Fairchild is overcome with lust. All four go out for the roll call
where Galy Gay answers to the name of Jip. Begbick tries to lure
Fairchild inside and tells him she wants to see him as a civilian. The

men pay Galy Gay off with 'five boxes of cheap cigars and eight bottles of brown ale', and he stays in the canteen to drink. Meanwhile, it has started to rain (5) and Wang tells the Sacristan to drag the palanquin indoors. He looks in it and discovers Jip, 'too drunk to recognise his own mother', and decides to 'make a god' out of him. The three soldiers arrive, but Wang baffles them with oriental paradoxes and they leave, grumbling. Back at the canteen (6) Galy Gay is asleep in his chair, 'like an Irish mammoth', and the soldiers decide to 'have a kip . . . it's all too depressing and it's really the fault of the rain'. Inside the pagoda (7) Wang has put up posters announcing his new god and 'religious ceremonies of some importance' – with dung balls and drumming – are going on. Jip wakes up, disorientated, and Wang brings him a beefsteak; he starts to eat it and persuades himself that he should not run away: 'It's all wrong that I should be sitting here, but this is good meat.' In the canteen (8) the soldiers are eating breakfast but Galy Gay is asleep. Wang comes in and buys beer 'for a white man'. The soldiers wake Galy Gay and try to persuade him to join them. He is only won over when they mention 'business', particularly the possibility of 'business involving an elephant'. When Galy Gay's wife comes to find him, he says that he does not recognise her; but Fairchild fancies her and follows her out. Uriah announces that Galy Gay can be turned into Jip: 'One man is like another. Man equals Man' and soon the drums and bugles give the signal for the departure to the Northern Frontier.

The Interlude consists of a brief speech by Begbick: 'Herr Bertolt Brecht hopes you'll feel the ground on which you stand / Slither between your toes like shifting sand.' Soon (9), the army is packing up the camp and Widow Begbick sings her 'Song of the Flow of Things'. Uriah announces that they are going to make Galy Gay sell an artificial elephant – which they then construct – and will arrest him for selling military property. Begbick agrees to play the buyer. Galy Gay arrives and is about to sell her the elephant when soldiers start to take down the canteen, leaving Jesse to explain to Begbick that everything is 'relative'. In I, The

Elephant Deal, Begbick is just about to buy the elephant when Fairchild interrupts them. In II, The Elephant Auction, Galy Gay sells the elephant to Begbick and is arrested for it. It soon runs away and Galy Gay is 'bound with cords and thrown into the latrine'. In III, The Trial of the Man Whose Name is Not to be Mentioned, the soldiers interrogate Galy Gay and conclude that he will have to be shot for stealing a phoney elephant. Soon, however, he says that he is Jip, not Galy Gay, but Uriah decides that they should scare him some more anyway and, in desperation, Galy Gay asks Begbick to cut off his moustache. In IV, The Execution of Galy Gay in the Military Cantonment of Kilkoa, Begbick shows Uriah the moustache and Galy Gay is dragged out of the latrine and led off, blindfolded. The countdown to his execution starts but, despite his protestations that he is not Galy Gay, Uriah shouts out 'three'. Galy Gay faints and the men shoot over his head. In IVa, Fairchild arrives in civilian clothes; he is drinking and boasting of his brutal past, but the soldiers abuse him, throw him into the bushes and deny his very existence. In V, Obsequies and Internment of Galy Gay, Uriah declares that 'our man has now been reconstructed' and Polly adds that 'all he needs now is a human voice'. The soldiers carry a crate, which they pretend is Galy Gay's body, and tell him that they are burying his body. They want him to give the address, but he is reluctant. Eventually he concludes that he should 'Close an eye to what concerns myself / And shed what is not likeable about me and thereby / Be pleasant'. Trains can be heard; Galy Gay is given his identity disc ('Jeriah Jip') and delivers a funeral oration. As the scene ends, Uriah mutters, 'He took his time, the swine. But we'll get him yet.'

On the train (10) the soldiers persuade Begbick to pretend that she has slept with Galy Gay; when he awakes he is confused about everything, but is eventually persuaded to stop thinking. Meanwhile, Fairchild is in despair: he is in civilian clothes and is no longer 'Bloody Five'. When Begbick mocks him for impotence, he goes and 'shoots off his manhood'. This inspires Galy Gay: 'Now I realise where such stubbornness gets you and what a bloody thing it is when a man is never satisfied with himself and makes so much fuss about his name.' They hear the 'roar of artillery' as the train nears the 'hills of Tibet'. On a hilltop facing the mountain fortress of Sir El-Djowr (11), Galy Gay is eager to go straight into battle ('charging on irresistibly like a war elephant'); he is followed by the three soldiers, 'groaning as they drag their gun'. The real Jip is waiting for them, but they all laugh at him and 'Jeriah Jip' (Galy Gay) gives him Galy Gay's paybook. Galy Gay loads the gun and Jip curses the others and leaves. As he starts to shoot, Begbick admires his manliness; on the fifth shot the fortress collapses and Fairchild threatens to kill him. However, 'Jeriah Jip' is acclaimed as 'the human fighting machine', and even when they hear that the fortress provided refuge for seven thousand refugees, 'most of them friendly, hard-working people', he marches on regardless:

> And already I feel within me
> The desire to sink my teeth
> In the enemy's throat
> Ancient urge to kill
> Every family's breadwinner
> To carry out the conquerors'
> Mission.

ABOUT THE PLAY

Brecht started thinking about his comedy of human transformation when he was just twenty-two. A note in his diary on 6 July 1920 describes how

> Citizen Joseph Galgei fell into the hands of bad men who maltreated him, took away his name and left him lying skinless. Everyone should look to his own skin.

Much later Brecht wrote, 'From what I learnt from the audiences that saw it, I rewrote *Man equals Man* ten times.'

The key literary influence on the play was the poetry and short stories of Rudyard Kipling (1865–1936), especially his *Soldiers Tales* (1896) in which he wrote sympathetically about ordinary British privates, trying to earn a living in imperial India. Brecht's own 'soldiers three' – brilliantly illustrated by George Grosz – are neither saints nor heroes. Instead, they are barrack-room debaters, casual racists, quite without moral scruple, keen to take their pleasures where they can find them, a true portrait of the common soldier let loose on unsuspecting natives in the service of empire.

The play's title is often translated as 'Man is Man' or 'A Man's a Man' (seemingly in homage to Robert Burns); John Willett, however, has rightly decided to follow Brecht's note in 1925, when he called the play *Galy Gay or Man = Man*. Although difficult to grasp at first, this reflects the play's fundamental meaning: that in certain circumstances one man is like another and that bourgeois notions of individuality are meaningless amid the anonymity of modern industrialised warfare. The philosophical premise is the Marxist view that character is dependent on circumstances and that people can be transformed by their environment. The positive implication of this is that 'human nature' does not stand in the way of progress and that people will behave better in a better world; the negative one is that such malleability can be exploited by those who want to bend people to their own will. *Man equals Man* applies this analysis to a military context and reflects on how civilised Europe descended into the barbarism of the First World War. It also acts as a chilling prophecy of the way the Nazis would brainwash millions of ordinary Germans into the most brutal kind of militarism. It is a message that has enduring relevance today.

Brecht's central figure, the Irish porter Galy Gay, is lazy and impressionable, unintelligent and vulnerable. He is described as being like an elephant: ponderous and clumsy until he has been goaded into action, at which point he becomes terrifying and unstoppable. Like so many of Brecht's greatest characters – Schweyk, Shen Teh, Mother Courage and Galileo – his is a story of survival in an alarming world. His initial reluctance to join the other soldiers is neither principled nor brave, and his acquiescence is ensured only by bribery and flattery. His eventual transformation into a human fighting machine is a disaster, not just for him but also for people like him. The Interlude tells us that 'Tonight you are going to see a man reassembled like a car'; the central point of the play is that human beings are made of such malleable stuff that under certain conditions this is possible.

Perhaps inevitably in a play that is a deconstruction of the notion of character itself, the other soldiers are hard to distinguish. Their names – Jeriah Jip, Uriah, Polly and Jesse – deliberately echo Kipling and Dickens, and their language has a jaunty, upbeat violence about it, literary in its extravagance but earthy in its directness. They are fantastical figures, whose ordinariness is painted in the most garish colours. Remorseless and determined, they are entirely alienated from their own better nature and only Jeriah Jip seems capable of human sympathy, as a result of his experience in Wang's temple. Yet Brecht refuses to comment: 'this is how it is' his deadpan style seems to be saying, adding that 'and for some people it's even fun'.

In keeping with his interest in the 'other ranks', Brecht does not present the senior officers who control these men's destiny. We do, however, meet Sergeant Fairchild, 'Bloody Five known also as Tiger of Kilkoa, the Human Typhoon'. The men find him terrifying: disciplined, military and impossibly unyielding. However, he has an Achilles heel: he is appallingly libidinous when it rains and loses all self-control. He too is subject to the process of change and is forced to dress in civilian clothes. His self-castration is borrowed from Jakob Lenz's *The Tutor* (1774), a play that fascinated Brecht all his life, and is the perfect metaphor for his melodramatic 'tragic fall', his transformation – the opposite of Galy Gay's – from manly bully to neutered coward.

Widow Begbick is the first in a long line of Brecht's canteen women: Begbick in *Mahagonny*, Mrs Kopecka in *Schweyk* and, above all, Mother Courage. She is a potent mix of the wise and the vulgar, the sentimental and the cynical, the mother and the whore. Her 'Song of the Flow of Things' echoes the Greek philosopher Heraclitus and expresses the central idea of the play:

> Don't try to hold on to the wave
> That's breaking against your foot: so long as
> You stand in the stream fresh waves
> Will always keep breaking against it.

However, she – like all the Europeans – is outclassed by the bonze, Wang, who turns Jeriah Jip into a god in order to make money out of him, and who hides his cynical tactics behind religious mumbo-jumbo. Like Schlink in *In the Jungle of the Cities*, Wang is a character from junk fiction, one of those wily oriental crooks who pursue their aims with pragmatic self-interest, and are detested by their equally cynical Western opponents for being insufficiently naive.

Brecht also wrote an interlude for the foyer called The Elephant Calf ('If you insist on seeing something full of meaning you should go to the gents'); it is a piece of inspired lunacy whose subtitle is The Demonstrability of Any Conceivable Assertion. Like The Elephant Calf, *Man equals Man* should not be taken too seriously; it was intended as a piece of theatrical knockabout, and its social and philosophical insights are scattered around in an entirely unsystematic fashion. The play is dense with quotations and self-conscious echoes, and rich with images from the circus – elephants and tigers, clowns and acrobats, magic tricks and high-wire acts. It also shows the influence of the political cabaret of the Bavarian clown Karl Valentin, whom Brecht knew and admired, and the slapstick comedy of one of his greatest heroes, Charlie Chaplin.

Of course, *Man equals Man* has a serious point, as Brecht wrote in a comic dialogue:

> You too can get caught up like that man in Bert Brecht's play so as
> to blot out your name and your self and your home and your wife
> and your memory, your laughter and your passion, your desire for
> women and your elevation to God; because you too can be lined up
> like that man in a formation one hundred thousand strong,

between man and man, dinner pail and dinner pail, just as millions of men have been lined up in the past and millions of men will be lined up in the future; because like that man you too can be hit by a red-hot lump of iron and blotted out of life and the world!!!

In the Preface to the radio version he explained that Galy Gay

becomes the strongest once he has ceased to be a private person; he only becomes strong in the mass. And if the play finishes up with him conquering an entire fortress this is only because in doing so he is apparently carrying out the determined wish of a great mass of people who want to get through the narrow pass that the fortress guards. No doubt you will go on to say that it's a pity that a man should be tricked like this and simply forced to surrender his precious ego, all he possesses (as it were); but it isn't. It's a jolly business. For this Galy Gay comes to no harm; he wins. And a man who adopts such an attitude is bound to win. But possibly you will come to quite a different conclusion. To which I am the last person to object.

The final note of this comment captures the play's remarkable quality: extravagant, playful and ironic, but also impassioned, committed and true.

In retrospect, *Man equals Man* is the key transitional work in Brecht's early development. Without sacrificing any of his formidable poetic and theatrical powers, Brecht wrote with a new kind of objectivity, a new degree of conscious political intent. In the three early plays his views are submerged and when they appear they tend to be maudlin and negative; here, his telling of the story leads us inevitably into asking more positive and radical questions about the way that the world operates. Thus, with *Man equals Man*, Brecht discovered his distinctive voice.

IN PERFORMANCE

Man equals Man was first performed on 25 September 1926, in simultaneous productions in Düsseldorf and Darmstadt. The former was a failure but the latter was a great success. It was directed by Jacob Geis, with scenery by Caspar Neher, and the director of the theatre, Ernst Legal, played Galy Gay, repeating his performance, with Helene Weigel as Widow Begbick, in the 1927 Berlin Radio version. Erich Engel directed the play at the Volksbühne Berlin on 5 January 1928, with Heinrich George as Galy Gay and Weigel as Begbick, with music by Edmund Meisel. Brecht directed his own ground-breaking production of the play at the Staatstheater Berlin in February 1931, with Peter Lorre as Galy Gay and Weigel once again as Begbick. The Russian playwright Sergei Tretiakov described this in vivid terms:

> Giant soldiers armed to the teeth and wearing jackets caked with lime, blood and excrement stalk about the stage, holding on to wires to keep from falling off the stilts inside their trouser legs.

This production featured music by Kurt Weill (now sadly lost), who had first encountered Brecht's work when reviewing the radio adaptation in March 1927.

The play's English-language premiere was on 6 September 1962 at the Living Theatre in New York. The London premiere was at the Royal Court Theatre in 1971 in a production directed by William Gaskill, and the play was revived by the RSC in 1975. It is very rarely performed today, despite its enduring relevance.

9 TWO MUSIC-THEATRE PIECES AND KURT WEILL

1924–1929

Brecht moved to Berlin in early 1924. He had met the left-wing Austrian actress Helene Weigel in the autumn of 1923 and she gave birth to their son, Stefan, in November 1924. In the winter of 1924 the German-American scholar Elisabeth Hauptmann was hired by Brecht's publisher to help complete three overdue books; she not only became his lover, but her extensive knowledge of English literature and selfless hard work provided him with essential research and secretarial support throughout his life. In addition, Brecht became involved with the young playwright Marieluise Fleisser (1901–74) and directed her second play *Pioneers in Ingolstadt* (1929) under a pseudonym. He also struck up friendships with the heavyweight boxer Paul Samson Korner (1887–1942), the painter and illustrator George Grosz (1893–1959) and the novelist Alfred Döblin (1878–1957).

The Berlin of the 1920s was a magnet for radical theatre artists from all over the world and it provided Brecht with an ideal base to explore his own ideas. In 1924 he worked as Assistant Director at Max Reinhardt's Deutsches Theater and directed a production of his (and Lion Feuchtwanger's) adaptation of Marlowe's *Edward II* at the Kammerspiele in Munich. In 1926 there were simultaneous premieres of *Man equals Man* in Darmstadt and Düsseldorf and, in 1927, Brecht joined the 'dramaturgical collective' of Erwin Piscator's ground-breaking Volksbühne, where he helped adapt Jaroslav Hašek's novel *The*

Good Soldier Švejk. The radio production of *Man equals Man* in the same year brought together the nucleus of Brecht's favourite actors, and his radio adaptation of *Macbeth* was the start of his lifelong interest in adapting Shakespeare. Brecht's volume of early poetry, *The Devotions*, was published in 1927 and in the same year he started work on *The Downfall of the Egotist Johannes Fatzer*, a fragmentary and experimental piece, which links his early expressionistic work with the more explicitly Marxist plays of the 1930s.

In March 1927 Brecht met the composer Kurt Weill. They soon started working together and their first project was the *Mahagonny Songspiel* – the sketch for the full-length opera that was to follow – which was premiered at the Baden-Baden Festival of New Music in 1927. This was followed by their great hit, *The Threepenny Opera*, at the Theater am Schiffbauerdamm in Berlin in 1928 and, exactly a year later, by its much less successful sequel, *Happy End*. The shouting SA men who picketed the Leipzig premiere of their only full-scale opera together, *The Rise and Fall of the City of Mahagonny* (1927–9), in March 1930 provided shocking evidence that the 'Golden Twenties' were over. Brecht's collaboration with Kurt Weill was to continue, however, on the *Berliner Requiem* (1929), *He Who Says Yes* and *He Who Says No* (1930), as well as the opera-ballet, *The Seven Deadly Sins* (1933), but nothing could compare with the glorious, catchy anarchy of *The Threepenny Opera*, or the dazzling intensity of *The Rise and Fall of the City of Mahagonny*.

THE THREEPENNY OPERA
[Die Dreigroschenoper]

Collaborators: Elisabeth Hauptmann, Kurt Weill
1928

THE STORY
In a fair in Soho, a ballad singer sings 'The Ballad of Mac the Knife'.

Act One opens in Peachum's outfitting shop for beggars (1), where Peachum sings his 'Morning Hymn' and tells us that his business is in trouble: people are too cynical to give to beggars any more. Even quoting the Bible does not work. A young man called Filch enters, looking for a job, and Peachum explains the techniques used, 'the five basic types of human misery'. When Peachum quizzes his wife about what their daughter, Polly, has been up to, she tells him that a captain asked the two of them to a dance. Peachum is appalled, drives Filch out and realises that Polly has been out all night, with 'Mac the Knife'! Together they sing the 'No they can't' song.

'Deep in the heart of Soho' (2) Macheath shows Polly into a 'bare stable'; she is in her wedding dress and this is where they are going to get married. His followers carry in a large amount of furniture that they have stolen to make the place feel grander. Four of them sing the first verse of the 'Wedding Song for the Less Well-off', they dress themselves in stolen suits, awkwardly congratulate the couple and give their presents – all of which are also stolen. Things quickly degenerate, Macheath knocks Matt to the floor and, over the wedding dinner, asks his men to sing a song. The reverend enters and the men sing the rest of the wedding song 'hesitantly, weakly and uncertainly'. In response, Polly sings the 'Song of Pirate Jenny', with its refrain: 'And a ship with eight sails and / All its fifty guns loaded / Has tied up at the quay.' Suddenly Tiger Brown, 'the Chief Sheriff of London, pillar of the Old Bailey', enters. The men start to creep away but Macheath welcomes him. Soon he and Brown sing the rousing

'Cannon Song' and, as he leaves, Brown assures Macheath that there is nothing on record against him at Scotland Yard. The men present the couple with their wedding bed and leave Macheath and Polly singing a romantic duet, beneath 'the moon over Soho'.

Back at her father's shop (3), Polly explains why she married Macheath. Her mother is about to faint and needs a drink. Five of Peachum's beggars come in, complaining about the standard of their equipment; he fires two of them. Polly's parents want her to get a divorce; when she refuses, they decide to get Macheath arrested. Peachum will visit the Sheriff – Tiger Brown – and his wife will go to see his 'tarts' to get them to betray him. All three sing the 'First Threepenny Finale, Concerning the Insecurity of the Human Condition': 'That's what you're all ignoring / That's what's so bloody boring / The world is poor, and man's a shit / And that is all there is to it.'

Act Two returns to the stable (4). Polly tells Macheath about her parents' intentions even though she has discovered the extensive charges against him. He decides to go into hiding and hands the business over to Polly. The gang enter, excited about the forthcoming coronation; they are unhappy to hear about Polly, but are easily convinced. Macheath bids Polly a tender farewell, but she knows the truth: 'Nice while it lasted, and now it is over / Tear out your heart, and goodbye to your lover! / What's the use of grieving, when the mother that bore you / (Mary, pity women!) knew it all before you?' In an Interlude in front of the curtain Mrs Peachum tells Low-Dive Jenny to betray Mac the Knife to the police; when Jenny doubts that he will visit her, Mrs Peachum sings 'The Ballad of Sexual Obsession'.

In the whorehouse in Turnbridge (5) the girls are enjoying a 'bourgeois idyll', comparing knickers and reading the paper. When Macheath arrives, Jenny shows him a copy of his arrest warrant and reads his palm – where she sees 'a woman's treachery'. As Macheath sings the 'Ballad of Immoral Earnings', she tries to betray him to Constable Smith. Macheath jumps out of the window, where he meets Mrs Peachum and other policemen, who 'escort the gentleman to his new home'.

In the cells at the Old Bailey (6) Tiger Brown is worried. When Macheath is brought in, Brown is devastated by his 'withering glance'. Macheath bribes Smith, but he is put into the cage all the same, where he sings 'The Ballad of Good Living' with its refrain: 'One must live well to know what living is.' Suddenly, Tiger Brown's daughter, Lucy, arrives: she wants to marry Macheath so she can 'become an honest woman'. However, Polly also turns up and she and Lucy sing 'The Jealousy Duet'. Lucy refuses to accept that Polly is married to Macheath and reveals that she is pregnant with his child. Mrs Peachum arrives and drags Polly away. Macheath tells Lucy that he loves her only and with her help manages to escape. Brown arrives and is relieved. Peachum comes in to collect the forty pounds reward, discovers Brown in Macheath's cage and warns him that he will be blamed for his escape. Macheath and Jenny sing the 'Second Threepenny Finale, What Keeps Mankind Alive?'.

In Act Three, late that night (7), Peachum and the beggars are preparing their campaign to 'disrupt the coronation by a demonstration of human misery'. Jenny and the other whores arrive, wanting their share of the reward for turning in Macheath. She tells the Peachums that Macheath has escaped and is now with Suky Tawdry, prompting Mrs Peachum to sing the third stanza of the 'Ballad of Sexual Obsession'. Peachum starts to send the beggars off to work and Brown arrives, determined to arrest them all. In reply, Peachum sings the 'Song of the Insufficiency of Human Endeavour': he points out the illogicality of Brown's position ('how will it look if six hundred poor cripples have to be clubbed down at the coronation?') and blackmails him into arresting Macheath. Brown sends Smith off to Suky Tawdry and Jenny sings 'The Solomon Song': only the person without wisdom, beauty, courage, inquisitiveness or sexuality can be regarded as fortunate.

In the Old Bailey (8) Polly wants to talk to Lucy and apologise for her behaviour the previous day. Lucy tells her that she should have stuck to her own 'class of people' and gives her coffee and cakes. She also confesses that she is not really pregnant and Polly says that she can have Macheath if she wants. Suddenly, however, Macheath is brought in again, this time to be hanged, and Mrs Peachum comes in with her daughter's 'widow's dress': 'You'll be a lovely widow. But you'll have to cheer up a little.'

It is early in the morning (9) and Macheath is about to be hanged. The bells of Westminster are ringing for the coronation, but the streets around Newgate are jammed with people wanting to see the execution. Brown comes to visit and Macheath tries to bribe him ('Life is short and money is sparse. And I don't even know yet if I can raise any'). Mournfully, he sings the 'Call from the Grave', but orders Matthew and Jake to get four hundred pounds from their savings account. Polly is allowed to visit but she does not have the thousand pounds Smith has asked for. As Macheath eats his 'last meal' – asparagus – Brown goes through his accounts, working out how much he owes him. The Peachums, Polly, Lucy and the whores come to say farewell, as do Matt and Jake – who have not been able to raise the money 'because of the terrible crush'. Finally, six o'clock strikes and Macheath takes his leave, singing the 'Ballad in which Macheath Begs All Men for Forgiveness'. After a solemn procession to the gallows Peachum declares, 'Since this is opera, not life, you'll see / Justice give way before humanity.' In the 'Third Threepenny Finale', the 'Appearance of the Deus Ex Machina', a royal official on a horse arrives, sets Macheath free and raises him to the 'hereditary peerage'. As the curtain falls, Peachum asks us to 'join in the hymn of the poorest of the poor':

> Injustice should be spared from persecution:
> Soon it will freeze to death, for it is cold.
> Think of the blizzard and the black confusion
> Which in this vale of tears we must behold.

ABOUT THE PLAY

Brecht's greatest hit is a fantastical vision of an imaginary

London: part eighteenth-century picaresque, part Victoriana, *The Threepenny Opera* also catches brilliantly the seedy, corrupt and unpredictable atmosphere of Weimar Berlin in the last years before Hitler.

The piece was commissioned by the young actor turned producer Ernst-Josef Aufricht, who, in early 1928, had secured private money to hire the Theater am Schiffbauerdamm. He had also engaged a director – Erich Engel – but had no idea what he wanted to put on there. Almost by chance he met Brecht who told him about the translation of John Gay's *The Beggar's Opera* (1728) that Elisabeth Hauptmann had written the previous year. When Aufricht expressed interest, Brecht insisted that Kurt Weill should be involved and in May both men, accompanied by Engel, Hauptmann and Weill's wife, the singer Lotte Lenya, went off to the South of France to work on a new adaptation.

Fundamental to the appeal of *The Threepenny Opera* is the quality of Kurt Weill's music which is astonishingly eclectic and thick with echoes and borrowings; it is also tremendously enjoyable. Weill said that *The Threepenny Opera* was 'largely about opera itself, an outdated upper-class art form now hopelessly out of touch with the modern theatre and its audience', and it is first and foremost a satire on operatic structure, operatic emotion and operatic manners. If the piece is also a stinging critique of 1920s bourgeois values, it is because of the central importance of opera in German bourgeois life. By parodying opera, Brecht and Weill were satirising society itself, as Weill made clear:

> The criminals showed, sometimes through the music itself, that their sensations, feelings and prejudices were the same as those of the average citizen and theatregoer . . . The tenderest and most moving love-song in the play described the eternal, indestructible, mutual attachment of a procurator and his girl.

The strength of Weill's music sometimes overshadows Brecht's text, which, for all its inconsistencies, occasional flat-footedness and awkwardness, is nevertheless an extraordinary achievement.

The story is simple – Polly Peachum elopes with Mac the Knife who is betrayed to the police three times and saved by royal intervention – and rather lacking in variety or dramatic tension. However, Brecht tells it in dialogue which is so witty and lively, and in a dramatic style which is so startling and energetic, that it sweeps all before it.

The Threepenny Opera is built around half a dozen characters. At the centre is Mac the Knife, a charming, sexually attractive rogue, who is as brutal and cynical as he is sentimental and sweet. He belongs to a long line of Brecht's antisocial, self-destructive anti-heroes, including Baal, Kragler, Schlink, Garga and Galy Gay. Unlike them, however, Macheath is genuinely attractive, and his energy, wit and defiance make a strong claim on our feelings.

Macheath's nemesis is Jeremiah Peachum, a larger-than-life caricature of bourgeois hypocrisy, who knows how to exploit religious sentiments for his own financial gain. His concern for propriety is unaffected by his greed and his religious morality does not stop him behaving quite improperly when it suits him. His wife, Mrs Peachum, is just as bad: apparently a model of feminine decency, her close connection with the whores of Turnbridge make us wonder about her past. Their daughter Polly is an independent-minded, middle-class young woman, whose common sense is undermined by her fatal attraction to Macheath, a man who most certainly 'was not a nice chap'.

If Brecht drew on Dickens for the Peachums, Tiger Brown ('Jackie' as Mac always calls him) is straight out of Kipling. The Chief Sheriff of London (an entirely invented title) is a retired soldier from the Raj. Still driven by carnal – and carnivorous – appetites, he spends much of his time lost in memories of his glory days. He is a powerful mixture of the sentimental and the cynical, both loyal and corrupt, a pillar of the establishment and a close friend of the criminals he polices. His daughter Lucy is only lightly characterised, but her relationship with Macheath further under-lines the extent of her father's involvement with London's criminal classes.

The Threepenny Opera features various supporting groups, who act like choruses in a classical opera: Peachum's beggars, Macheath's villains, the whores of Turnbridge and Tiger Brown's policemen. They are all corrupt and are only interested in improving their own lot. They do this with astonishing sangfroid and are utterly bourgeois in their aspirations. What the piece shows, in an entirely unsystematic fashion, is that criminals are not entirely wicked and that the charitable are not necessarily good. It also demonstrates that justice is elusive, sexual attraction is contradictory and love, friendship and loyalty are all relative. Brecht's youthful scepticism is fundamental to the piece's astonishing appeal.

In coming to any kind of assessment of *The Threepenny Opera* today, it is best to see it as a piece of brilliant juvenilia, written too quickly by a dramatist desperate for a hit, in a culture intoxicated by its own extravagance, and almost wilfully blind to the dangers that faced it. Its inconsistencies and its borrowings are as much the result of slapdash writing as of a conscious reaction against the romantic notion of the autonomous creative writer. Its cynical bravura barely disguises its lack of political logic, and nothing can hide the fact that its analysis of poverty and crime is laughable. Despite this, however, Brecht and Hauptmann's funny, imaginative, satirical text, matched by Weill's catchy, jazz-influenced music, make *The Threepenny Opera* not just the most important music drama of 1920s Germany, but the defining work of an entire culture dancing on the edge of catastrophe.

IN PERFORMANCE

The Threepenny Opera received its world premiere at the Theater am Schiffbauerdamm in Berlin on 31 August 1928, in a production directed by Erich Engel, with scenery by Caspar Neher, Lotte Lenya as Jenny, Carola Neher as Polly and Ernst Busch as the Street Singer. It was accompanied by the eight-piece Lewis Ruth Band (Weill later rescored it for twenty-three instruments). The rehearsals had been exceptionally troubled, the dress rehearsal was a disaster, and the first night looked like being a flop, until the 'Cannon Song' brought the house down. Soon, the piece became the biggest commercial success in German theatre history and was performed ten times a day during its first year, in fifty different cities across Europe. In 1934, while in exile in Denmark, Brecht wrote a not entirely successful retelling of the story in prose, *The Threepenny Novel*.

The US premiere took place on 13 April 1933 at New York's Empire Theater. The composer Marc Blitzstein produced an adaptation with Lotte Lenya again as Jenny, which opened off-Broadway on 10 March 1954 and became one of the longest-running musical shows in American theatre history. The piece was not professionally performed in Britain until Sam Wanamaker's production at the Royal Court Theatre in 1956. It is occasionally revived today: two recent versions include the National Theatre's (1986) and the Donmar Warehouse's (1994) – the latter with Jeremy Sams's updated lyrics. A large number of popular musicians, from Louis Armstrong to David Bowie, have recorded versions of 'Mac the Knife'.

Harry Buckwitz produced the first post-war German revival of *The Threepenny Opera* in Munich in 1949, with scenery by Caspar Neher, but, by common consent the greatest post-war production was by Giorgio Strehler at the Piccolo Teatro in Milan in 1956: Brecht wrote to Strehler saying, 'Passion and coolness, ease and precision distinguish this production from many that I have seen. You have given the work a true rebirth.'

G. W. Pabst made a film of *The Threepenny Opera* in 1931, which used many of the original cast. Brecht and Weill sued Nero Films for breach of copyright: Weill won and was awarded damages, but Brecht lost and eventually settled out of court.

THE RISE AND FALL OF THE CITY OF MAHAGONNY

[Aufsteig und Fall der Stadt Mahagonny]

Collaborators: Elisabeth Hauptmann, Caspar Neher, Kurt Weill
1927–9

THE STORY

'A large lorry in very bad condition breaks down in a desolate place' (1). Fatty and Moses do not know what to do but Madam Begbick says that they should found their city there: 'And its name is Mahagonny / Which means Suckerville!' It will be a place of extreme pleasure. Within a few weeks (2) the first 'sharks and harpies' are making themselves at home, and Jenny and six girls carrying large suitcases arrive, singing 'Oh show us the way / To the next whisky bar'. Soon (3) 'news of the founding of a new Jerusalem reaches the big cities' and Fatty and Moses implore 'the men who live in large dark cities' to join them. Over the next few years (4) 'the discontented from every country make their way to Mahagonny'. Begbick welcomes four men (5), including the famous Jimmy Gallagher, and introduces them to her girls ('Come out you beauties of Mahagonny! / We like to pay for what we like'). They soon see people leaving but this does not put them off. Walking through the city, Jenny asks Jim for 'instructions' on how he would like her to dress. 'Inside the As-You-Like-It Tavern' (7) Begbick is in distress: her business is in trouble and 'Our lovely Mahagonny / Has not brought in the business'. Newcomers have arrived: 'They looked like money to me / And maybe they'll spend it with us.' Soon Jimmy wants to leave Mahagonny (8) because it is so boring, but his friends persuade him to stay. Back in the tavern (9), Jimmy is still unhappy; he draws a knife and the others try to hold him back. Suddenly a hurricane threatens (10): 'We face utter destruction / A black, horrible end!' Everybody is awaiting it with grim foreboding (11), but Jimmy welcomes it and the others join in. News arrives that Pensacola has been destroyed: 'And the hurricane roars / On its raging way to Mahagonny.'

Amazingly (12), the hurricane changes direction only a minute from Mahagonny and everyone rejoices in their salvation. A year later (13) the city is booming and the men consume enormous amounts of food: Jake eats so much that he dies. Men queue up for Begbick's girls (14) – 'Lovers, stop waiting / Hurry, the juicy moon / Is green and slowly setting' – and Jenny and Jimmy sing a romantic duet. The men bet (15) on Moses and Joe slugging it out in the boxing ring – and Joe is killed. Prodigious amounts of alcohol are drunk (16) and the drinkers pretend that a billiard table is a ship, sailing through a stormy night to Alaska. Jimmy, however, cannot pay for his drinks and no one will give him credit, so he is clapped in irons and contemplates his fate. The others drink on: 'Don'ts are not permitted here.' Later that night (17) Jimmy, still in irons, curses the dawn that is breaking. The courtroom is a tent (18), Moses sells entry tickets and Begbick is the judge. Toby Higgins, a cold-blooded murderer, bribes Begbick and is acquitted; Jimmy tries to borrow money to do the same but is denied by his best friend. He is indicted for seducing Jenny and being cheerful in the face of the hurricane; Moses implicates him in the fatal boxing match and – 'the crown of our charges' – says that he did not pay for his drinks. For this, he is 'sentenced to death in the electric chair'. His execution (19) is a public affair. There is a tender farewell between Jenny and him, but his best friend Billy takes her in his arms straight afterwards. When Jimmy wonders if there is a God, the others stage a little play that shows that 'God came to Mahagonny / During the whisky'. As Jimmy is about to be executed, he says,

> When I came to this city, hoping that my money would buy me joy, my doom was already settled. Here I sit now and have had just nothing. I was the one who said 'Everyone must carve himself a slice of meat, using any available knife'. But the meat had gone bad. The joy I bought was no joy; the freedom they sold me was no freedom. I ate and remained unsatisfied; I drank and became all the thirstier.

Finally the city is in flames (20), created not by a hurricane, but by its inhabitants. In the last chorus everyone sings:

> You can't do anything to help a dead man
> Can't help him or you or me or no one.

ABOUT THE PLAY

In Brecht's collected works, *The Rise and Fall of the City of Mahagonny* is listed as an 'opera'. This is certainly how Brecht and Weill saw it, even declaring that it 'pays conscious tribute to the irrationality of the operatic form'. The piece has a more classical musical structure than *The Threepenny Opera* – it is *durchkomponiert* (through-composed) like nineteenth-century opera – and it is Brecht and Weill's most developed piece: an opera to be performed in opera houses by opera singers, with a classical orchestra and a conductor. Libretto and score are closely integrated and Kurt Weill was clear about the nature of his collaboration with Brecht:

> There is no ground whatsoever for the frequently voiced fear that any collaboration between literary figures of real stature must make the relationship between music and text into one of dependence, subordination or at best parity. The more powerful the writer, the greater his ability to adjust himself to the music . . .

In conceiving the text for *Mahagonny*, Brecht drew on his fascination with all things American, but combined this with an uncanny insight into its less attractive realities. The opera paints America as a mythical land, rich with its own biblical destiny, in which Mahagonny is one of the biblical 'cities of the plains'; it also satirises America's strange mixture of religion and sin, optimism and despair, pleasure and violence. In this, Jimmy's death in the electric chair for having no money is the logical climax to his pursuit of the American dream. The piece also pays unlikely homage to the American entrepreneurial spirit and the story of an entire city built in the desert and dedicated to hedonism – not unlike Las Vegas, founded in 1905 – is a testimony to American 'can do' optimism, as well as a parody of its darker forces.

In *Mahagonny*, Brecht seems more interested in creating atmosphere and describing a world than in drawing individual figures and the characterisation is fairly minimal. The men are all transfixed by the promised land that the new city offers and are involved in the same never-ending pursuit of money, sex and booze, while the women are committed to making as much money as they can out of the men's unleashed desires. If this strikes the modern reader as simplistic, it is worth remembering that the Wild West was notorious for its hedonism and that Brecht deliberately chose this location so he could write about working-class people, cut free from the conventions of bourgeois society, attempting, however disastrously, to build a new kind of world.

Brecht was keen to stress that *Mahagonny* was intended as 'a piece of fun'. At its heart, it tells an American folk tale, a story of impending disaster narrowly averted. Its emotions are heightened, its scenes are extreme and it is drenched in popular language and imagery. Uncannily, *Mahagonny* was completed just months before the Wall Street Crash of October 1929, and the hurricane is an uncanny prophecy of the economic and political disaster that was about to sweep the globe.

Brecht knew that *Mahagonny* carried its own explosive power and was particular about the theatrical form that it required:

> We had to make something instructive and direct of our piece of fun if it was not to be merely irrational. The form that suggested itself was that of the moral tableau. The tableau is depicted by the characters in the play. The text had to be neither moralising nor sentimental, but to put morality and sentimentality on view. The spoken word was no more important than the written word. Reading seems to encourage the audience to adopt the most relaxed attitude towards the work.

He also insisted on a new degree of objective coolness at all times:

Whatever is intended to produce hypnosis, or likely to induce improper intoxication, or creates fog, has got to be given up. Words, music and setting must become more independent of one another.

Thus *Mahagonny*'s strange mixture of the impassioned and the scientific, the bawdy and the pure, makes it the key transition between the popular extravagance of Brecht's plays in the 1920s and the political austerity of his work in the early 1930s.

Mahagonny's reputation as one of the musical masterpieces of the Weimar Republic is secure. What, however, are we to make of its libretto? Brecht's own judgement was severe:

It attacks the society that needs operas of such a sort; it still perches on the old bough, perhaps, but at least it has started (out of absent-mindedness or bad conscience) to saw it through . . .

Brecht was not to attempt opera again until *The Trial of Lucullus* in 1951 and in the 1930s Germany needed something more serious than even the most radical opera could provide. However, in 1929 Brecht and Weill wrote an extraordinary work which, with its astonishingly powerful music and its dramatic volte-faces, is one of the most intoxicating pieces of music-theatre ever written.

IN PERFORMANCE

The *Little Mahagonny* (also known as the *Mahagonny Songspiel*) was presented at the Baden-Baden Music Festival of New Music in 1927, with projections by Caspar Neher. Lotte Lenya played Jenny and she described how after the first performance

Suddenly I felt a slap on the back, accompanied by a booming laugh: 'Is here no telephone?' It was Otto Klemperer. With that, the whole room was singing the Benares Song, and I knew that the battle was won.

The full opera was first performed in Leipzig on 9 March 1930 in a production directed by Walther Brügmann with designs by Caspar Neher. This was picketed by Nazi protestors, but the piece was subsequently seen in a new production at the Kurfürstendamm Theater, Berlin, on 21 December 1931, co-directed by Neher and Brecht, and conducted by Alexander von Zemlinsky, with Lotte Lenya as Jenny. The sound of Lenya singing 'Show us the way / To the next whisky bar' has provided many with the best possible introduction to Brecht.

Mahagonny is particularly closely associated with Caspar Neher, who worked on the opera with Brecht from the outset. His extraordinary set – with its boxing ring, signs and texts, lorries, palm trees and hurricane charts – is an essential part of the opera's appeal and is fundamental to its extraordinary atmosphere.

Mahagonny received its London premiere at Sadler's Well's Theatre on 6 January 1963, where it was directed by Michael Geliot. This used the remarkable translation by W. H. Auden and Chester Kallman, which had been written for a planned American premiere in 1960 that never took place; Hannah Arendt said she knew of 'no other adequate rendering of Brecht into English'.

10 MARXISM AND THE THEATRE

1929–1933

Brecht's political views had been developing throughout the 1920s and in 1926, under the influence of Karl Korsch, he started reading Marx and Lenin. In 1927 he met the Marxist sociologist Fritz Sternberg, who became a close friend, and in 1929 both men watched the Berlin police, under Social Democrat control, attack banned May Day demonstrations and kill twenty-five protesters. This persuaded Brecht of the view that the Social Democrats were 'social fascists' and prompted his active involvement in Communism.

This political awakening was matched by significant aesthetic developments. In 1929 Brecht met the great Marxist philosopher Walter Benjamin, who helped him articulate his theatrical instincts. In the same year Elisabeth Hauptmann introduced him to Arthur Waley's English translations of Japanese Noh drama, which led him to write a series of small-scale, highly concentrated plays, much influenced by the oriental theatre, known as *Lehrstücke*, or learning plays. These had a didactic function directed at the participants as much as at the audience and tended to focus on questions of Communist tactics and discipline rather than critiques of capitalism. They were *The Baden-Baden Lesson on Consent* and *Lindbergh's Flight*, both premiered in 1929, *The Exception and the Rule, He Who Says Yes* and *He Who Says No* (all 1930) and *The Horatians and the Curatians* (1934). Most of these are lesser works; the exceptions are two of his greatest masterpieces, *The Decision* (1930) and *The Mother* (1930–1).

The *Lehrstücke* feature music by all four of Brecht's musical collaborators. As well as Kurt Weill, these included three important new figures: in 1927 Brecht was introduced to the film composer Paul Dessau with whom he struck up an immediate rapport; in 1929 he met the great, if apolitical, composer Paul Hindemith and participated in his festivals of *Neue Musik* at Donaueschingen and Baden-Baden; he also started working with the Communist composer Hanns Eisler, the most militant of Schoenberg's pupils, who provided him with a new kind of music that could illuminate his explicitly political plays, and move beyond the mordant wit and jazzy popularism of Kurt Weill.

It was in this astonishingly fertile period that Brecht also wrote the radio piece, the *Berlin Requiem* (1929), a cycle of poems set to music by Kurt Weill, the delicate and neglected *Keuner Stories* (1930), and one of his most ambitious plays, *Saint Joan of the Stockyards* (1930–1). In addition he completed *Round Heads and Pointed Heads* (1932), a largely unsuccessful adaptation of Shakespeare's *Measure for Measure*, which attempted to recast Nazi racial policy in the language of class war, as well as the screenplay for the great Communist film, *Kühle Wampe* (1932), both with music by Eisler. He was also involved in two landmark theatrical events: the premiere of *The Rise and Fall of the City of Mahagonny* at the Leipzig Opera House in 1930 and his own astounding production of *Man equals Man* in Berlin in 1931. His private life was equally lively: he divorced Marianne Zoff in 1927, married Helene Weigel in 1929 and their daughter, Barbara, was born in October 1930. In 1932 he met the young working-class Communist Margarete Steffin when she was playing a maid in *The Mother*, and she quickly became the closest of his many lovers as well as collaborating with him on several of his most remarkable plays.

The development of an explicitly Marxist revolutionary theatre is the key factor in Brecht's plays in the late 1920s and early 1930s. The best of them examine the demands of revolutionary change with consummate skill and artistry. As such they are crucial documents in the development of Communist art. Like all revolutionary art, however, they allow little room for humanism. The need for society to be changed comes above all other concerns and the plays pose uncomfortable questions about revolutionary means and ends. Furthermore, although he may have helped radicalise the many workers who participated in them, Brecht, like many other socialist artists and intellectuals, was more interested in raising revolutionary consciousness than in opposing the rise of Hitler. At times it feels as if Brecht set himself the wrong target: Fascism was the overwhelming danger to everything that he stood for, but it was not until the Nazis had swept into power and he had been forced into exile that he attempted to articulate the terrible danger that they represented.

SAINT JOAN OF THE STOCKYARDS
[Die heilige Johanna der Schlachtöfe]

Collaborators: Hans Borchardt, Emil Burri, Elisabeth Hauptmann
1929–31

THE STORY

The Chicago 'meat king and philanthropist', Pierpont Mauler (1), receives a letter: the meat market is depressed and he is advised to sell up. He tells his partner, Cridle, that he saw 'a big blond steer' being killed, and now intends to move out of meat. Cridle persuades Mauler to help engineer his rival Lennox's fall. Soon Lennox's plant has been shut down (2a) and Mauler is guarded by detectives (2b). Joan Dark launches a campaign (2c) to make God's voice 'resound in the stockyards', but when her Black Straw Hats (2d) start doling out soup, they quickly discover that the unemployed are more interested in jobs than morals. News arrives that Mauler and Cridle are shutting down their plants and Joan is determined to go and 'see this Mauler / Who's at the bottom of so much misery'.

Graham, a meatpacker, advises Lennox (3) to appeal to Mauler's better side. Cridle boasts of his new meat-processing machine, but Graham says the market is 'glutted'. Mauler and his broker, Slift, appear and Cridle discovers that he is in trouble because he bought Mauler's shares too expensively. Graham punches Mauler 'to see if he has a heart' and Mauler instructs Cridle not to buy 'a single can'. Mauler meets Joan, is amazed that she works for nothing and asks her whether she thinks he is right to sell up. He takes cash from his rivals' wallets and tells her to distribute it among the poor. When she wants him to do 'something that will really help', he tells Slift to show her the stockyards and see what the poor are really like. Triumphant, Joan declares that Mauler is 'the first / Our drums have flushed from the thickets of baseness'.

Slift takes Joan down into the stockyards (4). Luckerniddle, a worker, had fallen into a rendering tank four days previously and 'ended up with the leaf lard'; the foreman asks a young fellow to get rid of Luckerniddle's jacket and cap, promising him his job once the plant opens. When the young fellow puts them on, Joan feels sick; when Slift insists that he should tell Luckerniddle's widow where they come from, he is persuaded by the offer of 'a meal and a dollar'. Soon, Slift tells Mrs Luckerniddle that her husband has left town and that she can eat in the canteen free of charge, so long as she does not mention his absence. Elsewhere, Gloomb has lost a hand in the tin-cutting machine and is angry with the foreman; Slift tells him that if he can find someone else to take on his old job, he will be given a better one; Joan pretends to be looking for work and he recommends the job to her, despite the fact that she has bad eyesight and gets tired easily. Mrs Luckerniddle sits down to eat and admires the young fellow's cap which, he says, came from a man who 'fell into the rendering tank'; she feels sick, but asks the waiter not to take away her food. Joan tells Slift that he has not shown her 'the baseness of the poor but / The poverty of the poor' and invites him to see 'what suffering they endure'.

In the Livestock Exchange (5) the packers, wholesalers and breeders bewail their situation. Meanwhile, Mauler has been told that 'the whole meat ring will topple to the ground / And I'll be left with mountains of meat on my hands', and insists that his actions are driven by his conscience. Soon, however, a meat market crash is announced. Suddenly the Black Straw Hats enter, 'singing their battle hymn', and Joan insists that Mauler should listen to her criticisms. When she introduces the poor, Mauler faints; when he wakes up he refuses to open his eyes until they have left. They refuse to go and he starts to buy; suddenly there is work for all, but the businessmen are unhappy. Joan invites everyone to Sunday service and Slift says 'the market's going to hum'. The breeders admire Joan and join her.

In Slift's house (6), Mauler predicts the vengeance of the poor, but Slift cooks him a rare steak to 'bring him to his senses'. Mauler also realises that he has bought so much canned meat that he will be ruined; but he has been advised that now is the time to buy. The breeders confront Mauler too; they want him to buy from them. Mauler instructs Slift to see if Graham wants the meat, but suddenly decides to buy up everything himself – 'Two wrongs will make a right' – and everybody is delighted.

In the mission house (7) Snyder, the Black Straw Hats' major, is explaining to Mulberry, their landlord, how they are going to pay their rent: although the poor are 'most ungenerous', the rich will join them in their 'campaign against godlessness and materialism'. The packers arrive, grumbling about Mauler's latest initiative. Snyder says they have nothing to fear from the poor because he will tell them their poverty is a natural calamity – in exchange for eight hundred dollars a month. When Joan arrives the packers ask her to stop Mauler. She is shocked to see the poor receiving charity, despite the jobs that have been created, and discovers that the packers have not been employing anybody. She realises the depth of their 'exploitation' and drives them 'out of the temple'. Snyder is furious and strips her of her rank: 'Out into the snowstorm with your self-righteousness'. Meanwhile (8), Mauler and Slift plot to drive up the price of meat and Slift insinuates that Joan is Mauler's lover. She arrives in her own clothes and Mauler feeds her; when she asks him to pay off Mulberry, he demands her approval; she should respect money more, he says, but she refuses to listen. Her solidarity with the poor is such that she must go back to them.

Joan speaks of her dreams (9a): the poor of Chicago marched together and displayed their 'misery on the streets and squares'. Mauler (9b) demands 'immediate delivery of the / Canned meat our contract calls for' and the others are in despair. The Black Straw Hats try in vain (9c) to gather support and Joan can hardly bear to 'hear the words which / Were once such a joy and comfort to me'. Mauler is still insisting on his contracts (9d), but socialists are agitating for a general strike (9e). Joan offers to work for them: they see she is no 'stool pigeon' and give her letters to hand out at the Graham plant, assuring the strikers of wider support. The businessmen cannot pay Mauler what they owe him (9f) and Slift torments them with ever-rising prices; meanwhile, Joan is leading a huge crowd. As news arrives that the police have turned on them, Mauler is unable to control Slift's greed. Reporters (9g) cannot accept that Joan has left the Black Straw Hats, but the strikers stick together. The strike is working, when suddenly gunfire is heard. Joan urges the workers not to retaliate with violence and the strike is defeated. Mauler (9h) discovers that Slift's boldness has bankrupted him and decides to go down to the stockyards. Mrs Luckerniddle criticises Joan (9i), who is soon in despair, hears voices (9j) and realises the error of her ways.

Mulberry is repossessing the Black Straw Hats' mission (10) when Mauler arrives, dressed as a poor man, having given away his worldly wealth and repenting his sins. They are about to drive him out when the businessmen enter, 'chalky white': Slift's greed has brought down even the biggest banks. It has also brought Mauler to penury. A letter arrives which advises Mauler to come to an agreement with the suppliers, but he is racked with guilt. His solution is to burn half the stock; when Snyder asks why he does not just give the meat away, he explains that they are 'customers'. Endowments are promised to the Black Straw Hats, news arrives that the general strike has been broken and Mauler joins in the religious welcome offered to the poor and hungry. Elsewhere, labour leaders are carted off to prison (11a); one of them tells the soldiers that they are all on the same side. At the same time Joan is trying to keep the strike going. A group of workers (11b) admire her courage: 'There ought to be more of her.' Meanwhile, she has contracted pneumonia.

The Black Straw Hats are now rich (12). Joan comes in with a crowd of poor people and says that she is still going to deliver the letters supporting the strike. Snyder decides to canonise her and dresses her in her uniform again; but she regrets that 'when there was a chance to change the world / I wasn't there' and admits that she was 'just what the oppressors wanted'. The traders try to shout her down and when Joan denies the existence of God, the Black Straw Hats sing a hymn as loudly as they can. As news arrives of the great meltdown of the world financial markets, Joan dies and, with flags lowered over her body, Mauler and the businessmen speak solemnly of the dual nature of mankind.

ABOUT THE PLAY

Saint Joan of the Stockyards is one of Brecht's most ambitious plays. It combines many of his lifelong preoccupations – the value of 'goodness' in a wicked world, the contradiction between the wealthy's greed and their philanthropy, and the need for revolution if injustice and inequality are to be defeated. It also attempts to examine these issues with a new degree of philosophical and analytical objectivity. The result is an ambitious failure, which nevertheless marks an important milestone in Brecht's development.

The play is Brecht's most sustained attempt at describing high capitalism. He had been trying to write a play about the Chicago wheat industry for some time (originally called *Wheat*, it was also known as *Joe P. Fleischhacker from Chicago*), but was hindered by his ignorance about economic affairs, as a poem from the 1930s shows:

> Years ago when I was studying the ways of the Chicago
> Wheat Exchange
> I suddenly grasped how they managed the whole world's
> wheat there
> And I did not grasp it either and lowered the book.
> I knew at once: you've run
> Into bad trouble . . .

However, Brecht's reading of Karl Marx's *Das Kapital* in 1926 gave him the analysis he needed.

The play's literary influences are diverse. They include the popular novels of Frank Norris and Upton Sinclair, with their tales of the struggles of the Chicago poor to earn a living in the great

American metropolis. In addition, Brecht had been reading Bernard Shaw, particularly *Major Barbara* (1905), which examines the role of the Salvation Army in a tough world, and *Saint Joan* (1923), which retells the story of the French saint's war against the English. He also cannibalised Elisabeth Hauptmann's contribution to the disastrous sequel to *The Threepenny Opera, Happy End*. Finally, the play is dense with borrowings from German romantic drama, above all Goethe's *Faust* (1768–1829) with its portrait of the sacrifices a man makes for power and pleasure, and Schiller's *The Maid of Orleans* (1801).

Brecht's aim throughout the 1920s was to develop a kind of theatre that was sufficiently flexible to portray the complexities, contradictions and connections of the modern world: 'Petroleum', he quipped, 'resists the five-act form', and *Saint Joan of the Stockyards* is one of Brecht's formally most adventurous plays. In devising its theatrical style, he drew heavily on Erwin Piscator's remarkable work at the Volksbühne in Berlin in the 1920s, which portrayed the ordinary man being ground down by the faceless mechanisms of industrial society. Here, however, Brecht dramatises the system that lies behind the machine, the roller coaster of the stock exchange, and shows how the actions of a few rich and powerful men have a profound effect on the daily lives of thousands of working people. Inspired by Shakespeare, it is one of Brecht's first attempts to show the relationship between the individual and the masses.

Like *In the Jungle of the Cities, Saint Joan of the Stockyards* is set in Chicago. Here, however, it is a much more industrialised city, less exotic and considerably more frightening. Chicago's enormous wealth boom was built, above all, on the processing of cattle, and the image of innocent animals being ruthlessly slaughtered and turned into meat product provides Brecht with his central metaphor: high capitalism, the play implies, does the same with the poor.

At the centre of the play is Joan Dark, a portrait of instinctive goodness confronted by corruption and compromise. At the beginning, she has a simple-minded religious belief and is determined to right the wrongs of the world by the sheer force of her personality. She quickly becomes the leading figure in the Black Straw Hats, the Salvation Army to whom she has devoted her life, and is at first successful. Brecht's point, however, is that an instinctive desire to do good is insufficient and leads inevitably to the defeat of the cause it champions. Joan eventually sees the need for revolution, but this comes too late, and she dies bitterly disappointed by her own failure, cynically canonised by the twin forces of capitalism and religion.

Joan's polar opposite is the meat king Pierpoint Mauler, an extraordinary mixture of the monstrous and the tender, the brutal and the kind. Brecht wrote that the intention of the play was to demonstrate 'the present stage of development of Faustian man' and his portrait of Mauler shows a man who has sacrificed his 'soul' for money and worldly success. Brecht deliberately teases us with a classical conception of the great world historical figure but then implies that Mauler's tragic split is no more than an expression of the contradiction implicit in high capitalism, which has to be brutal to be kind, rewards the rich in order to keep the poor from starving and allows cut-throat competition to exist side by side with Christian charity.

The play teems with figures from all sectors of society: business managers, manual labourers, union leaders, newspaper reporters and so on. In his portrait of the Black Straw Hats, Brecht was keen not to mock religion and wrote:

> The aim of the play – to communicate a profound and practically active awareness of the great social processes of our time – would be distorted by blaspheming 'God' or showing the religious approach in a contemptible light.

Instead, he wanted to demonstrate the limitations of the charity that is offered in God's name. He also focused on a number of vividly drawn individuals: Luckerniddle's widow who, in the pursuit of financial security, finds herself cannibalising her own husband; the appallingly named Gloomb, who loses his hand in a tin-cutting machine but is happy to recommend his old job to Joan; Mauler's cynical and greedy broker Sullivan Slift, who is prepared to betray anyone for his own betterment; and the Black Straw Hats' entirely hypocritical landlord, Mulberry. If this rogues' gallery lacks realism, it does provide a mesmerising spectacle of a modern urban inferno.

Most of the work on *Saint Joan of the Stockyards* was undertaken in the South of France over the summer of 1930. Brecht was eagerly developing his theories of the epic theatre at the time and was clear that the play

> is a piece of non-Aristotelian dramaturgy. This is a dramaturgy that demands a quite specific approach on the part of the spectator. He has to be in a position to adopt a specific and learnable attitude, absorbing the events on the stage and grasping them, in their multiple relationships and complete progression. This with a view to a radical review of his own conduct. He is not allowed to identify himself spontaneously with particular characters in order merely to partake of their own experience.

Perhaps goaded by his debates with Lukács, Brecht was preoccupied with the question of whether the play could be seen as realistic, as these notes to the 1931 script indicate:

> Great sections of the working class, discontented with the prevalent social system, see the institutions in question as intellectually and organisationally bound up with a social order that denies them all possibility of life. And so they turn their backs on certain moral and religious trains of thought . . . Investigating the effectiveness of behaviour such as that of Joan and Mauler in our own time is unquestionably the enterprise of a realist, even where the field where it all happens is artificially constructed . . . Is *Saint Joan of the Stockyards* a realist work? Persons uncertain of the difference between realism and materialism are unlikely to consider this a realist work. It is even doubtful if they would describe it as a materialist one. The formal aspect alone might well mislead them.

Despite these protestations, Brecht's achievement in *Saint Joan of the Stockyards* is more formal than analytical, and his insistence on the play's realist credentials feels somewhat overstretched.

After the clearly defined limits of the *Lehrstücke*, Brecht wanted to write a large-scale play for the popular theatre. His attempt at a Shakespearean panorama of capitalism is an impressive undertaking; unfortunately, much of the play feels merely experimental and its rambling structure, unfocused dramatic action and abstract characterisation are largely unsatisfying. Furthermore, the timing was wrong for such a piece and Brecht's assault on capitalism was overshadowed by the much more sinister phenomenon of Fascism. It was exile that gave him the dramatic discipline that *Saint Joan of the Stockyards*, for all its laudable ambition, fails to achieve.

IN PERFORMANCE

It was impossible for Brecht to secure a production of such a large-scale play in Germany in the early 1930s and the only pre-war performance was on Berlin Radio in 1932. This featured a virtual roll-call of Brecht's greatest actors – Carola Neher as Joan, Fritz Kortner as Mauler, Helene Weigel as Mrs Luckerniddle, Ernst Busch as Foreman Smith and Peter Lorre as Sullivan Slift – and the radio critic of a Berlin newspaper declared:

> One day it will rank among the most memorable, and at the same time disgraceful landmarks of modern cultural history that the theatre had to leave it to the radio to communicate one of the greatest and most significant plays of our time.

Ruth Berlau and the Copenhagen Revolutionary Workers Theatre staged scenes from the play in the mid 1930s, but a full production was impossible. Paul Dessau wrote songs for the play in exile in Paris in 1936.

In 1949 Brecht wrote to Gustaf Grundgens (the model for Klaus Mann's novel *Mephisto*), who had been Intendant at the Prussian State Theatre under Hitler and who was now at the Düsseldorf Schauspielhaus:

> You asked in 1932 for permission to perform *Saint Joan of the Stockyards*. My answer is yes.

Despite sending an enthusiastic reply ('scared to death – but delighted you remember'), Grundgens did not get round to directing the play for another ten years, this time at the Deutsches Schauspielhaus in Hamburg, with scenery by Caspar Neher and Hanne Hiob, Brecht's daughter by his first wife Marianne Zoff, as Joan.

The play was produced by Benno Besson, first in Stuttgart in 1961 and then in Lausanne in 1962, by the Haiyuza Theatre in Tokyo in 1965, the Berliner Ensemble in 1968 and Giorgio Strehler's Piccolo Teatro in Milan in 1970. The play's English-language premiere was at the Gaiety Theatre in Dublin in September 1961, and it was first seen in London in June 1964. It was revived at the Citizens' Theatre in Glasgow in 1974.

THE DECISION
[Die Massnahme]

Collaborators: Slatan Dudow, Hanns Eisler
1930

THE STORY

Four Communist agitators (Prelude) tell the Control Chorus that they have to report the 'death of a comrade'. When asked how, they say, 'We killed him. We shot him and threw him into a lime pit.' The Chorus asks them to show how it occurred and says that they will inform them of their verdict. In The Teachings of the Classics (1) the agitators report on their meeting with a Young Comrade on the Chinese border. He declares his support for the cause ('My heart beats for the Revolution. The sight of injustice made me join the ranks of the militants. Man must help man. I am for freedom. I believe in the human race. And I support the decisions of the Communist Party, which is fighting for the classless society against exploitation and ignorance') and asks them what they have brought with them: 'We have nothing for you. But for the Chinese workers across the frontier in Mukden we have the teachings of the Marxist classics, the ABC of Communism. For the ignorant, to shed light upon their situation; for the oppressed, to teach them class-awareness; and for the class-conscious, the experience of the Revolution.' Together they go into Mukden, 'spreading the teachings of the Communist classics: the World Revolution'. In The Obliteration (2), the Director of the last Party house before the border insists that they hide their faces and obliterate their individuality ('empty pages upon which the Revolution writes what it has to say'). The Control Chorus speaks of how those who fight for Communism 'must know how to fight and how not to fight; to tell the truth and not to tell the truth; to be servile and also how not to be servile . . .' The agitators say they 'had no bread for the hungry, merely knowledge for the ignorant, and so we spoke of the causes of poverty: did not abolish poverty itself but spoke of abolishing its causes'. In The Stone (3) the agitators talk about watching coolies pulling a barge. They had told the Young Comrade to 'make propaganda among them' but not feel 'sorry for them'; but in the melancholic 'Song of the Rice-Barge Haulers', the Young Comrade does feel sorry for them and lays a stone to help a coolie from slipping and being whipped. As a result, the agitators are discovered and it is impossible for them to proceed. The Control Chorus sings a canon based on a Lenin quotation: 'He's not wise who never makes mistakes / He is wise who makes mistakes but puts them right.'

In Justice (4) the agitators report on the Young Comrade's attempt to hand out leaflets at the factory gates. A policeman is about to arrest a worker for reading one of the leaflets when the Young Comrade intervenes: as a result of assaulting a policeman the workers will 'never be able to go back to the factory, and it's all your fault'. When the Control Chorus asks whether it is not 'correct to stop injustice wherever it occurs', the agitators reply, 'He stopped a small injustice, but the big injustice was the strike-breaking, and that continued.' In By the way, What is a Man? (5) the agitators report on a mission the Young Comrade was sent on, to persuade a rich businessman to arm the coolies for a fight against English merchants, but actually for revolutionary purposes. The merchant welcomes him, offers him rice and asks him about the 'price of a man'; when the Young Comrade refuses to eat with him, he is thrown out 'and the coolies were not armed'. When the Control Chorus asks him if it is not 'correct to put honour above else?' the answer is a simple 'no'. In The Betrayal (6) the agitators describe being confronted by the Young Comrade, who wants the unemployed to storm the barracks immediately. He asks 'if the classics [of Marxism] accept the supreme importance of giving immediate help to any individual in misery'. When they say 'no', he declares that 'the classics are crap' and tears them up. In Extreme Persecution and Analysis (7) they describe how the Young Comrade's actions endangered the mission, just at the moment of greatest revolutionary potential. Finally, in The Decision (8) they explain why the Young Comrade had to be shot and 'thrown into a lime pit'. They enact the last conversation, which ends with the Young Comrade giving his agreement ('For the sake of Communism / Agreeing with the advance of the proletarian masses of all countries / Saying yes to the revolutionising of the world'). The Control Chorus supports them, declaring that 'only studying reality's going to / Help us alter reality'.

ABOUT THE PLAY

Brecht's most contentious *Lehrstück* is usually translated as *The Measures Taken*. John Willett's preferred title, *The Decision*, reflects the fact that the play is not about 'tough measures' so much as about a difficult decision. It is a crucial distinction, on which hangs any evaluation of the play as a whole.

Brecht described *The Decision* as 'not a play in the normal sense. It is an event put on by a mass chorus and four players.' It takes the form of a report to the Central Committee of the Communist Party (a mass choir) by three agitators. From the outset they declare the climax of their story – the killing of one of their comrades who jeopardised the success of the mission. The drama lies in an explanation of their action and a demonstration of what made them do it; the piece ends with the verdict that the committee eventually reaches.

Like Brecht's other *Lehrstücke*, *The Decision* draws on the techniques of the oriental theatre and reports an event that took place in pre-revolutionary China. Its means are exceptionally simple – a rope, some leaflets, a bowl of rice, four masks – and its points are made in the clearest way, unhindered by illusion of any kind. It uses reportage, songs, accompanied recitative, direct address and pared-down dramatic action. It requires three actors and a tenor, who take it in turns to play the Young Comrade (so as to avoid 'identification'). The action is punctured by a series of choruses, with titles such as 'Praise of the USSR', 'Praise of Illegal

Activity', 'Song of the Rice-Barge Hauliers', 'Alter the World, It Needs It' and 'Praise of the Party'. These encourage the audience to step back from the personal issues raised by the story and see it within the broader context of the revolutionary cause. The piece also features several solos for the tenor, including the merchant's 'Song of Supply and Demand', with its repeated refrain:

> Don't ask me what a man is.
> Don't ask me my advice
> I've no idea what a man is
> All I have learnt is his price.

When performed with Eisler's full score, the piece has all the power of a Bach Mass (later, Eisler spoke of having played passages from the *St Matthew* and *St John Passions* to convince Brecht 'how magnificently Bach can set a report'). It also has a curious – if unexplored – relationship with Heinrich von Kleist's *The Prince of Homburg* (1811), one of the finest play of German romanticism, about a young dreamer whose eagerness jeopardises the well-being of the group and their mission.

For all its great qualities, *The Decision* is a deeply contentious piece. The awkward question that it does not adequately resolve is this: was the Young Comrade sacrificed because he endangered the mission, or because he disagreed with the classics of Marxism? Furthermore, if he was killed because he jeopardised the mission, was this a sacrifice human beings should ever be expected to make? Thus, for all its dramatic and musical qualities, the dark shadow of 1930s Stalinism, with its brutal suppression of any dissidence, its show trials and its executions, inevitably hangs over the piece.

We should not imagine, however, that Brecht and Eisler's grappling with such questions was merely intellectual: Eisler's brother and sister, Gerhart and Ruth, had been Communist agitators in China, and Brecht and Eisler were both involved in the struggle of the German Communists in the years before Hitler. Their commitment to this shines through:

> Sink into the mire
> Embrace the butcher
> But change the world, it needs it!

Perhaps the best way to see *The Decision* is as a parable of faith and sacrifice, of the need for both if society is to be changed. At its heart is the almost Christian notion that individuality must be subsumed for the good of the community and that the cause demands sacrifice. Of course, the cause is very particular – the spread of the 'World Revolution' – and the piece is only tolerable if we can accept the necessity of this goal.

The Decision poses the modern liberal with the toughest of questions: namely, if you believe that the world should be changed, are you prepared to use all means, however dishonest, and do you accept that violence, however regretful, may sometimes be necessary? These are question that continues to resonate in surprising ways in the modern world.

A few days before he died Brecht was asked which of his plays represented the theatre of the future: his answer was *The Decision*. With the distance of history, it increasingly looks like one of Brecht's most formidable achievements.

IN PERFORMANCE

The Decision was first performed at the Grosses Schauspielhaus, Berlin, on 10 December 1930, in a production directed by Slatan Dudow, with Helene Weigel, Ernst Busch and the Workers' Choir of Berlin, conducted by Karl Rankl. It was revived the following year at the Philharmonie, Berlin, by the Workers' Singers Union, with changes suggested by the Communist Party.

Brecht and Eisler wrote that performances of *The Decision* should be 'realised by those they are meant for, who alone have a use for them: by workers' choruses, amateur dramatic groups, school choruses and school orchestras, in other words those people who neither can pay for art nor are paid for art, but just want to take part in it'. The aim was that the piece should teach everybody involved, not just the audience, and question-naires about Communist tactics were circulated at the first performance.

Under the title *The Expedient*, the piece was first performed in Britain in 1936 by the London Labour Choral Union in the Westminster Hall and on tour. There is a tantalising letter in the same year to Lee Strasberg – the father of American 'method' acting and often assumed to be Brecht's polar opposite – in which Brecht wrote,

> Unfortunately we had to cease rehearsals on the *Massnahme* for political reasons. It is a great pity, because I had the impression that we worked very well together. In general it is not very easy for me to express what I thought necessary for saving the theatre here from [a] bourgeois drug traffic and emotions racket. The few rehearsals with you and your group have at least shown me that a revolutionary pedagogic theatre is possible here too.

Nothing is known of these rehearsals.

Subsequent performances have been few and far between. In 1956 Brecht wrote in response to a request for permission,

> *Die Massnahme* was not written for an audience but exclusively for the instruction of the performers. In my experience, public perfor-mances of it inspire nothing but moral qualms, usually of the cheapest sort. Accordingly, I have not let anyone perform the play for a long time.

Evidently Brecht was aware of the complex resonances of the piece and felt that any performance would give comfort to his political opponents.

The Decision was eventually produced at the 1987 Almeida Music Festival, with the complete Hanns Eisler score and chorus, in a production directed by Stephen Unwin, conducted by Robert Ziegler, with Tilda Swinton, Stephen Dillane and the tenor Philip Doghan in the cast. This was the first full performance since the 1930s. It was subsequently broadcast on Radio 3. Some argued that the piece should not have been revived because it played into the hands of the right – or at least Brecht's detractors. Others felt that its artistic merits were such that it should be seen as an extraordinary work of art from a very different age.

THE MOTHER

[Die Mutter]

After Gorky

Collaborators: Hanns Eisler, Slatan Dudow, Günter Weisenborn

1930–1

THE STORY

Pelagea Vlassova would like to give her son, Pavel, better soup (1), but all he does is read and will not eat what she gives him: 'I try it this way and that. One day I scrimp on firewood, another day on clothing. But I can't manage. I don't see any answer.' He turns up with revolutionary workers (2) to use his mother's room to print illegal leaflets. She is worried about this: 'The result will be he'll lose his job.' One of the workers sings that the only way to fight is to 'turn the whole thing upside down for ever'. Suddenly the police arrive, smash up Vlassova's furniture and leave, with a warning: 'Better keep an eye on that son of yours. He's going down a bad road.' So when it is Pavel's turn to distribute leaflets, Vlassova insists she should do it instead and smuggles them into the factory by using them as wrapping paper for food and tobacco (3). A factory guard spots a man reading one and arrests him but, as Vlassova says, 'All he did was buy a gherkin.' She is perplexed (4) and is given her 'first lesson in economics' by the revolutionaries, who explain that although a chair can belong to an individual, a factory should be owned by the people who work in it. She argues that as long as they protest peacefully, it is 'nothing to do with the police'.

On May Day 1905 (5) the police demand that the demonstrating workers hand over the red flag. When they refuse, the man who is carrying it is shot dead and Vlassova picks it up. Soon Pavel has been arrested and one of the revolutionaries takes Vlassova to stay with his brother, a teacher (6). He is suspicious of their cause but gives her a job as his housekeeper. One evening the teacher comes home and finds her talking politics with a group of unemployed workers. He tries to teach them how to read; but all they want to learn are 'useful' words like 'class war' and 'exploitation'. When he says that 'Knowledge doesn't help. Goodness does', they sing 'In Praise of Learning'; slowly the teacher becomes radicalised and his brother says that he no longer recognises him. Vlassova visits Pavel in prison (7) where 'talk about politics is forbidden'. By pretending to be concerned only with maternal questions, Vlassova gets Pavel to give her a list of local peasants who support the workers. She goes into the countryside (8) where a group of peasants throw stones at her, thinking that she is a strike breaker. In the estate kitchen, however, she shows the domestic staff that their interests are identical with those of the peasants in the fields and soon they too have joined the strike.

By 1913 (9) Vlassova has become a leading figure in the revolutionary movement and installs a printing machine in the teacher's flat. He worries that it is noisy, so she goes to get some felt. Pavel arrives, having escaped from Siberia, and Vlassova returns, saying that the neighbour would not give her the felt she uses for her children's clothes, so she stole it instead. Together they start printing leaflets. As Pavel says, 'Fleeing from Siberia to Finland against the icy blasts of the north wind, the shots of his pursuers ringing in his ears, he finds no place to lay his head but in an illegal printing shop. And instead of caressing his locks, his mother gathers the pages.' Soon (10), however, the Chorus tells Vlassova that Pavel has been shot trying to cross the Finnish border, but consoles her with the fact that the people who 'did it were men of his own kind'. Three women arrive to express their Christian fellow feeling and give her a pot of food. However, when they say that it was God who took Pavel away, she challenges them, declaring that Pavel was not afraid of death: 'But he was very much frightened by the misery / Which is plain for all to see in our cities.' In the struggle that follows, their Bible is torn to pieces. When Vlassova falls ill (11) the teacher pays for a doctor, and when she hears that war has been declared she gets off her sickbed to help the party. Despite being beaten up by the police

(12), she reminds the others that the war is a distraction from the real struggle and that they must not give up. She joins a queue of women collecting copper for the war effort (13) and announces that she is handing over her little mug, 'so the war doesn't stop'. This puzzles the others and she explains how contradictory their actions are. She also recruits a young maidservant who joins her in a massive demonstration (14) with several thousand striking workers from fifty factories. In the last moments she declares,

> Whoever's been beaten must get to his feet.
> He who is lost must give battle.
> He who is aware where he stands – how can anyone stop him
>   moving on?
> Those who were losers today will be triumphant tomorrow
> And from never will come today.

ABOUT THE PLAY

Brecht's most explicitly revolutionary play has a single source, Maxim Gorky's novel *Mother* (1906), written in response to the failed Russian revolution of the previous year. A Soviet film of the novel was made in 1926, which gave the playwright Günter Weisenborn and the dramaturg Günther Stark the idea of adapting it for Erwin Piscator at the Volksbühne in Berlin. They approached Brecht – well known at the Volksbühne – because of his reputation for experimental political theatre and he quickly took over the project. One of his first decisions was to extend the action to 1917; Lenin had described 1905 as the 'dress rehearsal for the Bolshevik Revolution' and Brecht wanted to show how the one led inexorably to the other.

Brecht described *The Mother* as 'a sociological experiment' which tells a classic Marxist story: the raising of the political consciousness of a working-class woman, Pelagea Vlassova. The play does this in a series of clearly defined steps. At the beginning she fails to understand her son's point of view and is suspicious of his friends. Soon, however, her instinct for justice, as well as her desire to protect her son, leads her to hand out leaflets in the factory, where her natural curiosity awakens and her search for answers begins. She witnesses the violence of the ruling class at first hand and joins the revolutionary movement, where her acts of determined pragmatism win her a leading position. There she is confronted by the imprisonment and subsequent death of her son; however, despite worry and grief, she is prepared to lie, steal and suppress her maternal feelings for the good of the cause. What is more, she is prepared to lay down her life. Thus Vlassova is the prototype of a new kind of revolutionary woman and her actions are nothing less than a new kind of heroism.

Although Vlassova is the central figure of the play it is her son, Pavel, the radicalised factory worker, who is the main protagonist. He is a classical revolutionary figure: disciplined, serious and entirely focused on the task in hand. This leads inevitably to his imprisonment and early death. The play implies that however remarkable this commitment and self-sacrifice might be, it is his mother – transformed from a cowed, anxious woman worried only that her son is not eating enough, to the revolutionary leader carrying the red flag at the final demonstration – whose example will ultimately change the world.

The teacher has an important role to play. For Communists, the intelligentsia posed a particular challenge: their involvement was essential if the revolution was to be deep-rooted and transcend simple working-class resentment, but teachers and intellectuals were regarded as members of a different class, inevitably removed from manual labour, and their contribution had to be secondary. Brecht's teacher is a vivid portrait of how this contradiction can be resolved: his initial suspicion of Pelagea and his rejection of the workers whom she persuades him to teach, as well as his deep-rooted sense of bourgeois propriety, is both comic and touching, but eventually gives way to involvement and commitment. His radicalisation parallels Vlassova's own and the moment when he pays for her doctor is when it is complete: the teacher is being taught by his pupils.

The other characters in the play complete the revolutionary diagram. The police are the tools of the ruling class but, as members of the working class, they are also potential supporters of the revolution. The peasants, by contrast, are quite capable of revolutionary action – they are on strike – but are deeply suspicious of the proletariat; one of Vlassova's crucial achievements is convincing them of their shared interests. The women who try to comfort Vlassova after her son's death demonstrate the reactionary nature of Christian charity. The other revolutionary workers sometimes speak as individuals, most vividly in the scene when they are being taught to read; at other times they operate as a group, singing powerful choruses that interrupt the action at critical moments, helping the audience draw broader connections and see the narrative from new perspectives.

The Mother is one of Brecht's most consummate technical achievements. Much of it takes the form of simple, pared-down dialogue, full of wit and life, but concentrated on what needs to be made evident and free of extraneous chatter. It uses first-person reportage (for example, 'As we came along the Lyubin-Prospekt there were already several thousand of us. More than fifty firms were on strike, and the strikers joined us to demonstrate against the war and against Tsarist domination') as well as several songs and choruses. Brecht described his aims in the commentary attached to the 1933 publication:

> Written in the style of the didactic pieces, but requiring actors, *The Mother* is a piece of anti-metaphysical, materialistic, non-Aristotelian drama. This makes nothing like such a free use as does the Aristotelian of the passive empathy of the spectator; it also relates differently to certain psychological effects, such as catharsis. Just as it refrains from handing its hero over to the world as if it were his inescapable fate, so it would not dream of handing the spectator over to an inspiring theatrical experience. Anxious to teach the spectator a quite definite practical attitude, directed towards changing the world, it must begin by making

him adopt in the theatre a quite different attitude from what he is used to.

It is impossible to understand Brecht's most explicitly Communist play without recalling the Leninist insistence on 'the whole loaf, not just a slice' for the working class. It is the play's absolute conviction about the necessity of revolution that makes its discussion of tactics so compelling. Some have dismissed it as a fantasy about the Russian Revolution, all heroic workers striking poses and so on. However, it should be seen in context: with the Nazis on the very verge of power, Brecht was writing about subversive Communist activity in 1930s Germany, as much as agitation in pre-revolutionary Russia.

The Mother occupies a special place in Brecht's oeuvre: it is his first fully realised masterpiece, entirely free of expressionism and the florid exoticism of his early work, with a rigorously worked-out political analysis and a grippingly theatrical style. It is one of the great achievements of Communist art and if all that survived of Brecht's work were *The Mother*, we would still have a vivid sense of his unique genius.

IN PERFORMANCE

The Mother was first performed at the Theater am Schiffbauerdamm on 17 January 1932, on the anniversary of the assassination of Rosa Luxemburg, 'the great revolutionary' as Brecht called her. It was co-directed by Emil Burri and Brecht, with scenery by Caspar Neher and music by Hanns Eisler. Helene Weigel played Vlassova and Ernst Busch played Pavel. From there the production went to the Moabiter Gesellschaftshaus where industrial workers acted many of the parts. When performances were banned, public readings of the piece were given instead.

Ruth Berlau directed the play in 1935 with the Copenhagen Workers Theatre. It was presented in English by the Theatre Union at the Civic Repertory Theatre in New York on 19 November 1935 in a production directed by Victor Wolfson with scenery by Mordecai Gorelik; Brecht attended a dress rehearsal and said it had been 'badly butchered'.

Brecht directed *The Mother* in 1951 at the Deutsches Theater, with the recently formed Berliner Ensemble, and reunited the original 1932 team: Weigel as Vlassova, scenery by Neher and music by Eisler (but in a richer orchestration). This production had a more specifically Russian feel to it and it is striking to see from the photographs just how many naturalistic elements were used. It was revived by Manfred Wekwerth in 1957 and subsequently filmed.

One of the most remarkable productions of modern times was Peter Stein's at the Schaubühne-am-Lehniner-Platz in West Berlin in 1970. This featured the great actress Therese Giehse as Vlassova. Giehse – who played Mother Courage under Brecht's direction in Frankfurt in 1950 – said that Stein 'has much of the quality of Brecht and has the same way of working . . . As a director Stein is Brecht's immediate successor.'

In his *Diaries* Peter Hall describes his row with William Gaskill about Gaskill's desire to include *The Mother* in a season at Olivier Theatre in the recently built National Theatre; needless to say, Peter Hall won. The 'in-yer-face' British playwright Mark Ravenhill chose *The Mother* as his contribution to the 'Playwrights' Playwrights' season at the Royal Court in 2004.

11 OPPOSITION PLAYS

1933–1943

The Brechts left Berlin on 28 February 1933, the day after the Reichstag fire, and spent a few months in Zurich and Paris, where Brecht wrote the libretto for the opera-ballet *The Seven Deadly Sins*. In December 1933 he used the royalties from *The Threepenny Opera* to buy a large thatched house in Skovsbostrand in Denmark, looking across the Svendborg Sound towards Germany, and moved there with Weigel and their two children. Margarete Steffin soon joined them and lived there for most of the next six years. He also met the talented and beautiful Danish actress and journalist, Ruth Berlau, and started a deeply problematic relationship with her that was to last all his life. Many friends and colleagues, including Walter Benjamin, George Grosz, Fritz Sternberg, Hanns Eisler, Karl Korsch and Elisabeth Hauptmann, visited him there, and the 'Brecht circle' was alive and well, even in exile.

In 1934 Brecht wrote his last *Lehrstück*, *The Horatians and the Curatians*, a play for children, as well as the rather disappointing *Threepenny Novel*. In 1935 he started work on his great cycle of short plays about Hitler's Germany, *Fear and Misery of the Third Reich*, and, in 1937, following the outbreak of the Spanish Civil War, wrote *Señora Carrar's Rifles*. He also began work on one of his most remarkable collections of poems, *The Svendborg Poems* (1939), as well as starting to keep his extraordinary *Journals*, which he maintained until his death.

It is a mistake to imagine Brecht confined to his house in Svendborg. In 1934 he made a rather fruitless trip to London and in 1935 was invited by Piscator to Moscow, where he met the Soviet writer Sergei Tretiakov and the revolutionary film-maker Sergei Eisenstein; he also saw a one-man show by the Chinese actor Mei Lan-fang, with whom he spoke about the alienation effect in oriental theatre. Additionally, he was appointed honorary editor of *Das Wort*, the German-language anti-Fascist magazine published in Moscow. He spent three months in New York in 1935 to oversee the Theatre Workshop production of *The Mother* (which dismayed him) and went back to London in 1936. In 1937 he travelled to Paris for the premiere of *Señora Carrar's Rifles* – under the direction of Slatan Dudow and starring Weigel – and returned there the following year when Dudow directed eight scenes from *Fear and Misery of the Third Reich*.

The outbreak of the Spanish Civil War acted as a rallying cry for the international left, and many Communists and socialists went to fight in the International Brigades. Brecht did not go himself, but took part in the campaign in support of the Republic. At the same time, his attitude to the Soviet Union was increasingly sceptical but, like many on the left, he was reluctant to express his views openly – worried, above all, that any criticisms would be used by the enemies of socialism. He had, however, started to write the collection of highly coded but strongly anti-Stalinist aphorisms known as *Me-Ti* in 1936.

In April 1939, with the growing threat of Nazi invasion, the Brechts left Denmark and moved to a house on the island of Lindingø in Sweden. There he finished the first drafts of his two greatest masterpieces, *Life of Galileo* and *Mother Courage and her Children*. The shift from the austere *Lehrstücke* of the 1920s and the realistic plays of the 1930s to the great historical dramas of the late 1930s and 1940s reflects the growing maturity of Brecht's political and social analysis, as well as the refinement of his theatrical and poetic approach. The seven years in Scandinavia were perhaps the most creative phase in his life and his work in this period was Brecht at his very best.

Brecht's work in these years was motivated, above all, by his hatred of the regime that had taken root in his homeland, and his growing commitment to a 'popular front' against Fascism is a theme that runs through his work until 1945 – which is why two later plays, *The Resistible Rise of Arturo Ui* (1941) and *Schweyk in the Second World War* (1941–3), have been included in this section. If occasionally Brecht underestimated Hitler (he scornfully called him 'the housepainter'), he was only making the same mistake as much of the rest of pre-war Europe. The fact is that Brecht's opposition to Nazism was unshakeable and at no time did he give in to despair – at least not in public – or claim Hitler as malign 'destiny'. In the 1930s Brecht was a genuinely creative force, writing poems, plays, essays and letters, and trying to find some way out of the dark valley into which Europe had descended.

FEAR AND MISERY OF THE THIRD REICH

[Furcht und Elend des Dritten Reichs]

Collaborator: Margarete Steffin

1935–8

THE STORY

In One Big Family (1), two drunken SS officers find themselves in a working-class district late at night. They are terrified when they hear an old man calling for his wife and they start shooting in every direction; suddenly 'a terrible cry is heard. Someone has been hit.' In A Case of Betrayal (2), a lower-middle-class man and his wife are listening to their neighbour being dragged out of his flat. It is clear that they betrayed him for listening to foreign broadcasts, but they are shocked at the way the police rip his jacket. The Chalk Cross (3) is set in the kitchen of an aristocrat's house. A maid, a cook and a chauffeur are asking an SA man (the maid's fiancé) about his work, admiring his new boots, feeding him and giving him beer. The cook's brother, a worker, enters with a valve for the radio, and the SA man suspects his allegiances. The worker provokes the SA man by drinking his beer, who in return says that he will demonstrate how they mark out people in a queue who are grumbling. He persuades the worker to pretend to make complaints, but he does so in such an acted fashion that the SA man cannot work out whether it is real or not; eventually, the SA man slaps him on the shoulder, leaving a chalk cross on his jacket. When the maid asks the SA man to give her twenty marks from their savings account, he is suspicious; when she criticises him for the way he treated the worker, he becomes defensive and leaves. She tells the cook, 'I even feel like asking you to look at my shoulder and see if there's a white cross on it.'

In Peat-Bog Soldiers (4) political prisoners are mixing cement and singing. Their disagreements about tactics disappear when confronted by an SS man and his threats of solitary confinement. In Servants of the People (5) an SS man is exhausted by flogging a prisoner and tells him to flog the ground instead; when an officer appears, he is ordered to flog the prisoner on his stomach. In Judicial Process (6) a police inspector briefs a district judge about that morning's case: three SA men beat up a Jewish jeweller and looted his shop. He explains that the jeweller's daughter was involved in 'racial profanation' and that the SA men were 'provoked'. The Nazi Prosecutor rejects this, preferring to blame an unemployed Marxist. The maidservant brings breakfast, confident that the SA men will be found guilty; following the visit of a senior colleague, however, the judge realises how precarious his own position is and it soon becomes clear that the men will be cleared, the jeweller's Aryan partner will take over the shop and the Marxist will languish in a concentration camp. In Occupational Disease (7), a surgeon tells his assistants that they should take environment into account when examining a patient; it emerges that a new patient was beaten up in a concentration camp: 'another case of occupational disease, I suppose'.

In The Physicists (8) two scientists, X and Y, are comparing notes about their latest discoveries. When X mentions Einstein, Y is appalled and says very loudly, in the direction of where they thought they heard someone, 'What a typical piece of misplaced Jewish ingenuity. Nothing to do with physics.' In The Jewish Wife (9) Judith is sorting out what she will pack in her suitcases and is telephoning various friends and colleagues, ensuring that everything will be fine while she is away on 'a short trip'. She practises the call she will make to her husband, who is already in trouble at work because of his Jewish wife. When he turns up she tells him she is leaving; however, despite protesting that 'Things can't go on like this all that much longer', he does not offer to go with her, telling himself that 'it's only for two or three weeks'. In The Spy (10), a husband, his wife and their son have finished Sunday lunch. Friends ring up asking if they are at home, but the husband does not want to see them. He is restless ('It's intolerable, living in a country where it's a disaster when it rains') but she rebukes him. They are silent as the maid brings coffee but quarrel about politics once she has left: meanwhile, their son reads a newspaper report about Hitler's attack on the church. Suddenly they realise that he has left the apartment and discover that he has gone to the Hitler Youth. She is worried about how much he heard them say and he accuses her of having borne him a 'Judas'. The door opens and the boy enters, saying he went out to buy chocolates; his mother does not know whether to believe him.

In The Black Shoes (11) a thirteen-year-old working-class girl asks her mother for two pfennigs to contribute to the Hitler Youth, so she can go with them on a trip to the countryside, adding that she does not want to wear 'those old black shoes from the welfare' any more. Her mother promises to get her other shoes resoled – even though it will be 'so expensive' – but refuses to give her money for the Hitler Youth. In Labour Service (12), a rich student and a young worker are digging together in the Labour Corps (a Nazi scheme for eliminating class differences). The group leader arrives to gloat and both pretend to being productive. It is clear, however, that the student is paying the worker in cigarettes to do his work for him; left together, the student threatens the worker by saying there are 'an awful lot of people want cigarettes just as much'; the worker's reply is 'Yes, there are an awful lot of people like me. That's something we often forget.' In Workers' Playtime (13), a radio announcer is interviewing three factory workers. The older worker answers ambiguously, the woman worker recites clichés, but the younger worker says that he is paid less under the Nazis than he was before; he is pushed from the microphone and the announcer continues: 'In joyful cooperation the intellectual worker and the manual worker are tackling the reconstruction of our beloved German Fatherland. Heil Hitler!'

In The Box (14) SA men carry a zinc coffin into a working-class flat and leave. The child wants to look at her dead father (he died of 'pneumonia', the SA say) but his widow is worried that if they open the box the SA might come for his brother too, adding, 'We don't need to see him. He won't be forgotten.' In Release (15) a man and his wife are awaiting the return of their old comrade,

Max, from a concentration camp. The man does not know whether he will be able to trust him now, but Max quickly shows that he has not changed. In Charity Begins at Home (16) two SA men are delivering apples and money from the Winter Aid Organisation to an old woman. She is delighted and tells her daughter that this 'shows things aren't like your husband says'. The SA men hear this and arrest the daughter; the old woman vomits up the apple she has started to eat. Two Bakers (17) takes place in the yard of Landsberg prison. Two prisoners are comparing notes: one was sent there because he mixed potatoes and bran into his bread; the other, more recently, for refusing to do so. In The Farmer Feeds His Sow (18) a farmer tells his wife and children that he is determined to feed his cattle with his own grain, despite it being against the law: 'I'm supposed to deliver over my grain and pay through the nose for my cattle feed. So that that spiv [Hitler] can buy guns.' His children are posted on lookout as he mixes the pigswill: 'When a beast's hungry there ain't no State.'

The Old Militant (19) is set in a town square on a winter's morning. Customers are waiting outside the dairy. A young man complains about the way people grumble so much: 'D'you think we could have reoccupied the Rhineland with butter?' A dairywoman tells them that the SA came for the butcher's son the previous night for 'overcharging for meat', even though his father was such a keen Nazi: he had refused to hang a plaster ham in the window and argued against the government. Suddenly they see the butcher lit up in the shop window: he has hung himself and round his neck the slate says 'I voted for Hitler'. In The Sermon on the Mount (20) a fisherman is dying and asks the pastor if there is an afterlife. His 'life has been all toil and hardship', and he is unconvinced. His son is a Nazi supporter who refuses to believe in the Sermon on the Mount since 'it's written by a Jew and it doesn't apply'. When the fisherman presses the pastor for his opinion, the answer is: 'Render unto Caesar the things which are Caesar's; and unto God the things that are God's.'

The Motto (21) is set in a meeting room of the Hitler Youth. One of the boys does not have a gas mask. An overweight Sharführer ('Fatty') enters and asks the boy to recite the Motto. Eventually he manages it ('Beat, stab, shoot them so they fall / Be a German uncomplaining / Die for this, and give your all') and Fatty asks, 'Now what's so difficult about that?' In News of the Bombardment of Almeria Gets to the Barracks (22) two working-class boys are talking about the German attack on the Spanish town: 'It could lead to war.' They compare the food that they have been given: one boy – a committed Nazi – got two meatballs but the other only got one. In Job Creation (23) a worker comes home and finds his neighbour there. He has just got a new job in a factory making aeroplanes. His wife comes in with a letter: her brother, a pilot, has died in an accident in Stettin. The neighbour is surprised that he was not in Spain and the others realise that she is right. She also points out that he must have 'had an "accident" with one of the same things you're making in that factory'. He does not want his wife to wear black, because he will lose his job, but she refuses: 'Let them come and get me, then! They've concentration camps for women too. Let them just put me in one of those because I dare to mind when they kill my brother!' When he tries to get her to shut up, saying that 'it doesn't help', her reply is, 'What does help then? Do something that does!' In Consulting the People (24) two men and a woman are listening to the radio announcing Hitler's triumphant entry into Vienna. A rigged referendum is being offered ('You're German, are you in favour?'), in which all other opinions are banned. The woman reads out a letter from a condemned comrade to his son: 'Our task is very difficult, but it's the greatest one there is – to free the human race from its oppressors.' The men ask what should be in their leaflet. The woman's reply is simple: 'Best thing would be just one word: NO!'

ABOUT THE PLAY
Fear and Misery of the Third Reich takes the form of twenty-four short scenes describing everyday life in Germany in the first few

years following the Nazi election victory of 1932. Subtitled 'Germany – An Atrocity Story', the cycle provides an extraordinarily powerful panorama of an apparently civilised society set on course to barbarism.

The great strength of *Fear and Misery* lies in its lethal combination of human observation, pithy wit, dramatic tension and political anger, and the cycle includes some of Brecht's most moving work. Its style is predominantly naturalistic and most of the scenes are set in interiors – middle-class living rooms, working-class homes, factories, scientific institutes, barracks and town squares – although some are set in the early concentration camps, or the Nazi labour programmes. However, Brecht protested that the piece was formally inventive and complained that the great Marxist critic, Georg Lukács, who admired The Jewish Wife, had

> failed to notice the montage of 27 scenes [six additional scenes were composed] and the fact that it is just a table of gests: the gest of keeping silent, of looking over one's shoulder, of being frightened and so on: gestics under dictatorship . . .

What is remarkable is the way that Brecht combined his notions of the epic theatre – with its jump cuts and its self-conscious theatricality – with such a high degree of minutely observed naturalistic detail.

Several of the plays in the cycle – above all The Chalk Cross and Judicial Process – are substantial and have a wide range of precisely drawn characters, each with his own attitude, political allegiance and point of view. Others are little more than cabaret sketches, but none the less for that. The plays feature characters of all ages (the children are particularly affecting), all classes, a whole range of professions and none. Together, they chart the gradual erosion of an entire society – a highly cultured and sophisticated one – and the destruction of everything that made it decent. While Brecht sympathises with ordinary people victimised by the regime, he is merciless in showing the extent to which they allowed the disaster to happen. The effect is deliberately chilling, the tone is scientific and the analysis is utterly unsentimental throughout.

Essential to Brecht's response to the Nazis was exploring the extent to which they were not a natural – or unstoppable – form of evil:

> Anybody who talks about Germany becomes a deviner of mysteries. One favourite interpretation of the mystery which we have read goes like this: here is a country at the heart of Europe, a long established nursery of culture, which was plunged overnight into barbarism, a sudden horrible senseless outbreak of savagery. The forces of good were defeated and the forces of evil got the upper hand . . . In this interpretation the Third Reich is a natural event, comparable with a volcanic eruption which lays waste fertile land . . .

Instead, Brecht argued, the Nazis should be seen as something that could and should be opposed. Thus it is essential to stress that while *Fear and Misery* describes the Nazis' tightening grip, it also points to the existence of an opposition, however small, and that identifying and supporting such an opposition is the first step in defeating Fascism. When challenged that the result was too depressing, Brecht was uncompromising, if a little optimistic: 'It's not for us to preach the need to fight back, we show the fight going on. The final "no" seems enough to me.'

One of the most common criticisms of *Fear and Misery* is that it does not do justice to the appalling violence of the Third Reich, and that Brecht's economic and political analysis blinded him to the true monstrousness of the regime. It is important, however, to remember that the cycle was written several years before the outbreak of the Second World War and the implementation of the Final Solution. The great Swiss playwright, Max Frisch, sprang to Brecht's defence:

> A friend told me he felt that everything Brecht shows us here is more or less harmless by comparison with what came later.

Perhaps this is its greatest strength: we know the results, what we are looking for is the beginnings . . . If mankind had a memory surely things would start to improve? We would either shoot ourselves or change. Brecht hopes the latter. Hence the sober way in which he speaks to us, without ever being carried away or taking refuge in that vagueness which often masquerades as poetry; his poetry is his seriousness, his love of mankind. And his beauty, I'd say, lies in the dignity of his approach.

Few have articulated Brecht's particular genius with such eloquence. Furthermore, as the shock of the mind-numbing crimes of the Third Reich gives way to a more objective analysis of its origins, this great cycle of eloquent, dazzling short plays looks increasingly like one of anti-Fascism's most lasting monuments.

IN PERFORMANCE

Eight of the plays were performed in German at the Salle d'Iéna in Paris on 21 May 1938 under the title 99%, an ironic reference to bogus Nazi claims about their levels of support. Brecht co-directed this production with Slatan Dudow, music by Paul Dessau (his first collaboration with Brecht) and Helene Weigel as the Jewish Wife. The cycle was produced in New York – again in German – by Bertolt Viertel on 28 May 1942 and in June 1945 a selection of the plays were staged in English in New York and Los Angeles under the title Private Lives of the Master Race, translated by Eric Bentley. This featured new music by Hanns Eisler and a chorus of soldiers in an armoured troop carrier. Eisler described the production as 'a terrible failure'.

Brecht was adamant that Fear and Misery was conceived for the particular circumstances of the amateur theatre, for which its technical simplicity and emotional and political power seemed particularly suitable:

Censorship problems and material difficulties have hitherto prevented the available small workers' theatre groups from performing more than a few isolated scenes. Using simple indications of scenery, however, almost any theatre with a revolving or multiple set could resolve the play's technical problems . . . The play shows behaviour patterns typical of people of different classes under Fascist dictatorship, and not only the gests of caution, self-protection, alarm and so forth, but also that of resistance should be brought out.

Brecht showed no interest in reviving the cycle at the Berliner Ensemble and, sadly, subsequent professional productions have been few and far between.

The idea of a cycle of small, political plays has been widely imitated, and the East German playwright Heiner Müller's *The Battle* (1974) and the Bavarian Franz Xaver Kroetz's *Fear and Hope in the Federal Republic* (1983) and *I am the People* (1993) are three of the better-known examples.

SEÑORA CARRAR'S RIFLES
[Die Gewehre der Frau Carrar]

Collaborator: Margarete Steffin
1937

THE STORY

The play is set in a fisherman's cottage in Andalusia, one night in April 1937. Señora Teresa Carrar – the widow of a Republican hero who was killed at the front – is baking bread. Her fifteen-year-old son, José, is at an open window, looking at his brother Juan, out in a boat by himself, and is angry with him because he is not at the front. He shuts the window so he does not have to hear the radio which their neighbours, the Perezes, are playing: a general is broadcasting his threats and José curses it, but Teresa is just worried: 'We're poor; poor people can't make war.' Children run past the window singing that Juan is a coward and Teresa's brother, Pedro, a worker, enters in search of the rifles that belonged to her husband. He plays cards with José and teases him for his risk-taking – of other people's skins. A wounded man, Pablo, arrives in his militia uniform; Teresa changes his dressing, but he is worried about the front and leaves as soon as she has finished. The International Brigades are heard singing as they march by. Pedro is about to leave when Manuela, Juan's girlfriend, arrives, looking for him. When it emerges that Teresa sent Juan fishing so as to avoid a meeting at which he would be chosen for the front, Manuela leaves in rage: 'Tell your son I'm through with him.' The priest arrives. He is a pacifist, but Pedro argues that by supporting non-intervention he approves of 'every bloodbath the generals inflict on the Spanish people'; he has a Fascist leaflet, which promises to spare all Republicans who lay down their arms, and uses it to expose the priest's credulity. As Teresa shows him out, Pedro and José tear up a section of the floor and pull the rifles out. Teresa returns and grabs them back. When Pedro threatens to call Juan in from the sea, she stops him: 'I'm not for the generals and it's disgraceful to say I am. But if I keep quiet and watch my temper, maybe they'll leave us in peace. It's a very simple calculation.' Then she tears up the Republican flag that had been used as wrapping for the rifles.

Old Mrs Perez enters. Her daughter – a promising schoolteacher – was killed at the front the previous week and she has lost all her children, except for a son who is with Franco ('We don't talk about Fernando any more'). She has come to express her disapproval of the way that her family have treated Teresa. Although she recognises that both of them are poor, she implies that Teresa's sons should go to the front. Pedro says that if Teresa does not support the Republic, she is on the generals' side, and José announces that he is going to fight alongside his uncle. Teresa becomes increasingly desperate and in a struggle over the rifles, pretends that José has hurt her. Suddenly, however, the light on Juan's boat cannot be seen; she is convinced that he has been snatched by the Republicans and is furious: 'I didn't bring him into the world to ambush his fellow man behind a machine gun.' The door opens and two fishermen enter, carrying his dead body on a blood-soaked sailcloth: a Nationalist boat has gunned him down as it passed by. As Teresa realises what has happened, the guns in the distance draw nearer and the Nationalists have broken through. Teresa hands Pedro the rifles, takes the bread out of the oven and says that she is coming with them: 'For Juan.'

ABOUT THE PLAY

In July 1936 General Franco staged a military rebellion against the democratically elected Popular Front government in Spain. Thousands of workers and intellectuals from Europe and America went to Spain and fought for the Republic in the International Brigades, often with great distinction. Brecht himself never went – and has been criticised for it – but he did contribute his remarkable one-act play, *Señora Carrar's Rifles*, which was soon performed in socialist theatres throughout the world.

Teresa Carrar is the widow of a hero of the Republican cause and the mother of two young men, Juan and José. She is strong-willed and independent-minded. However, she is caught in a vivid contradiction: by striving so hard to protect her two sons, she loses the older one to the very forces that killed her husband. Eventually she realises that the only way she can save her younger son – and others like him – is to take up arms in the fight against the Fascists who would kill him.

At first, Señora Carrar is reluctant to become involved: she has already lost her husband, is only a fisherman's wife and believes that maintaining a low profile is the best way of keeping what she still has. The main action of the play, therefore, is the raising of her political consciousness embodied, above all, in her decision to reveal the whereabouts of her husband's rifles. Brecht charts this change with great precision. It is revealing, however, to read that, when advising on a post-war revival, Brecht stressed the sudden, dramatic nature of the moment when Carrar hands out the rifles. The argument is slowly ratcheted up, but the eventual decision is as impulsive as it is courageous.

Brecht gives a vivid portrait of Teresa's two sons. We only see Juan as a dead body, but sense that he has all the solitary caution of the eldest son, is in sullen rebellion against his father and pays the ultimate price for his lack of solidarity. José, by contrast, is impulsive and naive, proud of his father and angry with his mother and brother, and the death of his brother and his decision to join his uncle at the front mark his coming of age. Juan's girlfriend, Manuela, is intelligent and militant, attractive and passionate, and her presence in the play reflects the involvement of many such women in the Republican cause. Teresa's brother, Pedro, is the catalyst for the action: a peasant fighter against Fascism, he is cheerful and witty, and his attitude towards his sister is one of respectful patience – never berating her, but also never giving up on his clear-eyed commitment to the cause.

The Civil War caused deep divisions in Spanish society and Brecht is unsentimental about the atmosphere of hatred and betrayal that nearly destroys Carrar's family. The war has politicised everybody: Franco is heard broadcasting on the Perezes' radio but minutes later the International Brigades are heard singing as they march through the village; old Mrs Perez's instinctive sympathy and support is for the Republicans, but the war has taken away her children on both sides and divided her family. His view of the local priest is surprisingly indulgent, but in all his work Brecht was more interested in challenging the religious for their inaction than in criticising them for their beliefs. Brecht's portrait of these figures suggests the many complexities of the struggle.

Brecht wrote that *Señora Carrar's Rifles* was 'partly inspired' by J. M. Synge's *Riders to the Sea* (1904) and he recognised that formally it is one of the most conventional of his plays.

> The play is Aristotelian drama. The drawbacks of this technique can to some extent be made up for by performing the play together with a documentary film showing the events in Spain.

Such a film was not deemed necessary and the play's naturalistic form made it widely popular, particularly to the international supporters of the Republic. Following Franco's victory, Brecht wrote a new prologue for the play, set in an internment camp for Spanish refugees in Perpignan. This was intended as a way of bringing the play up to date: 'the battle may have been lost', it implies, 'but the struggle continues'.

Señora Carrar's Rifles is one of Brecht's most remarkable achievements, a dramatic miniature which makes its point with the utmost economy, but with a striking atmosphere and psychological and social realism. Brecht laid out his political intentions with almost shocking clarity:

> The little play we are talking about deals with an Andalusian fisherman's wife and her fight against the generals. I've tried to show how difficult it is for her to decide to fight them: how only the most extreme necessity makes her take up her rifle. It is an appeal to the oppressed to revolt against their oppressors in the name of humanity. For humanity has to become warlike in times like these if it is not to be wiped out.

He also hoped that the play would have a wider effect:

> At the same time it is a letter to the fisherman's wife to assure her
> that not everybody who speaks the German language is in favour
> of the generals and is despatching bombs and tanks to her country.
> This letter I write in the name of many Germans both inside and
> outside Germany's frontiers. They are the majority of Germans, I
> am sure.

If in retrospect this looks rather optimistic, it was at the time the
only logical position for a politically committed German writer in
exile.

The best efforts of a large number of international supporters –
not just intellectuals and artists but workers of all kinds – as well as
the enormous sacrifices of the Spanish Republicans themselves,
could not prevent Franco's victory of 1938. However, Brecht's
exquisite one-act play stands – along with Picasso's *Guernica* and
the great flowering of Spanish Civil War verse – as a testament to
the courage and vision of the first opponents to the Fascism that
was about to plunge Europe into darkness.

IN PERFORMANCE

The world premiere of *Señora Carrar's Rifles* took place at the Salle
Adyar in Paris on 16 October 1937, in a production directed by
Slatan Dudow with Helene Weigel as Carrar. Brecht was clear
about how he felt it should be staged:

> I imagine it being performed in a very simple style. Three-
> dimensional figures against lime washed walls, with the various
> groupings very carefully composed as in a painting . . . just calm,
> considered realism.

Brecht and Ruth Berlau co-directed the play in Copenhagen in
February 1938, again with Weigel, and in the same year Berlau
directed a Danish production (using the same set and stagings)
with the amateur actress Dagmar Andreasen. Brecht's essay,
'Different Ways of Acting' (1938), compares the two different

performances and contains a pithy summary of the alienation effect:

> She [Andreasen] must not just *be* a proletarian when she acts one, but show how a proletarian woman differs from a member of the middle or lower middle class. She must be conscious of everything that is special about a proletarian and portray this in a special way.

The Berliner Ensemble revived the play in 1952 in a production directed by Egon Monk, with Weigel recreating the part of Carrar, and Ekkehard Schall as José.

Perhaps because of its conventional form, student and amateur groups soon performed the play: as early as 1938 it was seen in Stockholm, Prague, New York and San Francisco. The London premiere was given by the Unity Theatre, London, on 13 September 1938, in a production which subsequently toured England. The play met with approval from traditional Communists who – to Brecht's dismay – praised its naturalistic form.

THE RESISTIBLE RISE OF ARTURO UI
[Der aufhaltsame Aufstieg des Arturo Ui]
A parable play

Collaborator: Margarete Steffin
1941

THE STORY

A Prologue introduces us to the key characters of this 'great historical gangster play' and assures us that 'Everything you'll see tonight is true / Nothing's invented, nothing new'.

The five directors (1a) of the Cauliflower Trust – Flake, Caruther, Butcher, Mulberry and Clark – are worried about the economy. Flake mentions that 'there's a fellow – Arturo Ui, the gangster – waiting in the lobby', who is offering help, but only with machine guns. The directors laugh, and Flake suggests that the city should give them a loan to build docks and get business going again. Dogsborough, 'the ward boss on the waterfront', is 'influential' but refuses to help, despite having been supported by the Trust in the past. The directors are in despair, but Butcher has a 'plan' and soon (1b) he and Flake try to persuade the shipyard owner, Sheet, to sell his shipyard to the Trust. Sheet, however, is obstinate and refuses to believe their promises of friendliness. Suddenly Arturo Ui, his lieutenant Roma and a bodyguard saunter past. Ui stares at Flake, as 'though expecting to be spoken to', and when Sheet sees in Flake a terrifying similarity to Roma, he hypnotises himself into selling the shipyard. When Flake says that he is 'crazy', Sheet's answer is, 'I only wish that that were true.'

In a back room in his restaurant (2) Dogsborough receives a visit from Butcher and Flake. He is adamant about turning down their proposition. When Butcher offers him 'the major share / Of stock in Sheet's shipyard for twenty thousand / Dollars, or less than half its value', Dogsborough becomes interested. After weighing up his position, he finally agrees. In a bookmaker's office (3) Ui and Roma are listening to the racing news on the radio. Ui is in a black mood:

'Two months without / A murder, and a man's forgotten.' Roma tells him that 'The boys are chafing too from lack of cash', but Ui insists that his own security comes first. A journalist arrives and teases Ui about his failure to progress, but is threatened by Ui's bodyguards and leaves. Soon Giri, one of Ui's lieutenants, arrives with Bowl, Sheet's old accountant until Dogsborough fired him, who tells them that Dogsborough had been a secret member of the Cauliflower Trust and that his loan was corrupt. Suddenly, Ui senses an opportunity.

Dogsborough (4) tells his son that he should never have accepted his new country house. Butcher phones to say that the City Council has 'voted to investigate the Cauliflower Trust's / Projected docks'. Dogsborough is appalled but is even more shocked by the arrival of 'the gangster' to see him. Ui tells his life story and asks Dogsborough to 'put a word in for me with the precinct', explaining that he wants to offer the Cauliflower Trust 'protection'. When Dogsborough threatens to call the police, Ui attempts to blackmail him with his involvement in the docks scandal, but also appeals to him for his help. As soon as Ui leaves, two city councillors, Goodwill and Gaffles, arrive and tell Dogsborough about the forthcoming investigation. As they are being shown round, Dogsborough decides to send a man to the investigation to testify for him. The directors of the Cauliflower Trust have assembled in the City Hall (5) where they are joined by Dogsborough – who is 'as white as a sheet' – the investigator O'Casey and reporters. News arrives that Sheet has been found dead and Ui, Roma and their bodyguards turn up. O'Casey asks to see the contracts for the builders of the new shipyard, but Ui declares that the city's funds were embezzled by Sheet – who, he says, must have committed suicide. O'Casey soon accuses Dogsborough of involvement, but his witness, Bowl, is shot by Ui's bodyguards, leaving Ui to congratulate Dogsborough: 'One way or another, I'll get things straightened out.'

Ui is in his hotel suite (6) with Givola, another of his lieutenants, who has arranged for a Shakespearean actor to teach him how to walk in the grand style, to stand with his arms folded in such a way that 'the backs of his hands remain visible' ('A trifling change, but the difference is incalculable') and to speak impressively: the scene ends with Ui reading Antony's oration from *Julius Caesar*. Ui soon puts this into practice in the offices of the Cauliflower Trust (7), saying that only his protection can save them from chaos. Prompted by Clark, Ui assures them that he will put an end to the 'teamsters' (the American trade unions) and praises Dogsborough for his 'sterling honesty / And incorruptible morality'. When Giri and Givola offer to take questions, some of the dealers say that 'things have been pretty quiet lately' and imply that they do not need protection. Givola produces Dockdaisy, who pretends to be Bowl's widow and expresses her heartfelt thanks to Ui; meanwhile, Giri (wearing Bowl's hat) leaves with a group of gangsters carrying gasoline cans. As a sentimental song is sung 'in memory of Bowl', the warehouse goes up in flames. Ui bellows, 'This should show / You men that no one's safe from the next blow!'

At the trial for the warehouse fire (8) Giri shouts at the accused, Fish, an unemployed worker, 'who is sitting in utter apathy' (8a). Giri has answers to all the defence counsel's questions, and 'fifty-two persons who are all ready to testify that they saw me'. Hook, a vegetable dealer, tells the defence counsel (8b) that he saw Giri go through the office of the Cauliflower Trust towards the warehouse with 'four men carrying gasoline cans'. The bodyguards get nervous, Young Dogsborough whispers something in the judge's ear and the court is adjourned: 'The defendant is unwell.' Hook is in the witness chair (8c) with bandages over his head and eyes. He admits to the prosecutor that his eyesight is poor, that he does not recognise Giri and that his warehouse does not adjoin the premises of the former Sheet shipyard. Dockdaisy (8d), as Mrs Bowl, 'mechanically' declares that she 'recognises the defendant perfectly because of his guilty look'. Givola (8e) declares that his bodyguard could not have been carrying gasoline because he was singing a song at the time. When the judge overrules the prosecutor's request for him to sing it in court, Givola protests against the scandalous bias of the court. The defence counsel (8f) can hardly get a coherent answer from Fish, who is desperately thirsty, and is accused of contempt of court when he protests. Eventually (8g), Fish is found guilty of arson and sentenced to 'fifteen years hard labour'.

A woman climbs out of a shot-up truck (9a); she is hit by machine-gun fire, and her last words are 'It's Ui! Ui did this job! / Where's everybody? Help! Who'll stop that mob?' Meanwhile (9b), Dogsborough is writing his confession: he knew everything that was going on, and 'All this / He tolerated out of sordid lust / For gain, and fear of forfeiting your trust'. In Ui's hotel suite (10) Givola is forging Dogsborough's will, leaving everything to Ui. Roma arrives; his boys have been getting trigger-happy. Roma and his bodyguards turn on Givola and Giri, complaining that Ui does not realise that they 'made Arturo what he is today'. Ui accuses Roma of lacking faith and tells him that he wants more than Chicago now – and is going to try out his new tactics in neighbouring Cicero, controlled by the Dullfeets. What is more, he has the support of the Trust. Roma offers to handle this, which will entail getting rid of Dogsborough. Soon Clark, Giri and Dullfeet's wife, Betty, arrive; although they have no objection to Ui's plans, they do object to Roma's involvement. When Giri warns Ui that war will be the outcome, his reply is: 'I know my duty and need no advice.'

In a garage at night (11), Roma and a young lad are waiting for Ui to arrive; Roma tells him that 'Arturo's so devoted to his henchmen / He'd rather sacrifice himself than them'. Suddenly a man announces the arrival of the cops and an iron shutter falls, blocking the garage door. A police car arrives; Ui and Givola enter, followed by their bodyguards who shoot Roma and his followers dead. In Givola's flower shop (12) Dullfeet is shocked by Ui's violence but his wife says that if he keeps his mouth shut, Ui will leave them be. Giri appears, wearing Roma's hat, to tell them that Ui is already inside. Ui and Givola come out and welcome the

Dullfeets, but Dullfeet tells Ui that Cicero would not welcome 'the ungodly bloodbath / That plagues Chicago'. Ui, however, asks them to see him as their friend and abstain from printing lurid stories. Ui shows Betty round the flower shop while Givola takes Dullfeet: he emerges from the tour 'deathly pale'.

Dullfeet mysteriously dies and is laid to rest in the Cicero funeral chapel (13). Clark and Mulberry appear and berate Givola and Giri, who accuse them of hypocrisy. Ui is sympathetic to Betty and offers her protection. She is appalled and accuses him of her husband's murder: 'The sight of blood delights you.' After telling her of his lowly origins, he reminds her of her defenceless position. Her determination starts to crumble; when he insists on 'friendship', she can only cry out, 'Never while I live!' and she runs out 'cringing with horror'. Soon, asleep in his hotel suite (14), Ui is visited by Roma's ghost, who prophesies, 'The day will come when all whom you struck down / And all you will strike down will rise, Arturo / And bleeding but made strong by hate, take arms / Against you.'

The Chicago vegetable dealers (15) are in shock. One of them says, 'This plague will sweep the country / If you don't stop it.' Others prefer to wait for God's help. Clark announces that Dullfeet's firm and the Cauliflower Trust have joined forces, and Ui steps up to the microphone to ask for their support. Betty asks them all to put their trust in Ui. When the vote is about to be taken, a man from Cicero asks permission to leave; as soon as he does so a shot is heard off stage. Unsurprisingly, the vote is unanimous and Ui makes a speech of thanks, which ends with his ambitions to extend his rule right across America.

ABOUT THE PLAY

Central to Brecht's view of the rise of Hitler was that it was a phenomenon that could be stopped. Instead of presenting it as a mysterious, inescapable force of nature, Brecht wanted to show Fascism as a 'resistible' extension of the distorting features of capitalism itself, susceptible to rational analysis and capable of being opposed. This approach lay at the heart of his great cycle of short plays, *Fear and Misery in the Third Reich*, and is the key to his brilliant satire on the rise of Hitler, *The Resistible Rise of Arturo Ui*.

Brecht conceived of *Arturo Ui* as a large-scale, theatrical event, full of big personalities, high emotions and spectacle. Its form is explicitly Shakespearean in ambition and the scenes are thick with echoes and quotations from *Richard III* and *Julius Caesar*. It is written almost entirely in iambic pentameters and bestrides the stage with tremendous robustness and directness of approach. Inspired by Charlie Chaplin's film *The Great Dictator* (1940), Brecht's aim was to show up Hitler's absurdity – his strutting, his rhetoric, his pomposity and so on – in the most accessible way he could. He drew on American popular art, especially stories and films about the high time of the Chicago gangsters. Less evident to most English readers is Brecht's pastiche of Goethe's *Faust* in the scene in Givola's flower shop.

Although Brecht argued that the play should not be seen as a simple *roman-à-clef*, his central characters are without doubt sharply drawn satirical portraits of the key figures in the Nazi hierarchy. At its centre is, of course, Arturo Ui himself. Like his real-life model, Ui's great strength is his command of language, his ability to convince by a kind of rhetorical style that carries all before it, even while offering an implicit threat. Like Richard III, his approach is deliberately theatrical, and his black moods and bouts of self-pity are calculated for effect, as are his repeated references to his working-class background and his long struggle for greatness. For all his absurdity, however, Ui is no clown and is almost as ruthless and manipulative as Hitler himself.

Ui's three lieutenants, Giri, Roma and Givola, are brilliant portraits of three key Nazis: Hermann Goering (one of Hitler's oldest associates), Ernst Röhm (the head of the SA) and Josef Goebbels (Hitler's propaganda chief). Giri is thuggish and obstreperous, vulgar and loud (he always wears his last victim's hat); Roma is highly sentimental, as naive and trusting as he is violent and crude, and he dies betrayed by the villain he adores;

and Givola is sophisticated and manipulative, untrustworthy and cruel. This unsavoury trio is surrounded by bodyguards and henchmen, the thugs and small-time crooks that were essential to the rise of Fascism.

Old Dogsborough is a portrait of the Weimar Republic's President Hindenburg: white-haired, venerated and highly conservative, he is also corrupt and deeply implicated in the rise of the forces that eventually overpower him. Dullfeet is modelled on the right-wing Austrian Chancellor Dollfuss and, like him, is cautious and worthy, complacent and ineffective. The Cauliflower Trust represents the Prussian landowning class – reactionary, ineffective and corrupt – and the vegetable dealers are the German petty bourgeois – small-minded, corrupt and looking out for their own interests. The play's action echoes a series of historical events (some better remembered than others) including the economic depression, the *Osthilfe* scandal, the Reichstag fire, the Night of the Long Knives and the annexation of Austria.

For all its popular appeal, *Arturo Ui* has often been criticised. The most cogent charge is that it trivialises the subject. Brecht, however, was quite aware of this and shortly before he died wrote a robust reply:

> The great political criminals must be completely stripped bare and exposed to ridicule. Because they are not great political criminals at all, but the perpetrators of great political crimes, which is something very different.

Many feel that subsequent history has made Brecht's satire look naive, if not inappropriate. Others argue that Brecht's 'parable play', as he called it, gives far too crude a historical analysis: Hitler was involved in something much more complex than simply a struggle for economic advantage and his ultimate ambitions cannot be subjected to the kind of rational analysis that Brecht preferred. Of course, the play only deals with Hitler's career up to the *Anschluss* – the annexation of Austria in 1938 – and although Ui's last speech threatens much bigger ambitions, Brecht never wrote what he called the 'utterly and universally unperformable' sequel. Again, Brecht was aware of the play's limitations:

> The play does not pretend to give a complete account of the historical situation in the 1930s. The proletariat is not present, nor could it be taken into account more than it is, since anything extra in this complex would be too much; it would distract from the tricky problem posed.

A more potent criticism is that the play occasionally strikes the wrong note. For example, it should be pointed out that some of Hitler's most committed opponents came from the object of Brecht's most savage satire, the Prussian landowners who provided the core of Germany's officer class. Then, the scene in which Roma appears to Ui in a dream as a representative of his victims is badly judged: of the many millions of Hitler's victims, Ernst Röhm was probably the least innocent of all. Finally, Brecht's portrait of the corrupt, blackmailed Dogsborough fails to reflect Hindenburg's naive attempts to use Hitler as a way of keeping the German Communists at bay.

Despite these reservations, *Arturo Ui* is an astounding achievement: a brilliant cartoon, which employs a whole range of different styles and tones to create a vivid and unified theatrical event, which shocks even as it teaches, entertains even as it appals, and does everything it can to mobilise opposition to the force that was in the process of threatening European civilisation itself.

The Epilogue – added after the defeat of Fascism – summarises the play's intentions:

> Therefore learn how to see and not to gape.
> To act instead of talking all day long.
> The world was almost won by such an ape!
> The nations put him where his kind belong.
> But don't rejoice too soon at your escape –
> The womb he crawled from still is going strong.

IN PERFORMANCE

Brecht never saw *Arturo Ui* on stage but was clear about the way that he thought it should be performed:

> In order that the events may retain the significance unhappily due them, the play must be performed in the grand style, and preferably with obvious harkbacks to the Elizabethan theatre . . . Pure parody however must be avoided, and the comic element must not preclude horror. What is needed is a three-dimensional presentation which goes at top speed and is composed of clearly defined groupings like those favoured by historical tableaux at fairs.

The play was first produced in Stuttgart on 10 December 1958, in a production directed by one of Brecht's former assistants, Peter Palitzsch. Palitzsch and Manfred Wekwerth then co-directed the play for the Berliner Ensemble in March 1959, with a dazzling central performance by Ekkehard Schall, scenery by Karl von Appen and music by Dieter Hosalla. This remarkable production visited the Old Vic Theatre in London and the Paris International Festival in 1965.

The play was first performed in English in 1967 with the comic actor Leonard Rossiter in the title role. Antony Sher played Ui at the National Theatre in 1991 directed by Di Trevis, and Jack Gold directed Nicol Williamson in an adaptation for BBC TV called *The Gangster Show* in 1972.

There have been two famous productions of the play in New York with leading American actors and radical British directors: Christopher Plummer played Ui at the Lunt-Fontanne Theater, New York, in November 1963, in a production directed by Tony Richardson, as did Al Pacino in 2002 directed by Simon McBurney, in a production intended as a satire on the emergence of President George W. Bush's neo-conservative US administration.

SCHWEYK IN THE SECOND WORLD WAR

[Schweyk im Zweiten Weltkrieg]

1941–3

THE STORY

The play opens with a Prologue in the Higher Regions, in which Hitler, Goering, Goebbels and Himmler are gathered round a globe. Hitler wants to know how the 'little man' views him, and the play attempts to provide an answer.

In the Chalice Tavern (1) in occupied Prague, an SS man is getting increasingly drunk, bragging of secret information about a failed attempt on Hitler's life, but the landlady, Mrs Kopecka, wants to avoid political discussions on her premises. Meanwhile Schweyk, a dog dealer, and his friend Baloun, a photographer, are having a drink and grumbling about their lives. Baloun is desperate to eat something decent, so he asks the SS man if the Germans are taking on volunteers for the Russian campaign. The SS man is delighted by this but Mrs Kopecka advises Baloun against. Meanwhile, young Prochazka is besotted with Mrs Kopecka; she wonders whether his love would 'stretch to two pounds of pickled pork'. When he promises to get it 'somewhere' she tells Baloun he will eat 'tomorrow dinnertime'. Brettschneider, the Gestapo agent, comes in with a paper describing the assassination attempt and is interested to hear their responses. Schweyk's amiable jokes lead to him getting arrested.

In Gestapo Headquarters (2) SS Lieutenant Bullinger interrogates Schweyk, who has already been 'knocked about' in his cell. His answers are evasive, light-hearted and apparently half-witted. When Bullinger discovers that Schweyk is a dog dealer, he tells him he wants him to get hold of a Pomeranian dog owned by a senior civil servant. Schweyk's doubts vanish when Bullinger draws his revolver, and he is set free.

Back in the Chalice (3) Baloun is waiting for his meal and shows his postcards of 'German cities' – all in ruins. Schweyk enters with

SS Man Müller, who wants to have his fortune read by Mrs Kopecka. She looks at his palm, praises him for his success with women, but predicts a heroic death for him and his unit; he is appalled and leaves. Meanwhile, Prochazka has returned – without Baloun's dinner. Brettschneider comes in and Baloun sings the savage 'Song of the Black Radish'. Back in the Higher Regions Hitler wants to know if the 'little man' will work for his war. In the gardens by the Moldau (4) Schweyk and Baloun meet two serving girls, one with the Pomeranian dog. As they chat them up, Schweyk steals the dog. Soon, however, a man from the Department of Voluntary Work, whose job, Schweyk jokes, is 'pinching men', arrests them both.

Baloun and Schweyk are working in the goods yard of Prague railway station (5). A German soldier guards them and Schweyk is impressed by German organisation. Mrs Kopecka arrives with a disappointing dinner of carrots and potato sausages. She is worried about keeping the stolen dog at the Chalice, but Schweyk is confident that Bullinger will pay up: 'business is business'. Baloun is jealous of the soldier's superior dinner and Schweyk tells the guard about a very complicated way of remembering the number of the goods wagons he is meant to be controlling. However, this makes him forget the number and, by the end, 'a wagonload of machine-guns may be on its way to Bavaria. But by that time perhaps what they'll need most in Stalingrad will be combine-harvesters and it'll be Bavaria's turn to want machine-guns.'

It is Saturday night at the Chalice (6) and Mrs Kopecka leads the guests in a noisy folk dance, designed to drive two SS men out of the bar. Baloun is depressed and foresees his own death. Schweyk turns up with a parcel of meat under his arm, which cheers up Baloun, but it is, in fact, the Pomeranian dog. Suddenly Bullinger arrives with a squad of SS men who turn the place over in their search for the dog. Brettschneider appears, has a furious row with Bullinger and Mrs Kopecka gets hit in the mêlée. Schweyk admits that the suspicious parcel belongs to him and, despite his nonsensical explanations, is dragged off by the SS. Baloun is again in despair, but Mrs Kopecka sings, 'The stones of the Moldau are stirring and shifting / In Prague lie three emperors turning to clay.' Meanwhile, in the Higher Regions, Hitler is told that Stalingrad is going to be no 'pushover'; his reply is that 'the little man shall salvage my battle'.

Schweyk is in a military prison (7) with other Czech prisoners, waiting for their medical. They are all pretending to be suffering and imagine that this will get them off the call-up. One of the prisoners is the Czech official whose Pomeranian dog Schweyk stole: he accused the SS of stealing it and was arrested for it. The 'Horst Wessel Song' can be heard outside and Schweyk leads the others in a subversive rewriting of the words. A German military doctor comes in and, without inspecting the prisoners, says they are all 'healthy enough to join the army'. Schweyk marches out of the cell door first saying, 'On to Moscow!'

Many weeks later (8), deep in the Russian snow, Schweyk has got lost on the road to Stalingrad and soon meets a patrol of German deserters, who mock him for his faith in Hitler. He dreams of the Chalice: Baloun is about to marry a servant girl and swears that he will never fight for the Nazis, while Mrs Kopecka is won over by Prochazka who has finally got hold of two pounds of pickled pork. Back in Russia, Schweyk comes across a drunken German Army chaplain searching for alcohol to use as petrol; together they head off towards Stalingrad where they think food will be found. They meet a family of peasants and the chaplain is killed when he tries to rob them, while Schweyk is hailed as a fellow Slav and a friend. He falls asleep in a snowdrift and once again dreams of the Chalice, where Baloun is being served pickled pork for his wedding breakfast. Baloun speaks tenderly about the wonders of food and Mrs Kopecka sings about the joys of friendliness. They also think of their friend Schweyk, 'out there in that icy cold'. Back in the snow, however, an armoured vehicle appears, full of defeated German soldiers singing the 'German Miserere'. As it disappears into the snowstorm, Schweyk finds a starving mongrel and calls it 'Ajax'.

In the Epilogue, Schweyk comes face to face with Hitler himself, who tries to explain why the invasion of Russia was necessary. Schweyk eventually finds himself unable to move forward in any direction and is buried in the snow. At the end a chorus of all the actors comes to the front and sings Mrs Kopecka's song:

> The stones of the Moldau are stirring and shifting
> In Prague lie three emperors turning to clay.
> The great shall not stay great, the darkness is lifting
> The night has twelve hours, but at last comes the day.

ABOUT THE PLAY

Jaroslav Hašek's novel *The Good Soldier Švejk* (1917) had been translated into German in 1926 and was one of Brecht's favourite novels. It had been dramatised by the Czech writer Max Brod (a close friend of Franz Kafka) and the German humorist Hans Reimann, but Erwin Piscator found their adaptation too conventional for his first season at the Volksbühne in Berlin and asked his dramaturgical team – of which Brecht was an occasional member – to rework it. Piscator's 1928 production – with a treadmill stage and projections of George Grosz's magnificent illustrations – was one of the most remarkable theatrical events of Weimar Germany. Piscator remained fascinated by the material, planning a film of the novel in the USSR in the early 1930s, as well as talking to a New York theatre about staging a revival in 1943.

Brecht wrote his updated version of *Schweyk* in May and June 1943. One of the few pieces of paid employment that he had managed to scrape together in Los Angeles was script work on Fritz Lang's film *Hangmen Also Die*, about the assassination of SS General Reinhard Heydrich – the architect of the Final Solution – in Prague in May 1942, and this may have drawn him back to Hašek:

> Once again I would like to do *Schweyk* . . . so people can see the
> ruling forces up top with the private soldier down below surviving
> all their vast plans.

This was certainly a good time to write about the growing
opposition to the Third Reich: by May 1943, after more than three
years of German victories, the defeat of Hitler's Sixth Army in
Stalingrad and the raising of the nine-hundred-day siege of
Leningrad seemed to indicate that the tide was finally turning.

At the heart of Brecht's play is the anti-hero Schweyk: conman,
beer drinker, professional coward and dog dealer. He is concerned
with one thing above all, his own survival, and central to the
comedy of the piece is his foolhardy oblivion to the great forces
that surround him. Brecht was clear about his intentions in
the *Journals*:

> Whatever happens Schweyk mustn't turn into a cunning under-
> handed saboteur. He is merely an opportunist exploiting the tiny
> openings left him.

Like Galy Gay, Señora Carrar or Mother Courage herself,
Schweyk is not an articulate critic of the system in which he finds
himself. Instead, this is history from the bottom up and Brecht's
aim is to provoke us into drawing conclusions from watching what
happens, not using a character to hector us with his views.

Schweyk himself is surrounded by a number of other Czechs:
his old friend Baloun, desperate for something to eat; the sharp-
witted landlady Mrs Kopecka who cannot stand the Nazis but
knows how to exploit their weaknesses; the romantic young
Prochazka, who is only taken seriously when he turns up with
some meat; the girls Kati and Anna whom Schweyk and Baloun
meet by the river; and the other habitués of the Chalice. These are
affectionately drawn portraits of real people, dedicated to the
ordinary pleasures of the world – having a drink in a local bar,
cracking jokes and getting something to eat – and trying to
survive. They are not heroes, but Brecht shows that their down-to-

earth materialism has its own rationality and dignity; it also carries its own unspoken criticism of the insanity of what is going on around them.

Much less convincing, however, is Brecht's portrayal of the Nazis, not so much Hitler and the high command, who are presented as larger than life satirical cartoons (Brecht said that the 'Interludes should be played in the style of a grisly fairy tale'), but the naturalistic portraits of the local Nazi hierarchy: Lieutenant Bullinger and his SS men, the Gestapo agent Brettschneider and the guard in the freight yard. These are comic figures, a long, long way from the staggeringly brutal occupation of Prague by the Nazis under Heydrich, whose assassination in May 1942 led to the destruction of Lidice and the murder of its five hundred inhabitants. More realistic – and much more haunting – is the vision of exhausted German deserters retreating through the snow from Stalingrad: these are working-class boys, led into war by the fanatics that have taken over their country, and their 'German Miserere' is Brecht at his most powerful – and politically coherent.

The play's formal diversity is one of its pleasures. The best passages – the scenes in the Chalice – are written as a piece of good-natured social comedy, reminiscent of the Austrian *fin de siècle* dramatists Johann Nestroy and Ferenc Molnár. This is interleaved by the savage, if rather abstract, political cartoon of 'the higher regions', and is punctuated by a series of remarkably moving and powerful songs. Brecht's inventive approach cannot, however, disguise the play's fatal flaw – the failure to describe the Nazis with any degree of historical verisimilitude – which, unfortunately, makes *Schweyk in the Second World War*, for all its great wit and charm, one of the less convincing of Brecht's full-length plays.

IN PERFORMANCE

The first performance of *Schweyk in the Second World War* took place in Polish on 15 January 1957 at the Teatr Dramatyczny in Warsaw. The German premiere was in Erfurt in 1958 directed by Eugen Schaub, with music by Hanns Eisler. It was not performed at the Berliner Ensemble until 1962 under the direction of Erich Engel. The early 1960s saw two important European productions of the play: by Giorgio Strehler at the Piccolo Teatro in Milan in 1961, and by Roger Planchon at the Théâtre Nationale Populaire in Villeurbanne in 1962.

The play's British premiere took place at the Mermaid Theatre on 21 August 1963, in a production directed by Frank Dunlop with Bernard Miles as Schweyk. Two more recent British productions include Richard Eyre's in 1982 at the National Theatre with Bill Paterson as Schweyk – and brilliant designs by the political cartoonist Gerald Scarfe – and Chris Honer's at the Manchester Library Theatre in 2003.

12 FIVE GREAT PLAYS

1938–45

Alarmed by the growing likelihood of war, the Brechts left Denmark
in April 1939 and moved to Lindingø Island in Sweden. There,
Brecht and Ruth Berlau collaborated on a production of *What's the
Price of Iron?*, his short satire on the Western Allies' lacklustre
response to Hitler's territorial aggression. More significantly,
following the German invasion of Poland in September 1939, Brecht
wrote one of his greatest masterpieces, *Mother Courage and her
Children*. In early 1940 he wrote his pacifist radio play set in ancient
Rome, *The Trial of Lucullus* and the short but revealing dialogue,
Conversation Among Exiles. With the worsening international
situation, the left-wing Finnish writer Hella Wuolijoki (1864–1954)
persuaded her Prime Minister to give Brecht asylum and on 17 April
1940 he and his entourage travelled to Helsinki. Three months later
they moved to a house on Wuolijoki's country estate, where Brecht
worked with Margarete Steffin on *Mr Puntila and his Man Matti*, an
original play loosely based on one of Wuolijoki's stories. In
September Brecht's friend, the great philosopher Walter Benjamin,
committed suicide rather than face arrest by the Gestapo. In the
spring of 1941 Brecht wrote *The Resistible Rise of Arturo Ui*, his satire
on the rise of Hitler, and on 15 May 1941, a month before the
German invasion of the Soviet Union, the Brechts left Finland for
America, via Moscow and Vladivostok. Tragically, Margarete
Steffin died of tuberculosis in Moscow on 4 June, but the rest of the
party arrived safely in Los Angeles in late July 1941.

Brecht soon met one of his heroes, Charlie Chaplin. He also joined a circle of eminent German exiles, including Arnold Schoenberg, Theodor Adorno, Max Horkheimer and Thomas Mann, and participated in the debate about the future of a liberated Germany. He completed *The Good Person of Szechwan* in 1941 (started in 1938) and the following year wrote *Hangmen Also Die*, a screenplay for the great German film director Fritz Lang about the assassination of Reinhard Heydrich in Prague earlier that year. In 1943 Brecht spent several months in New York, where he met up with old colleagues from Germany, including Erwin Piscator, Wieland Herzfeld, Ernst Bloch and George Grosz. He was also introduced to the English poet W. H. Auden, an early champion and translator of his work, and was reunited with the composer Paul Dessau. Returning to Los Angeles, he wrote two plays set in occupied Europe, *The Visions of Simone Machard* (1942–3) with Lion Feuchtwanger (rights for this were sold to MGM, but the film was never made) and *Schweyk in the Second World War* (1943).

Brecht spent much of the first half of 1944 writing his most popular play, *The Caucasian Chalk Circle*, which he finished on 6 June 1944 – D-Day. He also adapted with W. H. Auden John Webster's *The Duchess of Malfi* (not staged on Broadway until 1946, and then disastrously) and started working with the English actor Charles Laughton (1899–1962) on a translation of *Life of Galileo*. In 1942 he wrote a superb cycle of short poems, *The Hollywood Elegies*, which were set to music by Hanns Eisler, and completed the remarkable *War Primer*, a set of photographs cut out of newspapers, each accompanied by a satirical verse quatrain.

Brecht's time in America was complicated: he did not understand America and America did not understand him. It was difficult for him to write properly about Hitler's Germany among the palm trees of southern California and by choosing to go to the United States instead of the Soviet Union he had distanced himself from 'actually existing' Communism. Furthermore, not only was he unable to visit Switzerland for the premieres of *Mother Courage* and *Life of Galileo* but, with the notable exception of the 1947 production of *Life of Galileo*, it was impossible for him to get his mature work staged in the commercial world of the American theatre. The truth is that Brecht in America was a fish out of water.

The result was a temporary retreat from political engagement and a concentration on questions of theatrical style. It was in America that Brecht honed the idea of the parable form and it was there that he first glimpsed the grandeur of vision that characterised his best work at the Berliner Ensemble. The global reach of the war brought out his internationalism and encouraged his almost obsessive interest in contradiction. It was in America that Brecht's theatre finally came of age: it needed his return to a Europe at peace for his vision to be put into practice.

LIFE OF GALILEO
[Leben des Galilei]

Collaborator: Margarete Steffin

1938–9, 1945–7

THE STORY

Galileo is in his study (1). As he washes himself he shows his housekeeper's son, Andrea Sarti, a wooden model of the Ptolemaic astrological system. He tells him that just as society is opening up, so the solar system is full of movement. He demonstrates the orbit of the earth by sitting Andrea on a chair and carrying him around the room, and shows the working of gravity by sticking a splinter of wood into an apple. Andrea's mother, Mrs Sarti, announces the arrival of the rich young Ludovico, who want lessons from the great man. He quickly agrees to Galileo's price and tells him about the new invention in Amsterdam: the telescope. The Procurator arrives and says that the University will not increase Galileo's salary, advising him to undertake work which is more 'useful'. At the arsenal in Venice (2), however, Galileo soon presents the Doge with his new 'invention'; the Procurator praises it for its military potential, but Galileo knows that he can use the telescope for his own purposes too. The Doge protests that he needs a pretext before he can award Galileo any more money and Ludovico, who is interested in Galileo's daughter, Virginia, says he is 'starting to learn a thing or two about science'.

Late at night (3), Galileo and his old friend Sagredo are looking at the moon through the telescope. Galileo realises that the bright part is reflected sunlight and that the dark part glows with light from the earth: 'What you're seeing is the fact that there is no difference between heaven and earth . . . Today mankind can write in its diary: Got rid of Heaven.' The Procurator visits: he has found out that the telescope was invented ten years before and feels betrayed. Soon, however, Galileo is discovering Jupiter's moons;

when Sagredo points out that Galileo's conclusions could get him executed, Galileo declares his belief in 'reason's gentle tyranny' and tells Mrs Sarti to wake Andrea – 'He's to see something nobody but us two have seen since the earth was made.' He also asks her to judge whether the greater goes round the smaller, or the opposite; her common-sense answer shows that people 'grab at the truth'. Galileo says that he wants to move to Florence, where he can discover his proofs; Sagredo advises against – Florence is run by monks – but Galileo is determined. The last page of his grovelling letter to the nine-year-old Grand Duke appears on a screen.

In Florence (4) the Grand Duke arrives for his lesson: he wants to see the telescope and brawls with Andrea over the two different models of the solar system. Galileo invites a group of professors to trust the evidence of their own eyes, but they are more interested in formal disputes ('Can such planets exist?'), conducted in Latin. Andrea is dismayed, while Galileo appeals to empirical proof: 'Truth is born of the times, not of authority. Our ignorance is limitless: let us lop one cubic millimetre off it.' It is soon time for the court ball and the professors leave – without looking through the telescope. Galileo hears that Father Clavius, the chief astronomer in Rome, will look into his discoveries.

Galileo is working (5a) and Virginia runs in to announce that the plague has arrived in Florence. The Grand Duke has sent a carriage to take Galileo to Bologna, but he refuses to go, saying that he must not abandon his work. Andrea and Virginia leave, but Mrs Sarti stays behind. Soon (5b) Galileo hears that Mrs Sarti has caught the plague. Andrea appears – he jumped off the carriage – and Galileo tells him about his latest discovery: Venus is a planet. Two masked men appear with long poles and bread, and Galileo asks one of them to fetch him a book; he laughs ('As if a book could make any difference'), so Andrea goes to get it.

In the hall of the Collegium Romanum (6) there is great hilarity that 'the earth spins round like a marble in the gutter'. Two astronomers, however, are concerned that Clavius is taking too long examining Galileo's theory. A little monk says that if Galileo's theories are accepted the social order itself will collapse. A very old cardinal attacks Galileo, saying that he is at the centre of a divinely ordained universe; then, overexcited by mankind's indestructibility, collapses. Finally, Clavius announces, 'He's right.' The little monk tells Galileo that he has won; his response is that 'reason has won'.

At a ball in Cardinal Bellarmin's house (7) Virginia is dancing with Ludovico, who is now her fiancé. She is very beautiful, but in the distance madrigals are being sung about the transience of youth. Galileo, however, is puzzled by two secretaries playing 'old-style chess'. Cardinals Bellarmin and Barberini arrive, and have a learned conversation with Galileo about his discoveries. Eventually, Bellarmin tells him that the Holy Office has decided that the doctrine of Copernicus is heretical and suggests that he should temper his conclusions. The Inquisitor asks the secretaries to give him a transcript of the conversation and is surprised to hear that Virginia is not interested in her father's work; but he is delighted to hear that she is accompanying her father: 'He will need you; perhaps you cannot imagine this, but the time will come.'

Galileo is visited by the little monk (8), who cannot reconcile the decree with his own observations. Nevertheless, he recognises the 'dangers for humanity in wholly unrestricted research'. He also explains why he has given up astronomy: his parents are peasants and without God their poverty would make no sense. Galileo's response is forceful: 'You're right, it's not about the planets, it's about the peasants,' adding, 'The only truth that gets through will be what we force through: the victory of reason will be the victory of people who are prepared to reason, nothing else.' The little monk is soon absorbed in a bundle of manuscripts and when he does not understand a point, Galileo offers to explain it; at the same time Galileo is worried about his own endurance.

Having kept silent for eight years (9), Galileo has gathered his pupils in his house in Florence. Mucius, a scholar, complains that Galileo has condemned his refutation of Copernicus unheard. Galileo drops a stone and praises Mucius for 'saying that this stone has just flown up to the ceiling'; while Mrs Sarti thinks a 'proper astronomer at the university' should be asked to cast Virginia's horoscope. Andrea wants Galileo to investigate sunspots, but he will only experiment on floating bodies, adding that he cannot 'afford to be roasted over a wood fire'. Soon, however, their investigation reveals new observations, prompting Galileo to exclaim, 'One of the reasons why the sciences are so poor is that they imagine they are so rich.' Ludovico arrives and says that everyone is interested in sunspots now. Galileo is encouraged to hear that Barberini is likely to become Pope and tells Andrea to set up the sun reflector. Ludovico says the peasants do not care about discoveries, but Galileo says he might get them interested. Ludovico storms off in a fury saying that he does not want to see Virginia any more; she enters in her wedding dress, realises what has happened and faints. Galileo tells his pupils to 'Take the cloth off the telescope and point it at the sun'.

In the Carnival of 1632 (10) a ballad singer attacks Galileo's 'horrible doctrine and opinion', which is bringing about the collapse of the 'Great Order of Things'. This is followed by a procession, which satirises the 'new age' and includes a huge puppet of 'Galileo Galilei, the Bible-buster!'. The following year (11) Virginia and Galileo are in the Medici Palace in Florence and she is concerned that he has returned to his heretical ways. Vanni, an iron founder, tells him how much businessmen support science and offers him his coach to take him to Venice. Galileo shrugs this off saying, 'Every Tom, Dick and Harry with an axe to grind wants me to be his spokesman.' Eventually, the Inquisitor enters, followed by the Grand Duke, who is concerned about Galileo's eyes, but rejects his new book. Virginia is scared and Galileo admits that he has an escape plan. An official informs him that Florence no longer blocks the papacy's wish to interrogate him and that a coach awaits.

The new Pope is being dressed (12) and the Inquisitor tells him that 'a terrible restlessness has descended on the world' and that Galileo is undermining people's faith in God. When the Pope points out how famous Galileo is, the Inquisitor says that 'He is a man of the flesh. He would give in immediately.' The Pope says that 'His thinking springs from sensuality' and, now dressed, agrees, 'At the very most he can be shown the instruments.'

Galileo's followers (13) are outside the Florentine ambassador's palace in Rome, waiting for news. Federzoni, the working-class lens grinder, and the little monk are convinced that Galileo will never give in, while Virginia is praying that he will. A lackey tells them that he will recant at five and that the proclamation will be accompanied by the bells of St Mark's. Anxiously they wait, muttering that 'no force will help them to make what has been seen unseen'. Still the bell does not ring and they embrace each other: 'Such a lot is won when even a single man gets to his feet and says No.' At which point the bell tolls and the recantation is proclaimed. Galileo enters, 'so completely changed by his trial as to be unrecognisable', and Andrea says, 'Unhappy the land that has no heroes.' Galileo's reply is simple: 'No. Unhappy the land where heroes are needed.'

Galileo is a prisoner of the Inquisition in Fiesole (14). He is old and half blind, and is looked after by Virginia. He is allowed to undertake limited experiments but anything he writes must be given to the monk who guards him. Andrea – now a man in his middle years – turns up and is appalled at the way he has sold out. Galileo, however, has been writing his *Discorsi* secretly and is hiding a copy inside his globe. Andrea is overwhelmed – 'You were hiding the truth. From the enemy. Even in matters of ethics you were centuries ahead of us' – but is furious when Galileo admits that he recanted because he was afraid of physical pain. He declares that the role of science must be 'to lighten the burden of human existence' and admits that had he stood firm the scientists might have developed a vow to 'use their knowledge exclusively for mankind's benefit'. However, when Andrea asks him if he 'no longer believes that a new age has started', his answer is 'On the contrary', adding, 'Look out for yourself when you pass through Germany, with the truth under your coat.'

At the Italian frontier (15) a guard asks Andrea about his reasons for leaving Italy, while three boys argue with each other about a witch who lives nearby. He opens a box with Andrea's books in it – and a copy of the *Discorsi* – but goes off to collect taxes instead. Andrea picks up the box and one of the boys says the witch has stolen it; Andrea tells him to use his eyes, adding:

> People can't fly through the air on a stick. It'd have to have a machine on it, to say the least. But there's no machine like that so far. Maybe there never will be, as a human being's too heavy. But of course one never knows. There are a lot of things we don't know yet, Giuseppe. We're really just at the beginning.

ABOUT THE PLAY

Brecht worked on *Life of Galileo* for nearly twenty years. In November 1938, while writing his first draft (the version performed by the Zurich Schauspielhaus in 1943), he wrote in his *Journals*:

> Amid the darkness gathering fast over a fevered world, a world surrounded by bloody deeds and no less bloody thoughts, by increasing barbarism which seems to be leading irresistibly to perhaps the greatest and most terrible war of all time, it is difficult to adopt an attitude appropriate to people on the threshold of a new and happier age.

In March 1944 he met the great actor Charles Laughton in Los Angeles and started working with him on a translation of this first draft. Then, after the dropping of the atomic bomb in August 1945, Brecht brought the play's examination of the uses of science up to date:

> Most of the time we are still working on *Galileo*, which Laughton's audience in the military hospital listen to with quite extraordinary

interest. The atom bomb has, in fact, made the relationship between society and science into a life-and-death problem.

Their translation – published alongside the Methuen edition of the final version – is rich with Shakespearean cadences and was performed in Los Angeles in 1947. Finally, following his return to Europe, Brecht translated this new text back into German and prepared it for his planned production with the Berliner Ensemble.

Life of Galileo draws on Brecht's growing interest in Shakespearean historical theatre and marks a shift away from the explicitly anti-Fascist plays of the 1930s, towards a new and more sophisticated kind of historical and intellectual drama. The play is formally consistent and although the scenes are linked by elegant quatrains, which provide essential information about place and time, Brecht eschews the use of songs to interrupt the action.

In writing a play about seventeenth-century Italy, Brecht drew heavily on the Marxist reading of the Early Modern period as a time of rapid change, in which novel economic conditions revolutionised the structures of society, and new technology transformed the way people lived and thought. The play's original title was *The Earth Moves*, to reflect its central interest in the relationship between the dynamic movement of the heavenly bodies and the possibility of similar such movement in society. The play also has a more difficult subject – the murky relationship between science and society – and shows that claims about the benevolence of science are not always as straightforward as they seem.

Galileo himself is one of Brecht's greatest and most con-tradictory characters. We watch his journey, from brilliant scientist at the peak of his powers, overthrowing centuries of superstition by the rigorous application of the scientific method, to an elderly prisoner in his own house, fatally circumscribed as to what he can work on, trapped and compromised by the difficult realities of the world, but still, despite it all, committed to science and revealing the truth. In creating the part, Brecht was alert to the dangers involved:

It's important you shouldn't idealise Galileo: you know the kind of thing – the stargazer, the pallid intellectual idealist.

Brecht's Galileo is very different: a man of sensuous physicality and robust appetites, whose extraordinary scientific ability is underpinned by the most rigorous empirical method:

Galileo, of course, is not a Falstaff. He insists on his physical pleasures because of his materialist convictions. He wouldn't, for instance, drink at his work; the point is that he works in a sensual way. He gets pleasure from handling his instruments with elegance. A great part of his sensuality is of an intellectual kind: for instance, the 'beauty' of an experiment, the little theatrical performance with which he gives shape to each of his lessons, the often abrupt way in which he will confront somebody with the truth, not to mention those passages in his speeches where he picks good words and tests them like a spice.

Some have seen Brecht's self-portrait in his characterisation of Galileo. Certainly, with his emphasis on the material and suspicion of the abstract, as well as his mixture of intellectual courage and physical cowardice, he is a familiar figure. Brecht's motives, however, are more than mere autobiography.

Brecht was careful not to present Galileo simply as a hero – or at least not as a hero all the time. On the one hand he admired the way that his vision of the solar system provokes a sceptical attitude towards the social order; on the other he knew that such challenges have an impact on those at the bottom of society, as much as those at the top. Furthermore, while Brecht celebrates Galileo's intellectual independence, he refuses to condemn him for recanting: the scientist is, after all, a human being, for whom the physical is as real as the intellectual. Brecht understood that 'pure science' is a relative concept and that scientific research is dependent on money and power; he also saw that the benefits of science are monopolised by the ruling class and that its inventions are often used to repress and to control. Most provocatively, Brecht suggested that, under current conditions, science fails to alleviate the living conditions of the poor; it can even cause their destruction. It is a mark of his genius that in his portrait of the great scientist he was prepared to entertain such a profound contradiction:

> I hope this work shows how society extorts from its individuals what it needs from them. The urge to research, a social phenomenon no less delightful nor compulsive than the urge to reproduce, steers Galileo into that most dangerous territory, drives him into agonising conflict with his violent desires for other pleasures. He raises his telescope to the stars and delivers himself to the rack. In the end he indulges his science like a vice, secretly, and probably with pangs of conscience. Confronted with such a situation, one can scarcely wish only to praise or only to condemn Galileo.

Galileo is surrounded by a number of secondary characters, all drawn with their own individual energy and life. Galileo's housekeeper, Mrs Sarti, is a highly practical woman, more worried about paying the bills and not getting into trouble than in understanding the new world that her master is discovering; despite appearances to the contrary, however, she is utterly devoted to him. Her son, Andrea, grows from an enthusiastic young boy, taught the rudiments of science in exchange for running errands, into a dedicated, questioning, but bitterly disappointed disciple of the great man – rewarded, in the last scene of the play, by smuggling the *Discorsi* out of Italy. Galileo's daughter Virginia is a conventional young woman who goes to church, wants to get married and enjoys her youth and beauty; her tragedy is that her prospects are ruined by her father's single-minded commitment to science.

This great historical epic is populated by a vast panorama of other figures – Galileo's old friend Sagredo, the lens grinder Federzoni, the nervous Procurator of the University, young

Cosimo di Medici, the mathematician Cardinal Barberini (Pope Urban VIII) and dozens of peasants, monks and other clerics. Brecht was particularly keen to emphasise that his portrayal of seventeenth-century Catholicism was intended as a criticism of the Church's social conservatism and rigid hierarchy, not as a satire on religious faith.

Writing against the background of the Second World War – in which the products of science were used to kill people on an industrial scale – Brecht wanted to show that Life of Galileo is not a human tragedy. Instead, he said, 'the hero of this work is not Galileo but the people' and that it 'shows the dawn of a new age and tries to correct some of the prejudices about the dawn of a new age'. The play demonstrates that even the most remarkable individual is shaped and restrained by the historical conditions in which he finds himself. The result is widely hailed as Brecht's finest achievement and is one of the crowning glories of twentieth-century drama.

IN PERFORMANCE

Life of Galileo was premiered at the Zurich Schauspielhaus on 9 September 1943, in a production directed by Leonard Steckel, with Steckel himself playing Galileo and scenery by Teo Otto. Brecht never saw this production nor lived to see the Berliner Ensemble's great production at the Theater am Schiffbauerdamm, which opened in January 1957. He had attended many rehearsals but, following his death in 1956, the production was finished by Erich Engel. Ernst Busch, one of Brecht's actors from the 1930s, played Galileo and the scenery was by Caspar Neher.

Brecht was closely involved in the English-language premiere of the play at the Coronet Theater in Los Angeles in 1947. This was directed by Joseph Losey and Brecht, with Charles Laughton as Galileo and music by Hanns Eisler; it had been translated by Laughton and Brecht together. The first night was attended by Charlie Chaplin (who complained that it was 'not dramatic'). It was an extraordinary achievement for all involved but was badly received by the critics. It was taken to Broadway where it opened at the Maxine Elliott Theater on 7 December 1947.

The British premiere of the play took place in 1960 when Bernard Miles played the part at the Mermaid Theatre in London. John Dexter directed it at the National Theatre in Howard Brenton's translation with Michael Gambon in 1980 and Richard Griffiths played Galileo at the Almeida Theatre in a new translation by David Hare in 1994.

THE GOOD PERSON OF SZECHWAN

[Der gute Mensch von Sezuan]

A Parable Play

Collaborators: Ruth Berlau, Margarete Steffin

1939–41

THE STORY

Wang, the water seller, is eagerly awaiting the arrival of the gods. When they turn up, however, no one will give them a bed for the night and Wang runs away in shame. A prostitute, Shen Teh, says she will put them up, but confesses that she does not know how to be good. They give her money, which she uses to buy a tobacconist's. Her neighbours take advantage of her generosity (1), cadge cigarettes, invent debts and smash up the shop. Wang, meanwhile, is hiding in terror from the gods, who visit him in his dreams and tell him to 'show some interest' in Shen Teh. The next morning (2) the shop is full of 'sleeping bodies' when suddenly Shen Teh's 'cousin' Shui Ta (Shen Teh in disguise) arrives and, to the policeman's approval, throws them all out. That evening (3), in a public park, Sun, a 'young man in tattered clothes', shakes off the attention of two prostitutes. Shen Teh sees that he wants to hang himself: he says he is an unemployed pilot and she quickly falls in love with him. It starts to rain and Wang sings about trying to sell water in the rain. That night, again in a dream, Wang tells the gods that Shen Teh is in love and that she has become the 'Angel of the Slums'. They want to hear about Shui Ta: 'What has business to do with an upright and honourable life?' Shen Teh returns (4), only to discover that Wang has been driven out of the baker's shop and that his arm has been broken. She rages against the onlookers for being silent. Sun's mother arrives and asks Shen Teh for five hundred dollars so that he can fly again: she gives her two hundred dollars but says that Shui Ta will have to raise the rest. She sings about how 'The good / Cannot remain good in our country'. Sun comes to visit her (5) to get the remaining three hundred dollars, but is confronted by Shui Ta, who raises the money by selling the shop; in the process she discovers that Sun does not love her for who she is. It also emerges that Wang had lied about his arm to get compensation. Shui Ta tells the baker – who is interested in Shen Teh – that she is a bankrupt, but nevertheless arranges a romantic meal for two. When Sun hears about this, he persuades Shen Teh to run away with him after all.

On the way to her wedding, Shen Teh describes her fear but also her hopes. In a cheap restaurant (6) she and Shen Teh drink to their future. As they wait for Shui Ta, their 'special guest', Sun gets drunk and treats Shen Teh badly, particularly when she asks for her two hundred dollars back, which she wants to give to the old couple. Left alone together, they sing a desperate song about waiting until the moon is green for a 'new world to be born'. In a dream, Wang asks the gods if Shen Teh is too good for this world. They reply that suffering ennobles and that all will end well. However, Shen Teh is bankrupt and Sun has vanished (7). The baker appears, keen to help and offers a blank cheque which she refuses. She still loves Sun and reveals that she is pregnant by him. When Wang turns up with a boy who has been abandoned, Shen Teh takes him in, but tells Wang to fetch his father. The old couple arrive, dragging sacks of tobacco that they want to keep in the shop. Shen Teh reluctantly accepts, but when she sees a child scavenging for food in the dustbin, declares her determination to treat her own son better: 'Henceforth I / Shall fight at least for my own, if I have to be / Sharp as a tiger.' Wang returns with the child's father and two other children, but Shui Ta says that from now on they must all work to earn his generosity – and claims the sacks of tobacco as his own.

In a dream, Wang tells the gods that he imagines Shen Teh committing suicide, but his proposal to make their principles easier to fulfil is rejected. Shui Ta has turned the store into a tobacco factory (8); he has also employed Sun, who has done so well that he has become a typically demanding overseer: 'Sun is a different person from what he was three months ago,' his mother says. Shui Ta tells everybody (9) that he has no idea when Shen

Teh will return. Sun appears and complains to Shui Ta about the way the firm is being run. Wang arrives, wishing that Shen Teh would return, and announces that Shen Teh told him before she left that she was pregnant. Sun is furious and threatens Shui Ta if he will not let him see her. A property dealer would like to employ Sun and the baker wants him out of the way, so Shui Ta announces that his firm will open twelve new branches and all the profits will be given to his cousin. The policeman arrives, charging Shui Ta with keeping Shen Teh under 'illegal restraint'; he soon discovers Shen Teh's clothes and Shui Ta is escorted off to the magistrates' court. Once again the gods appear to Wang in a dream. They are crestfallen: they have found hardly any good people, except for Shen Teh, who they say 'was good and has not become evil, but has disappeared'.

In the courtroom (10), the gods are disguised as magistrates. The policeman defends Shui Ta, as does the baker and the property dealer. The poor, however, including Wang and the old couple, take the opposite view: 'He ruined us! He bled me white! Led us into bad ways!' Shui Ta's defence is that he was simply protecting his cousin's interests. Sun says that Shui Ta could not be a murderer, because he heard Shen Teh crying in the back room. Wang swears that Shen Teh was good and pressurises Shui Ta to tell the truth. He agrees – but only if the court is cleared first. Then he reveals the truth and explains his motives. The gods are shocked and cannot accept that the world needs to be changed, so they ascend to heaven on a pink cloud, telling Shen Teh: 'Only be good and all will be well.' The others re-enter and are amazed at the sight of the vanishing gods. Shen Teh 'stretches desperately towards them as they disappear upwards, waving and smiling'. An Epilogue apologises for the play's lack of resolution:

> There's only one solution that we know:
> That you should now consider as you go
> What sort of measures you would recommend
> To help good people to a happy end.

> Ladies and gentlemen, in you we trust:
> There must be happy endings, must, must, must.

ABOUT THE PLAY

The Good Person of Szechwan was inspired by two plays from pre-war Berlin, both with a distinctly Chinese flavour. First, one of Brecht's friends from Munich, the poet Klabund, had adapted the fourteenth-century Chinese playwright Li Hsing-tao's *The Chalk Circle* (*c*.1350), which was a great success for Elisabeth Bergner at Max Reinhardt's Deutsches Theater in 1924. Second, Brecht had seen Friedrich Wolf's play *Tai Yang Wakes Up* (1930), a deliberate corrective to Klabund's sentimentality, which had been staged brilliantly by Piscator in 1932.

Brecht found his parable of human identity difficult to write. In the late 1920s he had imagined a play on similar lines set in Berlin. Ten years later, in the spring of 1939, Brecht finally got round to writing it, but this time decided on an oriental setting. He did not complete the play, however, until early 1941 in Los Angeles. In its setting as much as in its theatrical style, it drew on his long interest in Chinese theatre. However, Brecht had moved beyond the austere formality of the *Lehrstücke* and his new interest in naturalistic elements raised its own aesthetic challenges:

> We are still mulling over the problem; bread and milk or rice and tea for the Szechwan parable? Of course there are already airmen and still gods in this Szechwan. I have sedulously avoided any kind of folklore. On the other hand the yellow race eating white French bread is not intended as a joke.

Brecht's Szechwan is neither medieval nor Maoist: it is capitalist through and through, and is driven by the energies and desires of the emerging middle class – much like a city in modern China, in fact:

> The city must be a big, dusty uninhabitable place . . . some

attention must be paid to countering the risk of Chinoiserie. The vision is of a Chinese city's outskirts with cement works and so on. There are still gods around but aeroplanes have come in.

This deliberate juxtaposition of the old and the new, the traditional and the contemporary, the international and the provincial, is fundamental to the play's flavour.

Contradiction is at the heart of Brecht's conception of character, but nowhere more acutely than in *The Good Person of Szechwan*. Here his central character, the honest, good-hearted prostitute, Shen Teh, needs to assume an identity diametrically opposite to her own, the ruthless businessman Shui Ta, in order to survive in the cut-throat world of capitalism. The contrast between the two could not be more extreme. Brecht wrote that the play shows 'The fatal effects of bourgeois ethics under bourgeois conditions' and Shen Teh's disguise as Shui Ta is a perfect metaphor for that deformation.

Brecht's portrait of her lover, the pilot Sun, is a remarkable achievement. When we first meet him he is a sympathetic figure – alone in the park, turning down prostitutes, out of work, down on his luck – and we can understand why Shen Teh falls in love with him. However, Brecht is not writing romantic drama and the play increasingly reveals another side: as soon as he is employed by Shui Ta he becomes no different from the neighbours, friends and family members who descend on Shen Teh the moment she buys the tobacconist's shop. He is transformed from an unemployed pilot into a small-time capitalist, a member of the new class for whom loyalty and community are meaningless, and everything is governed by the iron law of the market.

The water seller, Wang, is different. His utter poverty is made clear by his futile attempts to sell water during a rainstorm. He is a dreamer who refrains from appealing to Shen Teh for charity when she has become rich. Although he talks directly to the audience and helps narrate the action, Wang should not be seen as a mouthpiece for the writer. Indeed, with his respect for the gods, his social conservatism and his powerful instinct for self-preservation, Wang is another of Brecht's apolitical proletarians, the single biggest hindrance to the transformation of society that would help them the most. Like the other poor people in the play, he testifies against Shui Ta for his exploitative brutality, but revolutionary action is beyond him.

The arrival of the gods is the catalyst for the action. Dramatically, they form a deus ex machina, but Brecht is careful to show them in the most concrete human terms, as thinly disguised members of the ruling class, disappointed by their subjects and determined to discover that there is still 'goodness' on earth; furthermore, like the ruling class, they do not understand anything about the society that prevents such goodness. As so often in Brecht, it is not faith that is being mocked, it is organised religion's unspoken alliance with the ruling class and its complacency in the face of injustice. It is hardly surprising that the magistrates in the final scene turn out to be the gods in disguise.

The Good Person of Szechwan is one of Brecht's most remarkable achievements: sophisticated and poetic, but also robust and popular. Its weakness is its length (it cries out to be cut when performed) and the occasional repetitiveness of its argument. Brecht was quite aware of this, as he wrote in his *Journals* on 25 January 1941,

> Since the play is very long I want to work in some poetic touches, a few verses and songs. This may make it lighter and more entertaining, since it cannot be made any shorter, the play proves that the new drama requires a shorter working day. It may well be that even the hours at midday will have to be kept free for it. Classical Greek drama used the hours of daylight, the Elizabethans too, and this meant they had more intelligence and freshness at their disposal. – one sees that there are some hindrances which it takes a world war to clear away.

This last comment reminds us that Brecht wrote the play in the very worst year for the anti-Nazi cause.

Brecht said that the play 'uses certain techniques that are as old and as new as war itself' and he was acutely aware of the technical challenges he had set himself ('Interesting how with this thin steel structure the slightest miscalculation takes its toll'). Sometimes it feels as if he has not quite managed to weld his material into a coherent whole. Nevertheless, the resulting 'parable play'– as he himself dubbed it – confronts one of the great contradictions of modern life – the impossibility of being good while participating in the market – with tremendous wit and style. It does not say how this contradiction can be resolved: it does imply, however, that a radical solution is the only one worth considering.

IN PERFORMANCE

The Good Person of Szechwan was premiered at the Zurich Schauspielhaus on 4 February 1943 in a production directed by Leonard Steckel, with scenery by Teo Otto and music by Paul Dessau. Brecht described it as a 'falsification' of his play, even though he was not able to see it himself.

Szechwan was the subject of several aborted proposals in the United States: a plan to work with Piscator on it in New York came to nothing, as did Brecht's desire to set it in Jamaica with a Negro cast. Kurt Weill's proposal to turn the play into a musical was somewhat more fruitful in that it led to Brecht's 1943 Santa Monica version with its explicit reference to opium addiction and a considerable reduction in length. However, Brecht failed to persuade Christopher Isherwood to translate it and he never directed it himself. He asked Elisabeth Bergner to play Shen Teh at the Berliner Ensemble in 1955, but she declined.

The post-war premiere took place at the Theater am Josefstadt in Vienna in March 1946. This featured none of Brecht's collaborators and was much mocked by Brecht in a letter to Eric Bentley:

> It may interest you to know that the notices I've received from Vienna, where *The Good Person of Szechwan* was played last

summer, are absolutely idiotic; the poor fools take everything symbolically, they interpret a conflict between Shen Teh and Shui Ta as an eternal, universally human conflict, etc. The difference between a symbol and a parable should be made clear once and for all. In a parable a passing historical situation (i.e. one that should be made to pass) is depicted realistically. The rending in two of Shen Teh is a monstrous crime of bourgeois society.

Harry Buckwitz directed the play in Frankfurt in 1952. Brecht attended rehearsals for a few days and although he praised Teo Otto's sets as 'light, elegant and beautiful', he said that he 'tried to give the production a little clarity and lightness'. Benno Besson directed it in Rostock in 1956 and at the Berliner Ensemble in 1957, both times with Käthe Reichel as Shen Teh and designs by Karl von Appen. Friedrich Simms directed the play in Cologne in 1957 with designs by Caspar Neher.

The London premiere took place on 31 October 1956 as part of the first season of the newly formed English Stage Company at the Royal Court Theatre, with Peggy Ashcroft as Shen Teh, directed by George Devine. The American premiere was at the Phoenix Theatre in New York on 18 December 1956, directed by Eric Bentley, with Uta Hagen in the title role. Both productions benefited from Teo Otto's scenery and Paul Dessau's music. In 1981 Giorgio Strehler set the play in an Italian shantytown and Deborah Warner directed Fiona Shaw in the title role at the National Theatre in London in 1990 in a new translation by Michael Hofmann.

MOTHER COURAGE AND HER CHILDREN
[Mutter Courage und ihre Kinder]
A Chronicle of the Thirty Years War

1939

THE STORY

It is spring 1624 (1) and a recruiter is grumbling to his sergeant about how difficult it is to find suitable men: 'it's too long since they had a war here'. Mother Courage's cart comes on, drawn by her two sons, Eilif and Swiss Cheese, with her dumb daughter Kattrin sitting on top. She introduces herself and her children, all born to different fathers. The recruiter insults Eilif and he challenges him; but she is more interested in selling than in fighting. When he tries to take Eilif, she draws a knife, declaring that 'we're doing an honest trade in ham and linen, and we're peaceable folk'. She offers to tell their fortune and the sergeant picks out a black cross; she makes her children draw black crosses too. As they are about to move off, the sergeant feigns interest in a belt buckle and the recruiter leads Eilif away. Kattrin gesticulates wildly, but when Courage comes back, Eilif has gone. The sergeant calls, 'Like the war to nourish you? / Have to feed it something too.'

The following year (2) Courage is outside the General's tent arguing with a cook over the price of a half-starved capon. Inside, the general praises Eilif and offers him dinner; Eilif boasts of his exploits, killing peasants and stealing their cattle, and the general listens to his advice. Courage rages against bad leadership – 'If he knew how to plan a proper campaign what would he be needing men of courage for?' – but the cook buys the capon. When Eilif sings 'The Song of the Girl and the Soldier', Courage adds a gloomy last verse; when he comes out she slaps him for being brave.

Three years later (3) Courage is haggling with an armourer over a sack of shot. He leaves with Swiss Cheese, who has been given responsibility for the regimental cash box. The camp whore, Yvette, tells Kattrin her life story (to 'put her off love'). The cook and the chaplain arrive and persuade Courage to give them a drink and, as they talk about the war, Kattrin tries on Yvette's hat and boots. Suddenly news arrives that the Catholics have broken through and Courage daubs Kattrin's face with ashes. Yvette returns, eager for business, as does Swiss Cheese with the cash box. As the chaplain changes clothes, Courage hauls down the flag. Three days later they are eating together; Courage says that defeat means nothing, but she is worried about the cash box. She also discovers that Kattrin has stolen Yvette's red shoes. Left alone with his sister, Swiss Cheese decides to hide the cash box; a man with an eyepatch frightens her and Swiss Cheese leaves with it under his tunic. Courage returns and realises that the man was a Catholic spy and the chaplain hoists a Catholic flag. Two soldiers bring in Swiss Cheese, and both he and Courage pretend not to know each other. Despite offers of brandy, Swiss Cheese is taken away. Later that evening the chaplain sings about the sufferings of Christ. Yvette arrives with 'an extremely ancient colonel', to whom she hopes Courage can pawn the cart. No sooner have they settled than Courage has second thoughts. As she prevaricates, Yvette tries to bargain on her behalf. Eventually Courage agrees to pay the missing two hundred out of her own funds, but it is too late: Swiss Cheese's body is brought in on a stretcher and his mother denies knowing him at all.

Courage is outside an officer's tent (4), talking to a clerk; she has come to complain about damage done to her cart. A young soldier enters, furious with the captain for stealing reward money, followed by an older soldier advising caution. Courage tells him that his anger 'is a short one and you needed a long one'. When the clerk says that the captain will be with them in a minute, the young soldier sits down obediently. Seeing this, Courage sings the 'Song of the Great Capitulation', adding, 'that's why I reckon you should stay there with your sword drawn if you're truly set on it and your anger's big enough, because you got grounds, I agree, but if your anger's a short one best leave right away'. He slopes off and when the clerk announces the captain's arrival, she leaves too: 'I changed me mind. I ain't complaining.'

Two years later (5), near a badly shot-up village, Courage refuses to give a victorious soldier a drink without him paying for it first. Nor will she give her officers' shirts to the chaplain to bandage up wounded peasants. Kattrin is outraged and threatens her mother with a plank; meanwhile, the chaplain steals the shirts and starts tearing them into strips. Kattrin picks up a baby that has survived and makes lullaby noises to it. As Courage tries to return the baby to its mother, the soldier makes off with one of her drinks; as he leaves, she snatches a looted coat off his back.

By 1632 (6) Courage has grown prosperous and is stocktaking. In the distance we can hear the funeral music for the fallen Field Marshal Tilly, but the soldiers are all drinking. Courage is sympathetic to the leaders, whose 'finest plans get bolloxed up by the pettiness of them as should be carrying them out'. The chaplain argues that the war will last for a long time, almost like a natural urge. This appals Kattrin who is sent off with the clerk to buy stock. The chaplain admires Courage and proposes marriage, but she turns him down and tells him to chop firewood. Kattrin returns with a wound above her eye; Courage bandages her up but Kattrin refuses to accept Yvette's red shoes. By the end of the scene Courage's response is anger: 'War be damned.'

Courage is at the peak of her career (7), her cart is 'hung with new wares' and she sings a song praising the war. Later that year (8) an old woman and her son turn up to sell a large sack of bedding. Suddenly they hear that peace has broken out; the old woman faints with joy and Courage admits that she is glad. The chaplain emerges from the cart – he has moved in with Courage – and decides to go to the camp. The cook arrives and tells Courage that Eilif is coming to see them. Over a brandy, she tells him that the peace is going to ruin her business. Dressed again in clerical garb, the chaplain calls her 'a hyena of the battlefield'. The cook advises her to sell up quickly before 'prices hit rock bottom'.

Yvette arrives, dressed in black, 'much older and fatter', followed by a manservant; she is surprised to see the cook who, she says, 'Got more girls in trouble than he has fingers'. Soon Courage goes off with Yvette. The cook is worried ('I'm fed up already with this bloody peace') when suddenly Eilif appears, followed by soldiers with pikes. He broke into a peasant's cottage and killed the wife; in wartime the same act had won him promotion, now it means death. They take him off and the chaplain follows. Soon Courage returns, excited that war has broken out again, and asks the cook to come with her; he fails to tell her about Eilif, and he and Kattrin harness themselves to the cart.

Two years later (9) the war is at its worst: 'Once fertile areas are ravaged by famine, wolves roam the burnt-out towns . . . Business is bad, so that there is nothing to do but beg.' Early one morning Courage and the cook draw up outside a half-ruined parsonage, hoping for charity. He tells her that he has inherited a tavern in Utrecht and that he wants to take her there. She tells Kattrin about the offer, but he says that she cannot come with them. When Courage objects, he sings a song about the way virtue and wisdom brought famous men bad luck. A voice in the parsonage offers hot soup and both go in to fetch it. However, Kattrin has overheard everything and is about to leave when her mother returns. Courage confronts her and throws the cook's stuff out of the cart. The two harness themselves to the cart and drag it off. The cook returns and realises what has happened. The next year (10) Courage and Kattrin pass a peasant's house and hear someone inside singing a song about 'home': 'Happy are those with shelter now / When winter winds are freezing.'

In 1636 (11) a surprise Catholic attack is planned on the Protestant city of Halle and soldiers order a young peasant to show them the path to the town. When he refuses, they threaten to kill his cattle and he gives in. The peasant's father climbs on to the roof and watches them go: he tells his wife that they can do nothing about it. They see Kattrin in the cart and ask her to pray with them. Instead, she climbs on to the roof, pulls the ladder up behind her and bangs away at a drum to warn the inhabitants. Neither the offer to spare her mother nor the threat to smash the cart can make her stop drumming and she is shot for it.

Before first light (12) the sound of marching troops can be heard in the distance. Courage sings a lullaby over the body of her dead daughter and the peasants have to convince her that she is dead. She pays for Kattrin's burial and accepts their condolences. Alone, she harnesses herself to the empty cart. Still hoping to get back into business, she heads off in pursuit of the ragged army.

ABOUT THE PLAY

Brecht did most of the work on *Mother Courage and her Children* in Sweden, during the first few months of the Second World War, between 21 September and 7 November 1939:

> As I wrote I imagined that the playwright's warning voice would be heard from the stages of various great cities, proclaiming that he who would sup with the devil must have a long spoon. This may have been naive of me, but I do not consider being naive a disgrace. Such productions never materialised. Writers cannot write as rapidly as governments can make war, because writing demands hard thought.

Brecht's instinct for prophecy was never more acute.

Mother Courage is set during the Thirty Years War, the extraordinarily complex and wide-ranging religious wars that swept across central and northern Europe from 1618, and were only ended by the Treaty of Westphalia of 1648. The play has clear literary antecedents, above all Friedrich Schiller's epic plays about the Thirty Years War, *Wallenstein* and *Wallenstein's Camp* (1798–9). Brecht also drew heavily on Hans von Grimmelshausen's picaresque novel *Simplicissimus* (1667), which gave him the name of his central character, and Breughel's *Dulle Griet* (described by Brecht as 'the fury defending her pathetic household goods with the sword') provided him with visual inspiration.

Anna Fierling (nicknamed Mother Courage) earns her living by driving a cart from camp to camp, flogging boots, rum, sausages and pistols to the soldiers, striking bargains, lying and cheating, and sometimes even thriving. She is a formidable operator, who can deal with anything that is put in her way. She is unsentimental, canny and shrewd. She is one of the 'little people', for whom religion and ideology are alien, and her aim, above all, is to find a way of surviving.

Mother Courage is deeply contradictory. Towards the end of Scene 6 she speaks about how it is a 'long anger' that is needed, not a short one; this, she hints, is the anger that changes the world. Then, not long after, when her business starts up again, she loses that insight and sets out once more to earn a living. The challenge that Brecht presents is that he has written a character of tremendous human interest and insists that we are critical of her. What he is asking is similar to the Christian notion of hating the sin but loving the sinner: Brecht wants us to admire Courage's toughness and shrewd wit, while criticising her for not recognising the contradiction she embodies. The fact is Courage lives off the war that surrounds her and she feeds it, and our understanding of this is fundamental to the play's purpose.

It is sometimes forgotten that the play's full title is *Mother Courage and her Children* and Eilif, Swiss Cheese and Kattrin play a crucial role. Eilif, her elder son, is strong and dashing; but he is too brave for his own good and is shot for doing the same thing in peacetime – breaking into a peasant's house – that won him praise and promotion in the war. Her second son, Swiss Cheese, is a simple soul: honest, reliable and stupid. His decision to hide the regimental cash box seems sensible at the time but leads to his early death, and his mother's refusal to acknowledge his dead body is one of the most chilling moments in the play. Courage's daughter Kattrin is one of Brecht's most inspired creations: in a world gone mad, the guardian of goodness is dumb, resorting in crisis to wild gesticulations and banging a drum. Her death is the play's astounding climax.

There are three other important characters. Firstly, the cook, whose conversations with Courage are as intimate as the play gets. With their experience of suffering, their pragmatism and materialism, the two are perfectly matched and their budding romance is brilliantly drawn. The cook's offer to take Courage to Utrecht is not cynical, nor is his refusal to take Kattrin cruel; Courage's decision to turn him down is, in the context of the war, a terrible mistake. The chaplain, too, has an important role. He is at his best in time of war, when high morals take second place to necessity; in peacetime, however, he is sanctimonious and hypocritical. As usual in Brecht, it is not religion which is being satirised; it is its double standards and denial of material reality. Finally, Yvette's story is one of the most extraordinary in the play: she is transformed from a pitiful camp whore into the wife of an old colonel and lady of leisure. Her cynicism is matched by her decency and she uses the one thing she has – her body – to escape the squalid world in which she started.

The greatness of the play, and the reason why it is one of Brecht's most enduring masterpieces, lies in something more than its astonishingly well-drawn central characters and its passionately held insights. For, like Shakespeare, Brecht's historical imagination, coupled with his startling dramatic technique, creates the illusion of an entire world, caught in a terrifying and endless struggle between two sets of interchangeable masters, disguising themselves as different religions, but supported by the very people whose participation – and suffering – keep the war going. The result is a twentieth-century riposte to the classical drama of kings and queens, a history 'written from the bottom up', and Brecht focuses in detail on real people – soldiers, peasants, tradesmen, prostitutes and even generals – finding ways of feeding themselves and trying to survive the insanity which surrounds them. His characters are often distorted and dehumanised by the world in which they live, but they are astonishingly true to life and recognisable.

In his extensive notes on the play, Brecht said that *Mother Courage* was meant to show that in wartime the big profits are not made by little people. That war, which is a continuation of business by other means, makes the human virtues fatal even to their possessors. That no sacrifice is too great for the struggle against war.

Brecht believed that it was not enough to observe the world, it was necessary to change it, and the restrained edginess of this note goes straight to the heart of his intentions. What it does not express is the extraordinary realism of Brecht's treatment. This realism tolerates no heroism and his analysis is merciless and unsentimental. At times his vision can seem too harsh and uncompromising, too difficult for an audience to be involved in the kind of 'complex seeing' that he was so keen to promote. However, when set against the background of a world collapsing into barbarism and war, *Mother Courage* is an extraordinary vision of the darkest moment of a very dark century. If the twentieth century saw the worst wars in history, Brecht's play is drama's greatest plea for peace – and against Fascism.

IN PERFORMANCE

Mother Courage received its premiere at the Zurich Schauspielhaus on 19 April 1941 in a production directed by Leopold Lindtberg, with scenery by Teo Otto and Therese Giehse in the title role. Although Brecht was not able to see it, he was unhappy with the critical response that described the play as a 'Niobe like tragedy' (in which the loss of the children is somehow inevitable) and rewrote several scenes as a result.

Brecht's own great production (co-directed with Erich Engel) opened at the Deutsches Theater in Berlin on 11 January 1949. Helene Weigel played the title role and Angelika Hurwicz was Kattrin; Teo Otto designed its skeletal sets and Paul Dessau wrote its extraordinary music. This was the finest example of Brecht's theatrical practice and was seen all over the world, establishing at a stroke his international reputation.

Despite the dominance of this production (whose details were lovingly recorded in the Model Book) the play has become one of the twentieth century's greatest classics and been performed throughout Europe and America. One of the marks of its greatness is how it has attracted other leading actresses and directors: Therese Giehse revisited the title role in three post-war productions: in 1950 (Munich, directed by Brecht himself), 1958 (Frankfurt) and 1960 (Zurich). Ruth Berlau directed the play in Rotterdam in 1950 and Erwin Piscator directed it in Kassel in 1960. Lotte Lenya played Mother Courage in 1965. However, no production has come close to the astonishing emotional power and theatrical flair of Brecht's own.

The English-language premiere was in Barnstaple in 1955, directed – and performed – by Joan Littlewood for Theatre Workshop. Flora Robson played Courage on BBC television in 1959 and Anne Bancroft performed it in New York in 1963. Other notable English-language productions include William Gaskill's National Theatre production in May 1965 with Madge Ryan, Howard Davies's production of Hanif Kureishi's version for the Royal Shakespeare Company (1984) with Judi Dench, and Jonathan Kent's Royal National Theatre production of David Hare's translation with Diana Rigg (1995). The Glasgow Citizens' Theatre presented the cart as a beaten-up car, and there have been versions in the United States that have set the play during the American Civil War.

Although respected in the English-speaking theatre, the play has never been a box-office hit, and the size of the cast, as well as the demands of the piece, makes revivals in Britain and America less and less common. It is still regularly performed in France and Germany.

MR PUNTILA AND HIS MAN MATTI

[Herr Puntila und sein Knecht Matti]

A People's Play

Collaborators: Margarete Steffin, Hella Wuolijoki
1940

THE STORY

A verse Prologue announces that we are going to watch a comedy that recreates 'a monster from a prehistoric age'. Puntila has been in the back room of a hotel in the local town (1) for two days. His friend, the judge, falls off his chair, drunk. Puntila's chauffeur, Matti, enters, wondering when they are going to go home, but his master does not recognise him. Puntila declares that they both have kind hearts, but confesses to worrying 'fits of sobriety'. They leave, with Puntila declaring that 'money stinks'. His daughter, Eva, is at home eating chocolate (2), bored by her fiancé, the attaché, who retires to bed just before Puntila, Matti and the judge return with a suitcase full of drink. Eva instructs Matti to take the case upstairs, which drives Puntila off into the night, desperate for more, leaving Matti and Eva alone together. Early in the morning (3), having crashed his car, Puntila wanders through the village, pretending that he needs alcohol for his sick cows. Sly-Grog Emma offers her illegal home-brew, but the vet hands him a prescription for medical alcohol instead. When the chemist's assistant gives it to him he proposes marriage to her. He also proposes to a passing milkmaid, a telephonist and Sly-Grog Emma herself. Later that day (4), at a hiring fair, Puntila tells Matti off for taking advantage of him, but says he wants to talk about his 'feelings'. He starts drinking, hands out cash (but no contracts) and denounces a fellow employer as a 'typical capitalist'.

Puntila and Matti return to Puntila Hall (5) and the 'red' labourer Surkalla is offered a job. In the sauna, Matti tells Puntila that he should not make an enemy of the fat 'capitalist'. As soon as Puntila sobers up, he starts to abuse Matti, sacks the labourers and disappears into the house. Eva tells Matti that she is unhappy about her engagement and Matti says that the best way to get out of it is to be discovered in the sauna with him. The attaché hears them laughing and when Eva emerges with her hair in a mess and a button undone, Puntila threatens Matti with the sack. Matti is reading the paper (6) when the judge and the lawyer appear, shocked by the sexual freedom of the peasants. Eva has decided not to marry the attaché and wants Matti instead, but soon criticises him for being an 'egotist'. Puntila insists that she marry the attaché and tells her to avoid Matti. Soon the four women from Kurgela arrive (7) and discover that they are all engaged to Puntila at the same time, but when he arrives he drives them off his land. On the way back to town (8) they exchange stories about the impossibilities of their masters. At a party at Puntila's (9) the local parson is in despair about the people's 'inborn wickedness' and the judge and the lawyer agree. Puntila gets very drunk, says that he does not like the attaché's face and throws him out; he also decides to betroth Eva to Matti, 'a human being', as he calls him. Eva is keen, but Matti is cautious: how could he show her to his mother? He sets up a game to test Eva's practical skills which, of course, she fails. Puntila is disgusted and disowns her. He also throws the others out and tells Matti that 'they're not human beings'. In the distance, Surkalla can be heard singing about love across the class divide. In the yard (10), Puntila and Matti urinate and Matti mocks Puntila's complacency.

Next morning (11) Puntila has a hangover. The parson and the lawyer are concerned because Puntila gave Surkalla money, instead of evicting him. The disgrace of this is so great that Puntila vows to give up drinking altogether. When Surkalla arrives with his children Puntila dismisses him – but is shocked at his refusal to shake his hand. Meanwhile, Matti has arrived and is cursed by Puntila, who soon starts to drink the alcohol that was to be thrown out. He tells Matti that he wants to climb Mount Hatelma – which Matti pretends to build out of broken furniture on top of the billiard table. Together they climb up it and Puntila speaks poetically about the beauty of the countryside: 'Tell me that your heart swells at the sight of it all.' The next morning, however, Matti leaves the house for ever: 'I can't take his familiarities after that business with Surkalla.' As he leaves, his last speech says it all:

> Let's waste no tears, there's nothing we can do:
> It's time your servants turned their backs on you.
> They'll find they have a master really cares
> Once they're the masters of their own affairs.

ABOUT THE PLAY

When Hitler's armies invaded Denmark and Norway in April 1940, Brecht and his family were in neighbouring Sweden. The left-wing Finnish novelist and playwright, Hella Wuolijoki, was a friend of the Prime Minister and persuaded him to admit them into Finland. Initially they stayed in Helsinki, but in early summer they moved to a house on Wuolijoki's own twelve-hundred-acre estate in Tavasthus. This released in Brecht a lyrical feeling for rural beauty not evident in his plays since *Baal*:

> It's not hard to see why people in these parts love their landscape. It is so very opulent and widely varied. The waters stocked with fish and the woods full of beautiful trees with their scent of berries and birches. The immense summers that irrupt overnight following endless winters.

Soon Brecht and Margarete Steffin started work on a new play, which drew on Wuolijoki's unperformed play *The Sawdust Princess* and her related short story 'A Finnish Bacchus'. They also enjoyed listening to her stories:

> She looks wise and lovely as she tells of the tricks of simple people and the stupidity of the upper crust, shaking with perpetual laughter and now and again looking at you through cunningly screwed-up eyes as she accompanies the various personages' remarks by epic, fluid movements of her lovely fat hands as though beating time to some music that nobody else can hear.

The result is one of Brecht's most intensely poetical works, heady with a very particular Scandinavian atmosphere, which celebrates the libido in the face of the constraints of society and analyses the realities of the class struggle with tremendous wit and clarity.

At the heart of the play is the landowner Puntila, and the play's central conceit is that when he is drunk he is imaginative and freethinking, generous with his money and promises the earth; when he is sober, however, he becomes brutal and intolerant, sacking people easily and sending them away empty-handed. One of the remarkable things about the play is just how extreme this contrast is. On one level it acts as a demonstration of Brecht's notion of the fluidity of the personality; on a deeper level it is a warning against liberal reform as merely the drunken ramblings of the rich and powerful, whose sporadic benevolence is not to be trusted. The climax of the play, the extraordinary scene in which the drunken Puntila climbs up on to furniture stacked on top of the billiard table, pretending that he is on Mount Hatelma, demonstrates in the most vivid way imaginable the illusory and changeable basis of his power.

Puntila's chauffeur, Matti, is the opposite: constant, manly and resolute, a model of dry wit and sobriety. However, the surface conceals a powerfully rebellious streak and although he successfully hides it most of the time, Matti despises the ruling class. His attitude is made abundantly clear in his dealings with Puntila's highly sexed daughter Eva, with whom he conducts an erotically charged flirtation. Even here, however, Brecht's Marxist intentions are clear: Matti should not be seen as Eva's 'bit of rough' and Matti is in control throughout. His test of her suitability as his wife (which, of course, he knows she will fail) is as remorseless as Petruchio's taunting of Kate in *The Taming of the Shrew,* and it demonstrates conclusively that the class divide is not easily bridged.

Although dominated by master and man, the play has much more to offer. Centrally important are the women of Kurgela – Sly-Grog Emma, the telephonist, the milkmaid and the chemist's assistant – described by Brecht as 'the noblest characters in the play', as 'biblical brides hoping for a dance and a coffee from their bridegroom on high'. They are drawn with great tenderness and individuality, and take it in turn to recount their sexual experiences – 'what my life is like' – in a wonderful scene (8) which gives the play a new dimension. The play also includes one of Brecht's most realistic portraits of a 1940s Communist, 'Red' Surkalla, and Puntila's decision (11) to lay him off is the turning point of the play, which makes plain how the brutality of the sober landowner quickly eclipses his generosity when drunk. The play also includes several satirical portraits of the ruling class: a foolish young attaché (Eva's fiancé), a parson, a judge, a lawyer and a doctor.

Puntila is built out of a series of powerful contradictions, above all the existence of the class struggle in paradise. The great achievement of the play is that Brecht managed to forge these contradictions into a coherent, delicate, thought-provoking whole. Brecht was acutely aware of such paradoxes in himself:

> *Puntila* means hardly anything to me, the war everything; about *Puntila* I can write virtually anything, about the war nothing. I don't just mean 'may', but truly 'can'. Interesting how remote literature as a practical activity is from the centres where the decisive events take place.

If the play does not rank as one of Brecht's very greatest works, it is an astonishing, unusual and rather neglected tour de force that still has the power to entertain and resonate when his more explicitly didactic plays have started to lose their potency. In the heart of the Finnish countryside, with Europe plunging into darkness, Brecht managed to produce an extraordinary comic parable about a world at peace, but riven by the stubborn realities of the class divide.

IN PERFORMANCE

Brecht was keen to stress the play's popular quality:

> *Puntila* is far from being a play with a message. The Puntila part therefore must not for an instant be in any way deprived of its natural attractiveness, while particular artistry will be needed to make the drunk scenes delicate and poetic, with the maximum of variety, and the sober scenes as ungrotesque and unbrutal as possible. To put it in practical terms: *Puntila* has if possible to be staged in a style combining elements of the old *commedia dell'arte* and of the realistic play of mores.

The play was first performed on 5 June 1948 at the Zurich Schauspielhaus, in a production directed by Kurt Hirschfeld and Brecht, with scenery by Teo Otto, and Leonard Steckel as Puntila. *Puntila* was chosen to open the Berliner Ensemble on 12 November 1949 at the Deutsches Theater in Berlin, in a production co-directed by Erich Engel and Brecht, with Leonard Steckel repeating his performance as Puntila, but this time with scenery by Caspar Neher and music by Paul Dessau. Brecht tried to avoid making the character of Puntila too attractive and used masks throughout. It is possible that in a less politically charged time, he would have trusted the play to express its contradictions in a more relaxed fashion, as he hinted at in the *Journals*:

> Certain alienation effects come from the storehouse of comedy which is 2000 years old.

The play had its English-language premiere at the Wilbur Theater in Boston on 4 May 1959. The London premiere was given by the Royal Shakespeare Company at the Aldwych Theatre on 15 July 1965 in a production directed by Michel Saint-Denis, with Roy Dotrice as Puntila, Patrick McGee as Matti and Glenda Jackson as Eva. The Almeida and the Right Size Theatre Company presented the play in 1999 in a new translation by Lee Hall, directed by Kathryn Hunter. It was widely praised, but some felt that it sold Brecht's political intentions short.

THE CAUCASIAN CHALK CIRCLE
[Der Kaukasische Kreidekreis]

Collaborator: Ruth Berlau

1943–5

THE STORY

The Struggle for the Valley (1) acts like a prologue. It is set in 1945, near a ruined Caucasian village, following the defeat of the Nazis. Two collective farms have met to settle the future use of a nearby valley. The Galinsk farm wants to move back and use it for goat herding, while the Rosa Luxemburg farm wants to grow fruit. An official from the State Reconstruction Commission is with them and they have a spirited discussion over goat's cheese and jokes. When an agronomist shows how a dam could be built to provide water for both groups, adding that the valley would need to be irrigated to make it financially viable, the goat herders cheerfully accept the logic and a play is announced, to be performed by the fruit farmers. It is called *The Chalk Circle*.

In The Noble Child (2), the singer introduces us to the play: there was once a city ruled by a rich Governor, married to a beautiful woman, with a healthy child, Michael. It is Easter and petitioners are asking the Governor for help. The fat prince is pleased to hear that the slum houses are to be pulled down to make way for a garden, but is concerned the war is not going as well as he hoped. Michael is coughing and the doctors are criticised. Grusha, a maidservant, is late for church because she had to fetch another goose for the banquet; she is stopped by a soldier, Simon Chachava, who says that he saw her washing herself in the river. Soon, an uprising has broken out, the palace has been surrounded and forces loyal to the prince capture the Governor. The servants are terrified and the doctors decide to abandon the 'little brat'. Grusha has been told to accompany the Governor's wife, but rumour spreads that the Palace Guard has mutinied. In the turmoil she agrees to marry Simon, but he soon leaves to fight in the war. The Governor's wife is planning her escape and tells the nurse to put Michael down and fetch her slippers. When she hears of her husband's death, she makes her escape. The nurse returns and asks Grusha to hold Michael while she goes after her mistress; but Grusha hides him and leaves. Meanwhile, the Governor has been executed, his head is fastened over a gateway and the Ironshirts are looking for Michael. Grusha picks him up and leaves; as the singer says, 'Like booty she took it for herself / Like a thief she sneaked away.'

The Flight into the Northern Mountains (3) opens with Grusha carrying Michael in a sack on her back. She goes to a cottage to beg, and haggles for milk from an old peasant. She tries to stay in a caravanserai with two aristocratic ladies, who are also on the run, but they discover that she is a maidservant – from watching the ease with which she makes a bed – and call the police. Two Ironshirts are hunting for Michael and the corporal tells off his subordinate for not having enough enthusiasm for the task. Grusha arrives at another cottage and puts Michael on the threshold. Despite her husband's protests, the peasant woman picks him up and goes into the house. The Ironshirts meet Grusha and scare her into running away, straight back to the peasant woman, whom she persuades to say she is Michael's mother. The soldiers arrive and the corporal makes advances to Grusha; when he sees Michael, she hits him over the head with a log of wood, picks up the child and dashes off. Finally, she arrives at a rotten footbridge spanning a deep glacier. Three merchants are too cautious to attempt it but, with the Ironshirts approaching, Grusha ventures across. As she carries Michael off into the snow, she sings him a song.

In the Northern Mountains (4) Grusha arrives at her brother's house exhausted and ill from the trek. Lavrenti is a wealthy peasant, married to a pious woman, who wants to know who Michael's father is: Grusha says he is a soldier in the war. When spring arrives, Lavrenti tells Grusha that she must marry a dying man, so as to make her respectable. They go to the man's house;

his mother is only interested in the dowry she can bring, and his neighbours assemble to pray for his soul. A monk performs a perfunctory wedding ceremony, the neighbours stuff themselves with funeral cakes and musicians strike up a dance. However, on hearing that the war is over, the dying man sits upright in his bed and drives the astonished guests out of the house. Soon he is complaining that Grusha is not treating him properly and all the while Michael is growing up. One day Grusha sees Simon Chachava on the opposite side of the river. She tells him what has happened and he walks off in despair. Suddenly, two Ironshirts capture Michael and take him back to the city.

The Story of the Judge (5) returns to the day the Grand Duke was overthrown. Azdak, a village clerk, gives shelter to a fugitive. The policeman, Shauva, comes to arrest Azdak for poaching. Azdak quickly realises that the fugitive is the Grand Duke himself, and he and Shauva take him to the city, presuming that the new regime is revolutionary. They soon discover, however, that the judge has been executed and the Ironshirts have put down a rebellion, and Azdak's instinctive sympathies nearly get him hung. The fat prince is the new ruler and proposes his nephew as judge, but Azdak suggests that a mock trial should be staged as a test of his suitability. In this, Azdak acts the Grand Duke and defends himself by saying that the war was started by arms traders like the fat prince; the fat prince then calls for Azdak's execution, only to see him made judge instead. During the next two years of civil war, Azdak judges a series of cases – blackmail, medical negligence, rape and theft – and in each manages to subvert the law so as to support the poor. However, once it is announced that the Grand Duke is going to return, Azdak realises that the opportunity for change has passed. He looks at the statute book – on which he has been sitting – and realises that he will be hung for drunkenness. When the Governor's wife appears, he promises to do as she wishes: return Michael to her and have Grusha executed.

In the final scene, The Chalk Circle (6), Grusha is about to appear before the court. The cook tells her that the trial will go her way if Azdak is drunk. Simon Chachava appears, prepared to swear that he is Michael's father, but is told that this is unnecessary since she is married already. The Ironshirts are worried because Azdak has fled. The Governor's wife arrives with her lawyers, who advise her to moderate her language until she knows who the judge is. The Ironshirts drag in Azdak in chains, pull off his legal robes and are about to hang him when a messenger arrives from the Grand Duke announcing that he is to be reinstated; he is then helped from the gallows, sat on the judge's chair and given a drink. The lawyers present their case, citing 'nature herself' as their ally. Grusha says she has brought up Michael according to her best knowledge and conscience. Simon claims that he is Michael's father, but admits that he is not Grusha's husband. Azdak provokes the two of them – he repeatedly fines them and is amazed at their failure to offer him a bribe – until she denounces him in public and says that she has no respect for him. Azdak says that he has lost all interest in the case and turns to an old couple who want to be divorced. He then asks Grusha, 'I've noticed that you have a soft spot for justice. I don't believe he's your child, but if he were yours, wouldn't you want him to be rich? You'd only have to say that he isn't yours and at once he'd have a palace, scores of horses in his stables.' She cannot reply, but he understands her silence. Michael is brought in and Azdak tells Shaura to draw a circle of chalk on the floor: 'Now each of you take the child by a hand. The true mother is she who has the strength to pull the child out of the chalk circle towards herself.' The Governor's wife pulls Michael out easily, but Grusha says she cannot 'tear him to pieces'. So Azdak awards him to Grusha, sends the Governor's wife packing and signs the divorce papers for the old couple. Simon and Grusha are united and a dance ensues, in the midst of which Azdak disappears. The singer draws the conclusion:

But you who have listened to the story of the Chalk Circle
Take note of the meaning of the ancient song:
That what there is shall belong to those who are good for it, thus
The children to the maternal, that they thrive;
The carriages to good drivers, that they are driven well;
And the valley to the waterers, that it shall bear fruit.

ABOUT THE PLAY

In October 1943 Brecht visited the great actress Luise Rainer in New York and asked her what she wanted to play on Broadway. Her first thought was *The Chalk Circle,* Klabund's adaptation of Li Hsing-tao's fourteenth-century Chinese play, which had been a hit for Elisabeth Bergner in Berlin in 1924. Brecht was an old friend of Klabund's and even claimed to have suggested the idea to him in the first place. He had certainly been brooding on the subject ever since and, in 1940, used it as the basis for a short story, 'The Augsburg Chalk Circle'. He was soon commissioned by an American producer and started his new version in April 1944. The first draft was completed on 6 June 1944.

Brecht found *The Caucasian Chalk Circle* hard to write. On the one hand he had a tremendously powerful narrative that could carry an audience along; he had also found a colourful setting that was full of character and atmosphere. On the other hand he was worried that the piece would degenerate into folklore if it was not populated by contradictory, three-dimensional characters, and did not pose fundamental questions about contemporary life. Although some feel that the play does not entirely avoid the sentimental, most agree that, for all its deliberately contradictory structures, it is one of Brecht's greatest achievements.

Brecht's first problem was Grusha. He felt that in his first draft she was too simple, too much an idealised portrait of heroic goodness in a bad world:

Grusha should be simple and look like Breughel's Mad Meg [in *Dulle Griet*], a beast of burden. She should be stubborn and not rebellious, submissive and not good, long suffering and not incorruptible. This simplicity must in no way be equated with a 'wisdom' (the well known stereotype), but it is quite consonant with a practical bent, and even with a certain cunning and an eye for human qualities – Grusha ought, by wearing the backwardness of her class openly like a badge, to permit less identification and thus stand objectively as, in a certain sense, a tragic figure.

He was at pains to stress that Grusha was 'a sucker' (he used the American phrase) and that 'the more she does to save the child's life, the more she endangers her own'. Thus he did everything he could to help us see that Grusha's actions – above all, taking Michael and trusting her brother – are unwise in the extreme. However, it is a measure of Brecht's complex vision that this 'alienation effect' does not stop us from seeing the warmth of Grusha's relationship with Simon Chachava, the depth of her maternal instincts or the rightness of Azdak's judgement in the last scene. It is this dramatic three-dimensionality that makes her one of Brecht's most satisfying and carefully written roles.

Brecht also found it just as difficult to write his Judge. At first glance, Azdak is a peasant version of the corrupt Judge Adam in Heinrich von Kleist's *The Broken Jug* (1806) – a play that Brecht liked and co-directed at the Berliner Ensemble in 1955. Again, however, Brecht was keen to avoid oversimplification:

> The problem of how to construct the figure of Azdak held me up for two weeks until I realised the social reason for his behaviour. At first all I had was his disgraceful handling of the law, under which the poor came off well. I knew I couldn't just show that the law as it exists has to be bent if justice is to be done, but I realised I had to show how, with a truly careless, ignorant, downright bad judge, things can turn out all right for those who are actually in need of justice. That is why Azdak has to have those selfish, amoral, parasitic features, and be the lowest and most decrepit of judges.

But I was still lacking some basic cause of a social kind. And I found it in his disappointment that the fall of the old rulers did not bring about a new age, but just an age of new rulers, as a consequence of which he continues to dispense bourgeois justice, but in a degenerate, subversive fashion, serving the absolute self-interest of the judge.

Thus it is quite wrong – though tempting – to see Azdak as a powerful friend of the peasantry. He does not dispense justice that is favourable to the poor because he is good or wise, but because he is drunk and corrupt. Brecht's point is that in a corrupt world the poor only stand a chance of receiving justice if it is being dispensed by a corrupt judge. Furthermore, by the end Azdak has become a sad figure, like one of those early Communists who had hoped that the revolution would usher in a new golden age, and who were now in despair at its betrayal:

> Azdak is utterly upright, a disappointed revolutionary posing as a human wreck, like Shakespeare's wise men that act the fool. Without this the judgement of the chalk circle would lose all its authority.

In conclusion Azdak, like the mature Brecht himself, is a richly contradictory figure, whose mysterious disappearance at the end asks as many questions as it answers.

These two central characters are surrounded by a vast panorama of vividly drawn figures. Brecht's portrayal of the ruling class – and their supporters – is tougher than ever: the Governor's wife is selfish, arrogant, greedy and vain; the fat prince is stupid and dogmatic, and the lawyers' legalistic arguments simply serve to disguise their clients' self-interest. The peasants, however, are no more affectionately drawn and Brecht shows their caution, self-interest and greed with the same degree of unsentimental objectivity: Grusha's cynical brother Lavrenti; his petit-bourgeois wife; the man who marries Grusha as he pretends to be dying; the peasant woman whose husband tells her to be cautious about taking in Michael when she discovers him on the threshold, and dozens of others. It is to Brecht's credit that these characters are drawn with such frank realism and individuality.

Grusha's young lover Simon Chachava is a remarkable young man: strong but gentle, brusque but patient, he is neither a romantic nor a cynic, and his resilient dignity is exceptionally moving. Most of his dialogue with Grusha takes place in a highly charged third person:

> SIMON May one ask if a certain person is still in the habit of putting her leg in the water when washing her linen?
> GRUSHA The answer is no. Because of the eyes in the bushes.
> SIMON The young lady is talking about soldiers. Here stands a paymaster.
> GRUSHA Is that worth twenty piastres?
> SIMON And board.
> GRUSHA (*with tears in her eyes*) Behind the barracks under the date trees.
> SIMON Just there. I see someone has kept her eyes open.
> GRUSHA Someone has.
> SIMON And has not forgotten.

Theirs is one of the most tender and erotic relationships Brecht ever wrote.

One of the best things about the play is the skill with which Brecht finally manages to bring his two parallel plots together. Brecht's favourite phrase from Hegel was 'the truth is concrete' and the final scene of *The Caucasian Chalk Circle* gives it the most dazzling theatrical realisation:

> The test of the chalk circle in the old Chinese novel and play, like their biblical counterpart, Solomon's test of the sword, still remain valuable tests of motherhood even if motherhood today has to be socially rather than biologically defined.

The climax makes concrete the point of the play: that the child should be given to the person who will protect it, just as the valley should be owned by those who can best look after it.

The play is almost a textbook example of Brecht's notion of the 'epic theatre'. The story is presented as a play-within-a-play, performed to celebrate the agreement reached between the two collective farms, and this helps us watch what is being shown with a greater degree of objectivity. The first scene, however, is problematic: Brecht was adamant that such a framing device was fundamental to the play, but the impression that the Soviet Union following the defeat of the Nazis was full of smiling, cooperative peasants is fanciful in the extreme and difficult to make convincing in the theatre.

Central to the play's form is the singer, who presents the story directly to the audience, interrupting the action, controlling the pace and shaping and moving our responses. Brecht was clear about his role:

> [The play] uses the fiction that the singer stages the whole thing, i.e. he arrives without actors, the scenes are just representations of the main episodes of his story. Nonetheless, the actor must act as if he were the director of a company: he strikes the floor with a little hammer before entrances, making it clear that at certain points he is supervising the proceedings, watching for his next cue, etc. This is necessary to avoid the intoxicating effects of illusion.

The play also shows the strong influence of American spectacular theatre and of the deep roots of its popular tradition:

> The play was written in America after ten years of exile, and its structure is partly conditioned by a revulsion against the commercialised dramaturgy of Broadway. At the same time it makes use of certain elements of that older American theatre whose forte lay in burlesques and 'shows'.

As ever, Brecht was happy to steal from everywhere.

The Caucasian Chalk Circle is Brecht at his most accessible. It tells an exciting, easily understood story, full of colour and human detail, with episodes of knockabout comedy as well as passages of tender, almost romantic lyricism. It is a highly dramatic spectacle which, in a good production, carries an audience along with its exuberant theatricality. It also makes a serious point: that even the most fundamental notions of property need to be torn up and that only a new order can create conditions in which true justice is possible.

IN PERFORMANCE

One of Brecht's most touching late poems is called '1954: First Half':

No serious sickness, no serious enemies.

Enough work.

And I got my share of the new potatoes

The cucumbers, asparagus, strawberries.

I see the lilac in Buckow, the market square in Bruges

The canals of Amsterdam, the Halles in Paris.

I enjoyed the kindness of delightful A.T.

I read Voltaire's letters and Mao's essay on contradiction.

I put on the Chalk Circle at the Berliner Ensemble.

The premiere of Brecht's great production took place on 15 June 1954, with scenery by Karl von Appen and music by Paul Dessau. Angelika Hurwicz played Grusha, Helene Weigel the Governor's wife and Ernst Busch Azdak. This was the Berliner Ensemble's first production at the Theater am Schiffbauerdamm – where *The Threepenny Opera* had been such a hit a quarter of a century earlier – and it, along with *Mother Courage*, established the Berliner Ensemble as one of the great theatre companies of the world, particularly following triumphant seasons in Paris in 1955 and London in 1956.

Brecht rehearsed the play for almost a year and wrote vividly of the personal qualities that the actors required:

Roles like Grusha and Azdak cannot be shaped in our times by the work of the director alone. No less than five years at the Berliner Ensemble were necessary to give Angelika Hurwicz the right foundation, and Busch's whole life, from his proletarian childhood in Hamburg, via the struggle in the Weimar Republic and the Spanish Civil War to the bitter experiences after 45, was necessary to bring about this Azdak.

Observers at these lengthy rehearsals commented on Brecht's insistence on dramatic tension and fluent, forward-moving action, perhaps in contrast to the theories of 'epic theatre' and the 'alienation effect' that were already beginning to circulate.

Curiously, the play's world premiere took place in English, in May 1948, performed by students at Northfield, Minnesota, in a translation by Eric and Maja Bentley. The British premiere took place at the Aldwych Theatre on 29 March 1962 in a production for the Royal Shakespeare Company by William Gaskill, designed by Ralph Koltai. This was translated by James and Tania Stern, with W. H. Auden responsible for the verse. Simon McBurney directed a production for Theatre de Complicite at the National Theatre in London in 1997 with Juliet Stevenson as Grusha and McBurney himself as Azdak, in a new translation by Frank McGuinness. The play has been performed more often in Britain than any other of his plays, especially by amateurs and students.

One of the most remarkable productions of modern times was by the Rustaveli Theatre Company from Georgia (USSR), directed by Robert Sturua in 1975.

The BBC broadcast a television version in February 1973.

13 A LATE MASTERPIECE

1945–1956

Brecht spent most of the immediate post-war period working with Charles Laughton and Joseph Losey on the English-language production of *Life of Galileo*, which opened in Los Angeles on 30 July 1947. Three months later he was summoned to appear before the House Un-American Activities Committee (HUAC) in Washington DC and bewildered his interrogators by his convoluted and evasive answers about the extent of his allegiance to Communism. The next day, 31 August 1947, he left America, never to return.

Brecht went straight to Zurich, the only city in Europe that had been able to produce his work during the war. There he worked on an adaptation of Sophocles' *Antigone* for a small theatre in Chur. This was premiered on 15 February 1948 in a remarkable production co-directed by Brecht and Caspar Neher, with Helene Weigel in the title role. It featured many of the theatrical practices that Brecht wanted to introduce once back in Germany. In June, he attended the premiere of *Mr Puntila and his Man Matti* at the Zurich Schauspielhaus and wrote 'The Short Organum for the Theatre', the most important statement of his mature theatrical aesthetic.

Brecht returned to Soviet-controlled East Berlin in October 1948. His priority was to set up a theatre company where he could stage the plays that he had written in exile, as well as produce adaptations of the classics from a socialist perspective. He immediately started work on his production of *Mother Courage* with Weigel in the title role, which opened to great acclaim on 11 January 1949 at Max Reinhardt's old theatre, the Deutsches Theater. Later that year, on a visit to Zurich in search of new actors, he wrote his last, difficult masterpiece, *The Days of the Commune*, as well as the neglected *Tales from the Calendar*.

With the success of *Mother Courage*, the new East German government was keen to welcome this internationally regarded left-wing writer and, after some wrangling, committed itself to supporting a new company, to be called the Berliner Ensemble, with Brecht as its Artistic Director and Helene Weigel as its Intendant. Both of them knew that the challenges would be considerable – 'It may not be easy to create progressive art in the period of reconstruction,' wrote Brecht – but worked hard, in the exceptionally difficult circumstances of post-war Berlin, to achieve it. The Ensemble's opening production was *Mr Puntila and his Man Matti*, co-directed by Brecht and Leonard Steckel – who also played Puntila – at the Deutsches Theater on 12 November 1949.

In 1950 Brecht directed his own adaptation of Jakob Lenz's *The Tutor*, as well as a new production of *Mother Courage* at the Munich Kammerspiele, this time with Therese Giehse – who had premiered it in Switzerland in 1941 – in the title role. In the same year he took Austrian citizenship, regarded by some as evidence of his rapid disillusionment with the DDR. In 1951 he worked with Paul Dessau on their opera, *The Condemnation of Lucullus* (which the Communist authorities interfered with), as well as directing a new production of *The Mother* for the Berliner Ensemble. He also wrote one of his least distinguished works, *The Report from Herrenburg*, for a World Youth Festival in East Berlin. The following year he adapted Anna Seghers's radio play *The Trial of Joan of Arc at Rouen*, started work on his version of Shakespeare's *Coriolanus* (which was not premiered until after his death) and advised the young director Egon Monk on his revival of *Señora Carrar's Rifles*.

The year 1953 was not Brecht's finest. As a privileged member of the East German establishment – with a chauffeur, comfortable accommodation and freedom of movement – he found himself in an increasingly complex relationship with the government. This reached its climax with the workers' uprising in June. Brecht wrote in his *Journals* that these events 'alienated all [his] existence' and he produced a poem satirising the government's attitude to the people. However, in a truncated letter to the *Neues Deutschland*, he called for greater communication between the two groups and supported the government. His enemies have cited this as evidence of his Stalinism – the same enemies who criticise him for not being a committed Communist. The truth is more complicated, but compromising nevertheless. Also in 1953, Brecht oversaw the Berliner Ensemble's first production of a new play not written by himself, Erwin Strittmatter's *Katzgraben*, and wrote his own somewhat confused satire on liberal intellectuals, *Turandot, or the Congress of Whitewashers*. The great exception to this unhappy year was the *Buckow Elegies*, a remarkable collection of poems which express with great tenderness Brecht's growing isolation in post-war East Germany.

In early 1954, possibly in recognition of Brecht's apparent support the previous year, the government gave the Berliner Ensemble stewardship of the Theater am Schiffbauerdamm. Benno Besson's production of Molière's *Don Juan* inaugurated this in March, followed by Brecht's own production of *The Caucasian Chalk Circle* in October. It was in these last few years that Brecht's international reputation as a director, and that of the Berliner Ensemble, began to soar, particularly after the Ensemble's triumphant appearance at the Paris International Theatre Festival in 1954: suddenly Brecht was hailed as the great white hope of the post-war European theatre.

In 1955 Brecht wrote *Trumpets and Drums*, an adaptation of George Farquhar's *The Recruiting Officer*. He also co-directed a production of Heinrich von Kleist's *The Broken Jug* and started rehearsing *Life of Galileo*, with his old comrade from the 1930s, Ernst Busch, in the title role. However, by early 1956 Brecht's health was failing and he was unable to accompany the Ensemble to Paris and London in the summer. He died of heart failure on 14 August and was buried in the Dorotheen Cemetery in Berlin. He had written in a poem that he wanted his gravestone to say 'he made suggestions, others carried them out'; instead it just carries the one word, 'Brecht'.

★

Brecht's first wife, Marianne Zoff, remarried and survived Nazi Germany, despite being half-Jewish. His second wife, Helene Weigel, ran the Berliner Ensemble until her death in 1971; she is buried in the same cemetery as Brecht, as are Paul Dessau, Hanns Eisler, Erich Engel and Slatan Dudow. Kurt Weill and Lotte Lenya stayed in America after the war; he wrote two successful Broadway musicals and died in 1950; she worked all over the world and died in 1981. Elisabeth Hauptmann married Paul Dessau in 1946 and became chief dramaturg at the Berliner Ensemble in 1954; she died in 1973. Ruth Berlau was banned by Weigel from visiting the Theater am Schiffbauerdamm and died in 1974, as unhappy as she had been all her life.

Brecht's four children have had very different lives: Frank joined the *Wehrmacht* and died on the Eastern Front in 1943; Hanne worked as an actress, at the Berliner Ensemble and elsewhere; Stefan stayed in America and wrote extensively on the theatre; and Barbara returned to East Berlin with her parents, married the actor Ekkehard Schall and oversaw the Brecht estate in Europe following her mother's death.

The Berliner Ensemble itself maintained its extraordinarily high standards for several years after Brecht's death, but lost its way in the 1970s and 1980s. Although the reunification of Germany in 1990 posed new challenges, the Ensemble has been artistically reborn in recent years and is once again one of Germany's leading theatres, producing not just plays by Brecht, but contemporary and classical writers from all over the world.

THE DAYS OF THE COMMUNE

[Die Tage der Commune]

Collaborator: Ruth Berlau
1948–9

THE STORY

Outside a café in Montmartre (1), a bourgeois gentleman is eating his breakfast. A worker, Jean, and his mother, Madame Cabet, arrive, haggling with some children about the meat they are trying to sell. Three National Guardsmen arrive with a captured German soldier and complain that the waiter will not give them free Pernod. The gentleman is shocked by their materialism, but they say that their colleagues are planning to hang the generals. He denounces them as traitors and leaves. Madame Cabet recognises one of the soldiers as her tenant and demands her rent; instead, they share the bourgeois gentleman's chicken casserole and head off to the Hôtel de Ville.

Six days later (2) Prime Minister Thiers is feeling ill and is about to have a bath. He tells his Foreign Minister, Jules Favre, that he wants the war to be over: he despairs of Bismarck's demands, above all for reparations. Favre is worried about the strength of the National Guard: 'We made a patriotic sacrifice and armed the mob against the Prussians. Now they have weapons for use against us.' When he says that they are defending Paris, Thiers declares, 'Paris doesn't belong to them.' However, Favre explains that Bismarck is proposing a deal which would force the mob to give up its weapons in exchange for food; furthermore, he says, Thiers will profit from the reparations, which will be financed by German bankers. The bath is run and Thiers is determined to get better.

Two months later (3a) Jean and François, a National Guardsman, are guarding a cannon on the Rue Pigalle that they have refused to hand over. Jean advises François about his private life, but he is more interested in his microscope. Next morning (3b) a group of women are queuing up outside the bakery, having heard that Thiers has made a deal with Bismarck and is distributing bread in exchange for 'order and stability'. Government soldiers arrive to reclaim the cannon, but the women turn on them. One of the soldiers points his rifle at his own brother, but they are persuaded to join their side and soon word comes that the whole district has kept hold of its cannons. By eight o'clock (3c) the baker is making his shop secure, convinced there will be trouble 'if they go ahead with the Commune everyone's talking about'. Papa, one of the Guardsmen, arrives: General Thomas was shot last night, 'after a trial by the people'; 'This is serious,' he adds, as he walks off in a bad temper.

The next evening, at the Hôtel de Ville (4), delegates of the Central Committee of the National Assembly are discussing how to respond to the government. One of them, Varlin, argues that those who started the war should pay the reparations. The mayors of Paris propose to strike a deal but leave defeated. Some of the delegates want to march on Versailles immediately; others say that the important thing is to get the Commune properly established. Varlin announces that 'the capital of France, declaring the revolt against this gang of adventurers to be legitimate, arms herself now and strides calmly and determinedly to the election of her own free and sovereign Commune', and a resolution is quickly passed.

Later that day, at the Gare du Nord (5), terrified bourgeois families are fleeing Paris. Civil servants are dragging cash boxes from the town hall. Jean tries to stop his brother Philippe from rejoining the army. An aristocratic woman bids farewell to de Ploeuc, Governor of the Bank of France. Newspaper sellers shout headlines and street traders flog their wares. Soldiers of the National Guard catch Jean as he tries to stop the cash boxes from being stolen. De Ploeuc wants him formally arrested, but he is released and leaves in despair at their lack of willpower: 'I voted. But not for your Commune. Your Commune will go under.' Soon, in Montmartre (6), the communards are celebrating their new freedom. They drink, eat and sing, and Papa declares, 'This is the first night in history that here in Paris there'll be no murder, no robbery, no fraud and no rape . . . The city is liveable in.' Pierre Langevin, a worker, is worried about the Commune's 'carelessness', but Papa and Jean try to reassure him, by improvising a little play that shows Thiers grovelling at Bismarck's feet, both terrified of revolutionaries of all kinds. François reads out a newspaper declaration and all toast, 'The Commune!'

It is soon the opening session of the Commune (7a). The assembly room is draped with red flags and laws are passed abolishing the army, creating a new constitution, demanding free education, collectivising the workplace and so on. Soon (7b), Langevin discovers that the civil servants in the Ministry of the Interior have all fled; they have made themselves 'irreplaceable'. Delegates arrive and realise just how complicated the challenges are: for example, the Commune pays the workers less than the Empire did. Langevin is cheered when Philippe says that they should break into the Bank of France. Meanwhile (8), de Ploeuc is planning to transfer ten million francs to Thiers in Versailles; but, unknown to the communards, he has over two billion francs in the bank. One of the delegates, Beslay, arrives insisting that the safes be opened, so that the National Guard, which is drawn up outside, can be paid. When he adds that the Guard is to be dissolved, de Ploeuc declares that the bank 'stands above all parties'; furthermore, Beslay's demand for ten million francs is soon reduced to six million, and when de Ploeuc offers to 'work together', Beslay says, 'for peaceful negotiations I am at your disposal'.

Back at the Hôtel de Ville (9a), the delegates are furious. Beslay says that the currency depends on trust, but Varlin argues that violence must be used to smash the apparatus of the state. Langevin proposes that the Commune should trade only with other communards, and another delgeate, Rigault, argues that the National Guard should march on Versailles. 'The delegates reject civil war', but the Chairman has received a message that will 'turn the work of this assembly in a new direction': newspapers declare (9b) that the Versailles government has attacked Paris. As the Commune passes laws (9c), a wounded officer argues that their principles are preventing the National Guard from defeating the enemy and Ranvier persuades the other delegates to accept his expert advice. A message of solidarity arrives from the German revolutionaries (9d): 'Workers of the world, unite!' Meanwhile, in Frankfurt, Bismarck is attending a performance of *Norma* (10) and tells Favre – who is signing the peace treaty – that it is time for the 'pacification of Paris'; he has handed over 150,000 prisoners to Versailles and payment of reparations can wait.

In the Hôtel de Ville (11a), Langevin regrets not marching on Versailles and says that all their ideas mean nothing in reality: 'We should have been prepared, as the members of a body fighting for its life, to forgo personal freedom until the freedom of all had been achieved', concluding that 'in this struggle the hands not blood-stained are the hands chopped off'. As the delegates assemble, gunfire can be heard in the distance (11b); one of them reports that the citizens should man the barricade: 'should our enemy succeed in turning Paris into a grave it will at least never be the grave of our ideas'. Female workers have arrived and announce that they refuse to be mediators between Versailles and the Commune; Varlin again criticises the delegates for being merciful and Rigault reminds them of the enemy's brutality. The delegates object – 'do you deny that the use of violence debases the man who uses it?' – and a motion is carried saying, 'The voice of reason, untainted with anger, will stop our murderers in their tracks.'

Soon, however, in the Place Pigalle on Easter Sunday (12), men, women and children are building barricades. Jean's girlfriend Babette is expecting a child. François defends Philippe for leaving Paris. Madame Cabet distributes bread rolls and Easter eggs. A woman's fiancé arrives, disguised as a nun, sent to spy on them; Papa is about to shoot him when Madame Cabet intervenes. They unroll a banner saying 'you are workers like us', which they hope will make the enemy 'think again'. The troops are drawing near the barricade (13); the Hôtel de Ville has been taken and the slaughter has begun. As the barricade is stormed, Madame Cabet desperately hands out soup.

From the walls of Versailles (14) the bourgeois watch the destruction of the Commune through opera glasses. A duchess says to Thiers: 'This will make you immortal. You have given back Paris to her true mistress, to France.'

ABOUT THE PLAY

Brecht's last and most complicated masterpiece was written in a highly charged political context: the Berlin airlift, the development of the Soviet nuclear bomb and the formation of both East and West Germany as independent states. Brecht and Weigel had returned to East Berlin from Switzerland in October 1948 and founded the Berliner Ensemble early the next year. In February 1949 he returned to Zurich to sort out various matters, including finding actors for the company. Looking for new material had led him to reread the Norwegian Communist Nordahl Grieg's play about the Paris Commune, *Defeat* (1937), which Margarete Steffin had translated into German in 1938. He described it as 'astonishingly bad, but I think it can be changed'. He was joined in Zurich by Ruth Berlau, who had played Madame Lasalle in *Defeat* in Copenhagen in 1937, and Caspar Neher. They drew on a wide range of source material, including Marx's *Civil War in France* (1871) and Lenin's *In Memory of the Paris Commune* (1904), and by April 1949 the play was finished to Brecht's satisfaction.

For Marxists, the short-lived Paris Commune (January–April 1871) is a key episode in revolutionary history. It was perhaps the first moment when, in a time of national crisis (the Prussian invasion of France), the industrial working class took possession of a city and had an army on its side prepared to defend it. The fact that the Commune was defeated – about 25,000 communards were slaughtered by government troops in the Bloody Week (*la semaine sanglante*) – provided subsequent generations with a crucial case study in failure. Many theories abounded, but the classical Marxist version was that the revolutionary working class had made the fatal mistake of shying away from using violence to secure their goals and were let down by a fatal alliance of the bourgeoisie and the government. The Marxist-Leninist conclusion was that the bourgeoisie should never be trusted again; this was certainly Brecht's view.

The Days of the Commune marks a new development for Brecht in that it was the first time that he wrote a play based on actual historical events. Like Büchner in *Danton's Death* (1835), he handled the epic sweep of action with great dramatic skill, and the play works as 'a slice of illuminated history'. If it lacks the central characters that make many of his other plays so memorable, it teems with a vast range of sharply drawn men and women, historical and imaginary, heroes and villains, an entire city caught in a moment of extraordinary upheaval. Each scene has its own unique flavour and is painted in tremendous detail, like the crowded political canvases of Delacroix or Géricault. Furthermore, the play has a vivid Parisian atmosphere, as well as a typically French sense of intellectual, culinary and physical pleasure. It revels in the communards' seizing of the capital of the European bourgeoisie, and their camaraderie and high spirits are exhilarating, even as we are prompted to question whether they are wise.

Some critics have dismissed the play because of its naturalistic form; others have criticised it for its uncomfortable message: that violence is required if a revolution is to last. Indeed, it could be said that Brecht's choice of form makes this message even harder to accept. It is almost as if, after his many explorations of exotic worlds and theatrical forms, Brecht had decided to write a specifically European study of the defeat of the cause to which he had dedicated his life: it is as if he is reminding his audience that the Nazis had triumphed over the German left, and that the new German Communist state needs to be careful if it is not to be similarly defeated.

Brecht knew that his conclusions were difficult; but he also knew that simple optimism was not enough. In November he wrote a letter to Eric Bentley, which is tinged with sadness but shows his commitment to a complicated and challenging truth:

It's probably true that the play cannot be accepted unless one accepts the Marxist point of view. But to take a classical example: to accept *Hamlet* or *Troilus and Cressida* mustn't one accept the attitudes of Montaigne or Bacon? . . . What the play can show is that the proletariat cannot counter the force of its adversaries unless it is prepared to use force.

This is a conclusion revolutionaries have reached the world over, with a wide range of consequences, both good and utterly disastrous; but it is a view their opponents ignore at their peril.

IN PERFORMANCE

Brecht felt that *The Days of the Commune* was too controversial to be chosen as the opening production for the Berliner Ensemble. Various delays meant that it was not staged until three months after his death in November 1956 in Karl-Marx-Stadt (Chemnitz), in a production directed by Benno Besson and Manfred Wekwerth, with designs by Caspar Neher and music by Hanns Eisler. It had a mixed reception. The Berliner Ensemble presented a new production by Wekwerth and Tenschert, in a radically revised text, in August 1961, which drew questionable connections between the communards' barricades and the Berlin Wall, which had been recently built. This production was performed at the Old Vic in 1965.

The play was seen at the Liverpool Playhouse in 1972. It was performed at the Aldwych in 1977 in an RSC production directed by Howard Davies, with Ian McKellen as Langevin, Richard Griffiths as Thiers, Bob Peck as Papa and Alfred Molina as Bismarck. It is hardly ever staged in Britain today.

14 LEGACY

Brecht's work has had such a broad impact – not just on the theatre but on aesthetics as a whole – that it is sometimes difficult to decide what is peculiarly 'Brechtian' and what is simply modern.

Brecht's greatest legacy was a dozen or so remarkable plays, five or six of which are recognised masterpieces, powerful portraits of the darkest and most complex half-century in European history. He also wrote several volumes of outstanding poetry and short stories, as well as hundreds of letters and his fascinating *Journals*. This material is all widely available and translated into many languages. In addition, Brecht was restlessly engaged with questions of theatrical form and left behind many essays and dialogues about the theatre and a new sense of what it could achieve. These, and the many surviving accounts of his remarkable work as a director, have changed the way that theatre has been made ever since.

Although in recent years Brecht's dominance in the German theatre has been questioned, he is still the key figure against whom the best compare themselves. His many disciples at the Berliner Ensemble included some of the greatest directors of post-war German theatre – Manfred Wekwerth, Peter Palitzsch, Joachim Tenschert, Egon Monk, Thomas Langhoff and Manfred Karge – all of whom acknowledged the central importance of Brecht's example. Though never part of the 'Brecht Circle', Peter Stein has been hailed as his natural successor and his pioneering work at the Schaubühne in Berlin in the 1970s and 1980s was often stubbornly Brechtian in style. Other leading directors, such as Peter Zadek, Klaus Peymann and George Tabori, have struggled with the inheritance of the Berliner Ensemble and Brecht has been instrumental in the development of many post-war German-language dramatists, such as Friedrich Dürrenmatt, Max Frisch, Peter Weiss, Franz Xaver Kroetz, Peter Handke and Heiner Müller.

Beyond Germany, Brecht's impact has been enormous, if different in kind. It was first felt in mainland Europe with French directors such as Roger Planchon and Patrice Chéreau at the Théâtre Nationale Populaire and the Italian Giorgio Strehler at the Piccolo Teatro in Milan all looking to learn from the Berliner Ensemble, especially in their approach to the European classics. In more recent years Brecht's work has inspired theatre in developing countries, and directors such as Augusto Boal in Latin America and Barney Simon in South Africa applied his theatrical approach to very different political circumstances.

Although most of Brecht's early plays were performed in pre-war Britain, his influence on the British theatre can be dated to the Berliner Ensemble's visit to London in 1956 with *The Caucasian Chalk Circle*, *Mother Courage* and *Trumpets and Drums*. The directors, designers and writers who were affected by this visit reads like a roll-call of the best in post-war British theatre: George Devine founded the English Stage Company at the Royal Court in 1956, and his commitment to work with a radical social content would have been impossible without Brecht's example; Joan Littlewood attempted to create a radical, popular theatre at the Theatre Royal, Stratford East, and acknowledged Brecht as her forebear; the National Theatre under Laurence Olivier pursued an approach to the classics which had absorbed Brecht's technique and concerns; and the best work of the Royal Shakespeare Company under Peter Hall – above all *The Wars of the Roses* – echoed Brecht's view of the political content and theatrical form of the Elizabethan and Jacobean theatre. The great British director Peter Brook has acknowledged the centrality of Brecht, whom he called 'the key figure of our time, and all theatre work today at some point starts or returns to his statements and achievement', and his productions of Peter Weiss's *Marat-Sade* (1964) and *US*

(1966) both used 'Brechtian' techniques; in recent years, however, Brook has produced work that, with its striving for 'universality', its search for a mystical notion of 'truth' and its lack of interest in history, is antithetical to everything Brecht believed in.

Brecht's influence was strongly felt by the large number of politically minded dramatists who flowered at the Royal Court after 1956: John Osborne, John Arden, David Storey, Arnold Wesker, Edward Bond, David Hare, Trevor Griffiths, Howard Brenton, Caryl Churchill and dozens of others. The Berliner Ensemble was also the key inspiration behind the British political theatre of the 1970s, especially cooperative companies such as John McGrath's 7:84, the Joint Stock Theatre Group, Belt and Braces, and Red Ladder. The visual impact of the Berliner Ensemble had a huge impact on British theatre design and Jocelyn Herbert, John Bury, Alison Chitty, Pamela Howard have all acknowledged the influence of Caspar Neher on their work.

With the advent of Thatcherism in 1979, however, Brecht's left-wing theatre started to look irrelevant – if not outmanoeuvred – and his British followers found themselves increasingly marginalised. In more recent years a growing interest in physical and visual theatre, let alone the celebrity-led theatre of late, has made Brecht's intellectual, literary ensemble plays feel almost exotic. Companies such as Out of Joint and English Touring Theatre produce work that shows the influence of Brecht, but do not often perform his plays. Today, his presence is most evident in the productions of contemporary avant-garde theatre artists such as Deborah Warner, Complicite, Robert Wilson and the Wooster Group, all of whom draw on Brecht's aesthetics and occasionally stage his plays, while usually ignoring – and occasionally decrying – his political analysis. Most recently Brecht's influence is evident in the growth of documentary drama.

Brecht's aesthetic theories have been more closely studied than his political analysis and have had a profound effect on post-war European cinema, particularly the left-wing Italian film directors of the 1950s and 1960s, such as Roberto Rossellini, Luchino

Visconti and Michelangelo Antonioni, as well as the leading figures of the French 'nouvelle vague', such as Claude Chabrol, François Truffaut and Jean-Luc Godard, and the gritty British realists Lindsay Anderson, Tony Richardson and Ken Loach. Perhaps the most explicitly 'Brechtian' films of all time is Gillo Pontecorvo's masterpiece, *The Battle of Algiers* (1967), arguably the greatest work of art about terrorism.

A number of blues and jazz singers, including Ella Fitzgerald and Nina Simone, have covered the songs of Kurt Weill, whose work had a dynamic effect on contemporary music, especially singer-songwriters such as Bob Dylan, Tom Waits and David Bowie, who have all acknowledged their debt. The influence of *The Threepenny Opera* can also be felt in the musicals of Kander and Ebb, especially *Cabaret* (1966) and *Chicago* (1975), and, to a lesser extent, Stephen Sondheim.

Brecht's legacy extends beyond the performing arts and the aesthetic revolution of 'Brechtianism' has penetrated the very fabric of contemporary life. It is evident in the fragmentary and self-conscious nature of much popular culture, and it is ironic that the most profound impact of Brecht's work has been on those aspects of modern life that he would have found most alien: advertising, television and newspapers. Furthermore, Brecht's emphasis on 'textuality' and quotation, on parody and distance, is fundamental to modern philosophy and the postmodernism of Roland Barthes, Jacques Derrida and Michel Foucault are all unthinkable without Brecht – even if his political commitment and pragmatic materialism carries its own stern reprimand to their intellectual and free-floating abstraction.

*

In the fifty years since his death, Brecht has gone in and out of fashion. The end of Communism in Eastern Europe in 1989 and the collapse of the Soviet Union in 1991 led some to argue that his identification with such a lost cause disqualified him from the first rank of dramatists. Furthermore, among theatre professionals, the 'alienation effect' has often seemed mechanistic and incapable of reflecting the subtleties of modern life, particularly private life, while the 'epic theatre', with its emphasis on history and the transformation of society, has appeared an inadequate instrument for addressing the fragmentary, individualistic nature of modern life. Finally, Brecht's reaction against Naturalism has been eclipsed by the ever growing reputations of Ibsen, Chekhov and their many followers. The result is that, in some theatrical circles at least, Brecht is regarded as 'old hat', as irrelevant to the modern theatre as a minor Jacobean dramatist, or 1960s performance art.

However, Brecht cannot so easily be dismissed. He is an iconic figure, one of that handful of artists whose work was only possible in the twentieth century and who tried to create a new kind of art capable of reflecting its momentous changes. More important, his work continues to reveal itself in novel ways and the challenges of the new century, whether it be the widening gap between the rich and poor, the re-emergence of religion as a powerful force, or the growing frustration of the excluded, will demand a new kind of politically engaged drama. Brecht's probing, ironic and poetic plays, and his hard-edged, witty and sophisticated attitude to the theatre, will continue to resonate wherever there is poverty, injustice and despair.

15 CHRONICLE

1898		10 February: Bertolt Brecht born in Augsburg
1914	Outbreak of First World War	17 August: first contribution to the *Augsburger Neueste Nachrichten*
1917	October: Russian Revolution	Matriculates as a medical student at Munich University
1918	November: Kaiser abdicates End of First World War	Military service as medical orderly in Augsburg Elected to Soldiers' Council as an Independent Socialist (USPD) during the November revolution Writes *Baal* and *The Ballad of the Dead Soldier*
1919	January: Spartacus Rebellion June: Versailles Treaty	30 July: birth of Brecht's illegitimate son Frank by Paula Banholzer 21 October: first theatre criticism for the *Augsburger Volkswille* Writes *Drums in the Night* and the one-act plays Takes part in the Munich political cabaret of Karl Valentin Meets Lion Feuchtwanger and Peter Suhrkamp
1920	February: Nazi Party founded March: failed Kapp Putsch	21 February: first trip to Berlin 1 May: death of his mother

1921
Leaves university without a degree

November: second trip to Berlin

Attends Max Reinhardt's rehearsals of Strindberg's *A Dream Play*

Meets Arnold Bronnen

Reads Rimbaud

1922 Mussolini comes to power in Italy

Treay of Rapallo between Germany and the USSR

Directs Arnold Bronnen's *Parricide*, but is taken off the production

Autumn: becomes Dramaturg at the Kammerspiele in Munich

30 September: premiere of *Drums in the Night* at the Munich Kammerspiele

3 November: marries Marianne Zoff, an opera singer

13 November: awarded the Kleist Prize

20 December: *Drums in the Night* at the Deutsches Theater

1923 French and Belgian troops march into Ruhr

German economic crisis

Failed 'beer-cellar' putsch

9 May: premiere of *In the Jungle* at the Residenztheater in Munich

12 March: daughter Hanne is born

August: co-directs Hans Jahnn's *Pastor Ephraim Magnus*

8 December: premiere of *Baal* at the Altes Theater, Leipzig

Meets Helene Weigel

1924 January: Death of Lenin

Dawes Plan

Stalin becomes General Secretary of USSR

Assistant Director at Max Reinhardt's Deutsches Theater in Berlin

19 March: directs *The Life of Edward II of England* at the Munich Kammerspiele

29 October: *In the Jungle (Downfall of a Family)* at the Deutsches Theater in Berlin

Meets Elisabeth Hauptmann

3 November: Stefan Brecht is born

1925	Franco–German treaties at Locarno	Meets the heavyweight boxer Paul Samson Korner

1926 Germany admitted to the League of Naitons

14 February: co-directs *Baal* at the Deutsches Theater in Berlin

25 September: simultaneous premieres of *Man equals Man* in Darmstadt and Düsseldorf

Starts to read Karl Marx's *Das Kapital*

December: premiere of *A Respectable Wedding* in New York

1927

January: publication of *The Devotions*

25 March: radio broadcast of *Man equals Man*

March: meets Kurt Weill

17 July: premiere of *Mahagonny Songspiel* at the Baden-Baden Music Festival

Works with the Piscator Collective at the Volksbühne

14 October: radio broadcast of his adaptation of *Macbeth*

2 November: divorces Marianne Zoff

Starts work on *The Downfall of the Egotist Johannes Fatzer*

December: *In the Jungle of the Cities* in Darmstadt

1928

5 January: *Man equals Man* at the Volksbühne in Berlin

23 January: premiere of the Piscator Collective's adaptation of Hašek's *The Good Soldier Švejk*

31 August: premiere of *The Threepenny Opera* at the Theater am Schiffbauerdamm in Berlin

1929 October: Wall Street Crash

April: co-directs Marieluise Fleisser's *Engineers in Ingolstadt*

10 April: marries Helene Weigel

1 May: witnesses Berlin police break up banned KPD demonstration

Summer: broadcast of *Berlin Requiem* on Berlin radio

Meets Walter Benjamin

Writes *Saint Joan of the Stockyards* and *The Exception and the Rule*

28 July: directs premieres of *The Baden-Baden Lesson on Consent* and *Lindbergh's Flight* at the Baden-Baden Music Festival

31 August: premiere of *Happy End* at the Theater am Schiffbauerdamm in Berlin

1930 September: Nazis become second largest political party in Germany	9 March: premiere of *The Rise and Fall of the City of Mahagonny* at the Leipzig Opera House

April: sees Meyerhold's production of Sergei Tretiakov's *Roar China*

23 June: directs *He Who Says Yes* in Berlin

Writes *He Who Says No* and the *Keuner* stories

18 October: birth of daughter Barbara

Screenplay for *The Threepenny Opera*

10 December: *The Decision* opens at the Grosses Schauspielhaus in Berlin

1931

30 January: Radio broadcast of adaptation of *Hamlet*

6 February: directs *Man equals Man* in Berlin

19 February: G. W. Pabst film of *The Threepenny Opera*. Brecht and Weill sue Nero Films for breach of contract; Brecht loses, settles out of court, but Weill wins

21 December: *The Rise and Fall of the City of Mahagonny* at the Theater am Schiffbauerdamm in Berlin

1932 July: Nazi election victory

17 January: *The Mother* opens at the Theater am Schiffbauerdamm in Berlin

30 May: opening of film *Kuhle Wampe*

11 April: broadcast of *Round Heads and Pointed Heads* on the radio

Meets Margarete Steffin and Sergei Tretiakov

| 1933 | January: Hitler becomes German Chancellor | 28 February: the Brechts leave Germany via Prague. Go to Paris and buy house on Fyn island, Denmark, overlooking the Svendborg Sound |

1933 January: Hitler becomes German Chancellor

27 February: Reichstag Fire

March: First concentration camp built at Dachau

Gestapo formed

Germany withdraws from the League of Nations

28 February: the Brechts leave Germany via Prague. Go to Paris and buy house on Fyn island, Denmark, overlooking the Svendborg Sound

Visits London

13 April: New York premiere of *The Threepenny Opera*

7 June: premiere of *The Seven Deadly Sins* at the Théâtre des Champs-Elysées in Paris

Autumn: meets Ruth Berlau

1934 Soviet show trials

October: visits London

Writes *The Horatians and the Curatians*

Writes *The Threepenny Novel*

1935 September: Nuremberg Laws passed

October: Italians invade Ethiopia

Spring: visits Moscow for International Theatre Conference

8 June: German citizenship renounced by the Nazis

October: Danish Revolutionary Theatre Group's production of *The Mother*

19 November: visits New York for the Theatre Union's premiere of *The Mother*

1936 Outbreak of Spanish Civil War

4 November: Danish premiere of *Round Heads and Pointed Heads*

12 November: Danish premiere of *The Seven Deadly Sins*

Becomes co-editor of *Das Wort*, literary magazine for German émigrés

1937

28 September: *The Threepenny Opera* at Paris World Fair

16 October: German-language premiere of *Señora Carrar's Rifles* in Paris

Starts writing *Life of Galileo*

19 December: Danish premiere of *Señora Carrar's Rifles*

1938 March: German
annexation of
Austria

September: Munich
Agreement

October: Germans
take over
Sudetenland

November:
'Kristallnacht'

21 May: premiere of eight scenes of *Fear and
Misery of the Third Reich* in Paris under the title
99%

23 November: finishes first version of *Life of
Galileo*

1939 March: Fascist
victory in Spain

August: Nazi-Soviet
pact

September:
Invasion of Poland
leads to outbreak of
Second World War

23 April: moves to Stockholm

May: *Svendborg Poems* published

20 May: death of Brecht's father

What's the Price of Iron? co-directed by Brecht and
Ruth Berlau in Stockholm

21 September–7 November: writes *Mother Courage
and her Children*

Writes *The Trial of Lucullus*

1940 Spring: Germans
invade Norway,
Denmark and the
Low Countries

June: Fall of France

Summer: Battle of
Britain

17 April: moves to Helsinki

July: moves to Hella Wuolijoki's country estate

Writes *The Messingkauf Dialogues* and *The Good
Person of Szechwan*

12 May: broadcast of *The Trial of Lucullus* on radio

Writes *Mr Puntila and his Man Matti* and
Conversations Among Exiles

1941 July: German
invasion of USSR

December:
Japanese attack on
Pearl Harbor

10 March–12 April: writes *The Resistible Rise of
Arturo Ui* with Margarete Steffin in Helsinki

19 April: premiere of *Mother Courage and her
Children* at the Zurich Schauspielhaus

15 May: leaves Finland for America, via
Leningrad, Moscow and Vladivostok

June: death of Margarete Steffin in Moscow

21 July: arrives in Los Angeles

Meets Charlie Chaplin

Starts *Schweyk in the Second World War*

1942 January: Wannsee Conference

Writes screenplay for *Hangmen Also Die* directed by Fritz Lang

November: German defeat at El Alamein

Meets Arnold Schoenberg, Theodor Adorno and Thomas Mann in Hollywood

August: rents a house in Santa Monica

Ruth Berlau works in New York

Works with Lion Feuchtwanger on *The Visions of Simone Machard* and sells rights to MGM

1943 January: German defeat at Stalingrad

4 February: premiere of *The Good Person of Szechwan* at the Zurich Schauspielhaus

September: Allied landings in Italy

Starts second draft of *Life of Galileo*

Finishes *Schweyk in the Second World War*

Visits New York for three months and stays with Ruth Berlau

Meets up with Paul Dessau again

9 September: premiere of *Life of Galileo* at the Zurich Schauspielhaus

November: death of son Frank on the Russian Front

1944 June: Normandy landings

Writes *The Caucasian Chalk Circle*

Adapts with W. H. Auden John Webster's *The Duchess of Malfi*

March: meets Charles Laughton and starts work on English verison of *Life of Galileo*

Writes *The Hollywood Elegies* with Hanns Eisler

Son by Ruth Berlau lives for only a few days

1945 January: Auschwitz liberated

June: *Private Life of the Master Race* (American adaptation of *Fear and Misery*) in San Francisco and New York

May: Defeat of Nazi Germany

July: Germany divided

August: Atomic bombs dropped on Hiroshima and Nagasaki, followed by Japanese surrender

1946 January: foundation
of the United
Nations

October:
Nuremberg Trials

15 October: opening of adaptation of *The Duchess of Malfi* on Broadway

Ruth Berlau taken to hospital after breakdown

1947

30 July: premiere of *Life of Galileo* with Charles Laughton in Los Angeles

30 October: appears before the House Un-American Activities Committee in Washington

31 October: leaves USA for Switzerland

7 December: *Life of Galileo* with Charles Laughton in New York

1948 Autumn: Russian
blockade of the
Allied sector of
Berlin

15 February: directs his adaptation of *Antigone* in Chur, Switzerland

Writes *Tales from the Calendar*

Writes 'A Short Organum for the Theatre'

May: world premiere (in English) of *The Caucasian Chalk Circle* in Northfield, Minnesota, USA

5 June: *Mr Puntila and his Man Matti* premiere at the Zurich Schauspielhaus

October: returns to East Berlin

1949 March: NATO
formed

May: West Germany
founded; Berlin
blockade lifted

September: USSR
develops atomic
weapons

October: East
Germany founded

Completes *The Days of the Commune*

11 January: directs *Mother Courage and her Children* with Helene Weigel at the Deutsches Theater

12 November: co-directs *Mr Puntila and his Man Matti* for the Berliner Ensemble at the Deutsches Theater

1950	Outbreak of Korean War	Takes Austrian citizenship
		15 April: directs his adaptation of Jakob Lenz's *The Tutor* for the Berliner Ensemble at the Deutsches Theater
		8 October: directs *Mother Courage* with Therese Giehse at the Munich Kammerspiele
1951		10 January: directs *The Mother* for the Berliner Ensemble at the Deutsches Theater
		17 March: *The Trial of Lucullus* tried out at the East Berlin State Opera
		August: *Report From Herrenburg* at the World Youth Festival, East Berlin
		12 October: *The Condemnation of Lucullus* rewritten and premiered at the East Berlin State Opera
1952		Adapts *Coriolanus* for the Berliner Ensemble
		16 November: revival of *Señora Carrar's Rifles* for the Berliner Ensemble at the Deutsches Theater
1953	March: Death of Stalin June: Workers' uprising in East Berlin and elsewhere, quickly suppressed	17 May: directs *Katzgraben* by Erwin Strittmatter with the Berliner Ensemble at the Deutsches Theater
		Writes *Turandot, or the Congress of Whitewashers* and the *Buckow Elegies*
1954	West Germany admitted to NATO	Berliner Ensemble moves into the Theater am Schiffbauerdamm
		March: *The Threepenny Opera* (English adaptation by Marc Blitzstein) opens in New York
		19 March: opening of adaptation of Molière's *Don Juan* for the Berliner Ensemble at the Theater am Schiffbauerdamm
		15 June: directs premiere of *The Caucasian Chalk Circle* for the Berliner Ensemble at the Theater am Schiffbauerdamm
		Mother Courage visits Paris International Theatre Festival

1955	Signing of Warsaw Pact	12 January: co-directs Berlin premiere of *Winter Battle* by Johannes R. Becher
		Berliner Ensemble's second visit to Paris International Theatre Festival with *The Caucasian Chalk Circle*
		Awarded the Stalin Prize
		Taken ill
1956	June: Krushchev's secret speech denouncing Stalin	The Berliner Ensemble visits London
		14 August: dies of heart infarct
	November: Soviet forces crush Hungarian Uprising	17 August: is buried in the Dorotheen Cemetery in Berlin